WHOEVER
FIGHTS MONSTERS

Best Wishes

Robert K. Ressler

For Bob Ressler with best wishes,

Francis Dolarhyde

No. B-11,064 / William Blake, 1757-1827 / *The Great Red Dragon and the Woman Clothed with the Sun*, c.1805 / watercolor
409 x 336 mm (16 x 13 1/4 in.) / Rosenwald Collection / National Gallery of Art, Washington

and Thomas Harris

WHOEVER
FIGHTS MONSTERS

ROBERT K. RESSLER
& TOM SHACHTMAN

A · THOMAS · DUNNE · BOOK

ST. MARTIN'S PRESS   NEW YORK

Frontispiece: *The Great Red Dragon and the Woman Clothed with the Sun,* © 1805, William Blake, 1757–1827, National Gallery of Art, Washington, D.C., Rosewald Collection.

WHOEVER FIGHTS MONSTERS. Copyright © 1992 by Robert K. Ressler and Tom Shachtman. All rights reserved. Printed in the United States of America. No part of this book may be used or reproduced in any manner whatsoever without written permission except in the case of brief quotations embodied in critical articles or reviews. For information, address St. Martin's Press, 175 Fifth Avenue, New York, N.Y. 10010

Design by Dawn Niles

Library of Congress Cataloging-in-Publication Data

Ressler, Robert K.
   "Whoever fights monsters" : a brilliant FBI detective's career-
long war against serial killers / Robert K. Ressler and Tom
Shachtman.
     p. cm.
   "A Thomas Dunne book."
   Includes index.
   ISBN 0-312-07883-8
   1. Homicide—United States.   2. Serial murders—United States.
I. Shachtman, Tom. II. Title.
HV6529.R473   1992
363.2'59523'092—dc20
[B]   92-4013
                                         CIP

First Edition: May 1992
10 9 8 7 6 5 4 3 2 1

ALSO BY THESE AUTHORS

Robert K. Ressler

Sexual Homicide (with Ann Burgess and John Douglas)

Tom Shachtman

The Day America Crashed
Edith and Woodrow
The Phony War
Decade of Shocks, 1963–1974
The FBI-KGB War (with Robert J. Lamphere)
The Gilded Leaf (with Patrick Reynolds)
Straight to the Top (with Paul G. Stern)
Image by Design (with Clive Chajet)
Skyscraper Dreams

To my close friend and brother-in-law, who during his thirty-three-year police career fought many monsters on the streets of Chicago.

Patrolman Frank P. Graszer
Chicago Police Department Badge Number 4614
Served July 13, 1953–May 11, 1986

Born October 3, 1928; Died December 24, 1990.

—Robert K. Ressler

CONTENTS

ACKNOWLEDGMENTS

I wish to acknowledge many people who have been of tremendous assistance to me in making this book possible. First of all, Mary Higgins Clark, who first asked me to speak to the Mystery Writers of America at their annual conference in New York in 1987. It was there where I met MWA executive secretary Priscilla Ridgway, who induced me to join their organization and later introduced me to Ruth Cavin, senior editor at St. Martin's Press, who urged me to write *Whoever Fights Monsters*. Mary, Priscilla, and Ruth kept the pressure on me and I finally began the project after leaving the FBI in August 1990.

Within the FBI, a few had the vision to support my efforts in the creation of an entirely new service within the Bureau. Those who were most helpful and supportive were Larry Monroe, Dr. Ken Joseph and James McKenzie, former Assistant Directors, and James O'Connor, former Deputy Assistant Director of the FBI Academy. All came to my aid on numerous occasions when I had to "fight monsters" within the bureaucratic structure.

Howard Teten and Pat Mullany were the orginal psychological profiling team and each tutored me at the FBI Academy and on the road in this futuristic concept of criminal investigation. Special thanks to my friends and colleagues in the FBI Behavioral Science Instruction and Research Unit and the VICAP Program with whom I worked so closely over the past years, in particular Unit Chief John Henry Campbell, Dick Ault, Al Brantley, Kathy Bryan, Bernadette Cloniger, Joe Conley, Connie Dodd, Terry Green, Joe Harpold, Roy Hazelwood, Jim Horn, Dave Icove, Ken Lanning, Cindy Lent, Ellen Maynard, Joyce McCloud, Winn Norman, Roland Reboussin, Jim Reese, Ed Sulzbach, and Art Westveer. Also, thanks to those field agents, John Conway, John W. Mindermann, John Dunn, Dick Wrenn, Jim Harrington, Neil Purtell, Charlie Boyle, Byron MacDonald, Laroy Cornett, Ralph Gardner, Karl Schaefer, Mary Ellen Beekman, Don Kyte, Dick Artin, Rich Mathers, Bob Scigalski, Dan Kentala, Candice DeLong, Don Zembiec, Joe Hardy, Hank Hanburger, Larry Sylvester, Pete Welsch, Tom DenOuden, Tom Barrett, Tom Diskin, Jane Turner, Max Thiel, Mel DeGraw, Bill Cheek, Chuck Lewis, Jim McDermott, Mickey Mott, Stan Jacobson, and Bill Haggerty. Most are still in the Bureau, some are retired, but all, and many still unnamed, were of great help to me in conducting research into the minds and crimes of monsters.

I would be remiss to pass acknowledgment to Bob Heck of the U.S. Department of Justice, John Rabun of the National Center for Missing and Exploited Children, and Roger Adelman, a Washington, D.C., attorney in private practice, with whom I worked in the John Hinckley presidential attempted assassination trial. Also special thanks to Ray Pierce, New York City Police Department, Eddie Grant, New York State Police, and Chief of Detectives Joseph Kozenczak, of the Chicago Police Department.

Those in the mental-health and professional academic field who have made very significant contributions to my career over the past seventeen years are Dr. Ann W. Burgess, Dr. Allen Burgess, James Cavanaugh, M.D., Park E. Dietz, M.D., Richard Goldberg, M.D., Derrick Pounder, M.D., Richard Ratner, M.D., Robert Simon, M.D., Dr. Robert Trojanowicz, and Richard Walter. A special gratitude is cited to the late Dr. Paul Embert and Dr. Marvin Homzie.

My military police and CID friends and colleagues must also be acknowledged, since my thirty-five years of military service far exceeded my FBI years: Major Generals (retired) Paul Timmerberg and Eugene Cromartie, former commanders of the U.S. Army Criminal Investigation Command, and Major General Pete Berry, current commander of USACIDC, Brigadier General Tom Jones, Col. Harlan Lenius, Col. Thomas McHugh, Lt.C. (ret.) John F. Jackson, MWO Ray Kangas, and far too many others to name here.

Finally, I wish to acknowledge special thanks to my wife, Helen, and my children, Allison, Betsy, and Aaron, who supported me over many years of absence from my home while I conducted my investigations and research with the U.S. Army and the FBI.

Whoever fights monsters should see to it that in the process he does not become a monster. And when you look into an abyss, the abyss also looks into you.

—FRIEDRICH NIETZSCHE,
Thus Spake Zarathustra

WHOEVER
FIGHTS MONSTERS

1

THE VAMPIRE KILLER

Russ Vorpagel was a legend in the Bureau, six four and 260 pounds, a former police homicide detective in Milwaukee who also had a law degree and was an expert in sex crimes and bomb demolition. His job as Sacramento coordinator for the FBI's Behavioral Science Unit took him up and down the West Coast, teaching local police about sex crimes, and he had a lot of credibility to do so, because cops and sheriffs appreciated the depth of his knowledge.

On a Monday night, January 23, 1978, that local police confidence had translated into a call to Russ from a small department north of Sacramento. A terrible homicide had been committed, one that was far beyond the ordinary murder in terms of the violence done to the victim. David Wallin, twenty-four, a laundry-truck driver, had returned to his modest suburban rented home after work, about six on the evening of January 23, and found his twenty-two-year-old, three-months-pregnant wife, Terry, in the bedroom, dead, with her abdomen slashed. He ran screaming to a neighbor's house, and that neighbor called the police. Wallin was so upset that he could not talk to the authorities when they arrived. The first policeman who entered the home, a sheriff's deputy, was similarly shocked. Later, the deputy said that he had nightmares for months from viewing the carnage.

As soon as the police had seen it, they called Russ for help, and he called me at the FBI Training Academy at Quantico. Disturbed though I was about the murder, I was also intensely interested, because the case seemed as if it would provide me with an opportunity to use the technique of psychological profiling to catch a killer almost as soon as he had struck. Most of the time, when a case was sent to the BSU, the trail was long cold. In Sacramento, it was very hot indeed.

Articles in the newspapers the next day reported that Terry

Wallin had apparently been attacked by an assailant in the living room of the house as she was preparing to take out the garbage. There were signs of a struggle from the front door to the bedroom; two bullet casings had been found. The dead woman was clad in a sweater-type blouse and a pair of pants; her sweater, bra, and pants had been pulled away from her torso, and her abdomen had been slashed. The officers at the scene told reporters that they could not determine a motive for the death, and that robbery had been dismissed as a motive because nothing had been taken.

In fact, the details were far worse than that, but, Russ told me, they were being withheld from the public so as not to cause a panic. Many people often think of the police as rather tough and heartless men who like to shove the public's nose into the dirt so taxpayers will know what the cops themselves have to deal with every day. Not in this instance; some details were kept in-house to spare the public unneeded agony and fright.

There was another reason for withholding information, as well: to keep private certain facts that only the killer would know, facts that might later prove valuable in an interrogation of a suspect. What the public was not told then were these details: The major knife wound was a gaping one from chest to umbilicus; portions of the intestines had been left protruding from it, and several internal organs had been taken out of the body cavity and cut. Some body parts were missing. There were stab wounds to the victim's left breast, and inside those wounds the knife appeared to have been moved about somewhat. Animal feces had been found stuffed into the victim's mouth. There was also evidence that some of the woman's blood had been collected in a yogurt container and drunk.

The local police were both horrified and mystified, and Russ Vorpagel was alarmed, too, because from what he knew of sexual homicide, it was clear to him—as it was immediately obvious to me— that we had to act quickly; there was a distinct danger that the killer of Terry Wallin would strike again. The high level of violence, reflected in the ghastly crime scene, made that almost a certainty. Such a killer would not be satisfied with one homicide. An entire string of killings might follow. I was due to go out to the West Coast to teach at one of our road schools on the following Monday, and we made arrangements that would allow me to arrive on the Friday before that (though on the same taxpayer nickel) and help Russ look into this crime. It was going to be the first time that I was able to go on-site with a profile, and I looked forward to it. Russ and I were both so convinced of the likelihood of the slayer striking again, however, that we shot back and forth a bunch of teletypes and I did a preliminary profile of the probable offender. Criminal profiling was a relatively young science (or art) then, a way of deducing a description of an unknown criminal based on evaluating minute details of the crime scene, the victim, and other evidentiary factors.

Here, in the original (and not entirely grammatical) notes written at the time, is how I profiled the probable perpetrator of this terrible crime:

> White male, aged 25–27 years; thin, undernourished appearance. Residence will be extremely slovenly and unkempt and evidence of the crime will be found at the residence. History of mental illness, and will have been involved in use of drugs. Will be a loner who does not associate with either males or females, and will probably spend a great deal of time in his own home, where he lives alone. Unemployed. Possibly receives some form of disability money. If residing with anyone, it would be with his parents; however, this is unlikely. No prior military record; high school or college dropout. Probably suffering from one or more forms of paranoid psychosis.

I had plenty of reasons for making such a precise description of the probable offender. Though profiling was still in its infancy, we had reviewed enough cases of murder to know that sexual homicide—for that's the category into which this crime fit, even if there was no evidence of a sex act committed at the scene—is usually perpetrated by males, and is usually an intraracial crime, white against white, or black against black. The greatest number of sexual killers are white males in their twenties and thirties; this simple fact allows us to eliminate whole segments of the population when first trying to determine what sort of person has perpetrated one of these heinous crimes. Since this was a white residential area, I felt even more certain that the slayer was a white male.

Now I made a guess along a great division line that we in the Behavioral Sciences Unit were beginning to formulate, the distinction between killers who displayed a certain logic in what they had done and those whose mental processes were, by ordinary standards, not apparently logical—"organized" versus "disorganized" criminals. Looking at the crime-scene photographs and the police reports, it was apparent to me that this was not a crime committed by an "organized" killer who stalked his victims, was methodical in how he went about his crimes, and took care to avoid leaving clues to his own identity. No, from the appearance of the crime scene, it was obvious to me that we were dealing with a "disorganized" killer, a person who had a full-blown and serious mental illness. To become as crazy as the man who ripped up the body of Terry Wallin is not something that happens overnight. It takes eight to ten years to develop the depth of psychosis that would surface in this apparently senseless killing. Paranoid schizophrenia is usually first manifested in the teenage years. Adding ten years to an inception-of-illness age of about fifteen would put the slayer in the mid-twenties age group. I felt that he wouldn't be much older, for two reasons. First, most sexual killers are under the age of thirty-five. Second, if he was older than late twenties, the illness would have been so overwhelming that it would already have resulted in a string of bizarre and unsolved homicides. Nothing as wild as this had been reported anywhere nearby, and the absence of other notable homicides was a clue that this was the first killing for this man, that the killer had probably never taken a human life before. The other details of the probable killer's appearance followed logically from my guess that he was a paranoid schizophrenic, and from my study of psychology.

For instance, I thought this person would be thin. I made this guess because I knew of the studies of Dr. Ernest Kretchmer of Germany and Dr. William Sheldon of Columbia University, both dealing with body types. Both men believed there was a high degree of correlation between body type and mental temperament. Kretchmer found that men with slight body builds (asthenics) tended toward introverted forms of schizophrenia; Sheldon's categories were similar, and I thought that on his terms, the killer would be an ectomorph. These body-type theories are out of favor with today's psychologists—they're fifty years old and more—but I find, more often than not, that they prove to be correct, at least in terms of being helpful in suggesting the probable body type of a psychopathic serial killer.

So that's why I thought this was bound to be a thin and scrawny guy. It was all logical. Introverted schizophrenics don't eat well, don't think in terms of nourishment, and skip meals. They similarly disregard their appearance, not caring at all about cleanliness or neatness. No one would want to live with such a person, so the killer would have to be single. This line of reasoning also allowed me to postulate that his domicile would be a mess, and also to guess that he would not have been in the military, because he would have been too disordered for the military to have accepted him as a recruit in the first place. Similarly, he would not have been able to stay in college, though he might well have completed high school before he disintegrated. This was an introverted individual with problems dating back to his pubescent years. If he had a job at all, it would be a menial one, a janitor perhaps, or someone who picked up papers in a park; he'd be too introverted even to handle the tasks of a delivery man. Most likely he'd be a recluse living on a disability check.

I didn't include some other opinions in the profile, but I did believe that if this slayer had a car, it, too, would be a wreck, with fast-food wrappers in the back, rust throughout, and an appearance similar to what I expected to be found in the home. I also thought it likely that the slayer lived in the area near the victim, because he would probably be too disordered to drive somewhere, commit such a stunning crime, and get himself back home. More likely, he had walked to and from the crime scene. My guess was that he had been let out of a psychiatric-care facility in the recent past, not much more than a year earlier, and had been building up to this level of violent behavior.

Russ took this profile to the several police departments in the area, and they started pounding the pavements looking for suspects. Several dozen policemen rang doorbells, talked to people on telephones, and so on. Media attention on the case was high, and focused on two questions: Who had killed this young woman and—even more puzzling—why?

More details continued to surface over the next forty-eight hours. Sacramento is the capital of California; Terry Wallin had been a state worker, on a day off. That Monday morning, she'd cashed a check at a shopping center within walking distance of her home, and there was speculation that the killer had seen her do that and had followed her home. Her mother had called Terry's home at one-thirty in the afternoon and had gotten no answer, and the coroner's office said Terry had been killed prior to that time. The coroner's office also was of the opinion that some of the stab wounds had been inflicted prior to Terry's death, but that fact was not told to the public. The men in charge of the investigation put out the word through the news media that the killer probably had had blood on his shirt as a result of the crime and asked anyone who had seen a man with blood on his shirt to call a special number.

On Thursday, the north Sacramento area was jolted with the news of more grisly murders. At about 12:30 P.M., a neighbor had discovered three bodies in a suburban home that was within a mile of the Wallin murder. Dead were Evelyn Miroth, thirty-six, her six-year-old son, Jason, and Daniel J. Meredith, fifty-two, a family friend; in addition, Miroth's twenty-two-month-old nephew, Michael Ferriera, was missing and presumed to have been abducted by the killer. All the dead had been shot, and Evelyn Miroth had been slashed in a manner similar to Mrs. Wallin. The killer had apparently escaped in Meredith's red station wagon, which was found abandoned not far from the crime scene. Once again, there was no apparent motive for the crime. The house was reported as not having been ransacked. Evelyn Miroth had been the divorced mother of three children; one resided with her former husband, and another child had been at school when the slaying occurred.

Sheriff Duane Low was quoted by the newspaper as calling the murders "The most bizarre, grotesque, and senseless killings I've seen in twenty-eight years," murders that had "terribly disturbed" him. Evelyn Miroth had been a baby-sitter for the neighborhood, and many of the children and mothers knew her well; other children had gone to school with the six-year-old boy. No one could think of any reason for anyone to have killed them. A neighbor who had been friendly with the dead woman told a reporter that she felt like crying, "but I'm scared, too. That's awfully close." Residents of the neighborhood watched the local television news to get what details were available, and then came out of their homes to gather in clusters on the street and discuss the matter. It was a foggy night, and, with the waiting patrol cars and emergency vehicles and the knowledge of murder in the air, many found it to be an eerie scene. Though the reports said shots had been fired, no one could be found who had heard any shots.

People were frightened. Although police were trying to keep the information about the killings from causing hysteria, enough of it had leaked out so that doors were being double-locked, window shades pulled down; some people were even loading up their cars, station wagons, and small trucks and moving out.

Russ Vorpagel called me as soon as he heard the news. We were alarmed, of course, but as professionals we had to put aside our sense of horror and decipher the puzzle—right away. From a crime-scene analyst's standpoint, the second group of killings provided important new information and verification of what we believed we already knew about the killer. At this second crime scene—again, these are details that were not immediately made public—the man and the boy had been shot but had not been molested. Meredith's car keys and wallet had been taken from him. In contrast, Evelyn Miroth had been even more badly molested than the first female victim. She was found nude on the side of a bed, shot once through the head, and with two crossing cuts on her abdomen, through which loops of her innards partially protruded. Her internal organs had been cut, and there were multiple stab wounds all over her body, including cuts on the face and in the anal area. A rectal swab showed the presence of significant amounts of sperm. In the playpen where the visiting baby was normally kept, a blood-soaked pillow and an expended slug were found. In the bath, there was red-colored water, as well as brain and fecal matter. Blood appeared to have been drunk at this location, too. Also important was that the stolen station wagon had been found not far away, with its door ajar and the keys still in the ignition. The baby had not been found, but the police were fairly certain from the amount of blood in the playpen that he would not be alive.

Using this new information, and with a mounting sense of urgency and the certainty that if not caught this man would kill again— and soon—I refined the profile that I had put together just a few days earlier. The sexual connection of the crimes had become more overt. The number of victims at a single crime scene was growing. The violence was escalating. I was more convinced than ever that the slayer was a seriously mentally disturbed young man who had walked to the crime scene, and walked away from the spot where he had abandoned the car. I translated these convictions into a revised profile that indicated the probable offender was "single, living alone in a location within one-half to one mile from the abandoned station wagon." To my mind, the slayer had been so disordered that he had no sense of hiding anything, and had probably parked the station wagon right near his own house. I also reinforced the notions as to his unkempt and disheveled appearance, and the slovenliness to be expected at his residence.

I also told Russ that I believed that before this man had murdered, he had probably committed fetish burglaries in the area, and that once he was caught, we'd be able to trace his crimes and difficulties back to his childhood. We characterize as fetish burglaries those breaking-and-entering cases in which the items stolen or misused are articles of women's clothing, rather than jewelry or other items of marketable value; often, the burglar takes these for autoerotic purposes.

With this new profile in hand, more than sixty-five police personnel hit the streets, concentrating on everything within a half-mile radius of the abandoned station wagon. It was a tremendous manhunt. People in apartments and homes and on the sidewalks were asked whether they had seen a youngish man who appeared quite disheveled and thin. The area of the search was further narrowed when the police received a report that a dog had been shot and disemboweled at a country club close to where the abandoned car had been found.

The police found two people who thought they had seen the red station wagon being driven in the neighborhood, but even under hypnosis these witnesses were able to recall only that it had been driven by a white male. The most promising lead came from a woman in her late twenties who had met a young man whom she had known in high school in the shopping center near the site of the first murder, just an hour or two preceding the attack on Terry Wallin. She had been shocked at her old classmate's appearance—disheveled, cadaverously thin, bloody sweatshirt, yellowed crust around his mouth, sunken eyes— and when he tried to pursue a conversation with her by pulling at the door handle of her car, she had driven away. When the police alerted the area to look for a man with blood on his shirt, she had contacted the authorities. She told the police that the man was Richard Trenton Chase, and that he had graduated from her high school in 1968.

By then, it was Saturday. The police learned that Richard Trenton Chase lived less than a block away from the abandoned station wagon, a mile north of the country club and a mile east of the shopping center. They staked out the area near his apartment and waited for him to come out. At this point, he was only one among a half-dozen likely suspects. He did not answer phone calls to the apartment, and toward late afternoon the watchers decided they would try a ruse to see whether they could lure him outside. They knew that the killer had a .22 revolver and was not afraid to take a human life, so they proceeded carefully. One went to the apartment of the manager of the project as if to use the telephone, while the other openly walked away from the front of Chase's apartment. Moments later, Chase appeared at the door with a box under his arm and started to make a run for his truck.

As soon as he began to run, the officers knew they had their man, and they ran to grapple with him. As they rolled about, the .22 came out of his shoulder holster. In their grasp, he tried to hide what was in his back pocket: Daniel Meredith's wallet. The box he carried was full of bloody rags. Chase's truck was near the apartment, and it was a dozen years old, in poor condition, and littered with old newspapers, beer cans, milk cartons, and rags. A locked toolbox and a twelve-inch butcher's knife were also in the truck, together with rubber boots with what appeared to be blood on them. In his apartment—as slovenly as could be—were some animal collars, three food blenders with blood in them, as well as newspaper articles about the first murder. Dirty clothing was strewn about the house, some with blood on it. Several dishes in the refrigerator had body parts in them, and a container held human brain tissue. In a kitchen drawer, there were several knives that turned out to have been taken from the Wallin residence. A calendar on the wall of the apartment had the inscription "Today" on the end-of-January dates of the Wallin and Miroth-Meredith murders; the same inscription was on forty-four more days spread out over the remainder of 1978. Would there have been forty-four more murders? Thankfully, we'll never know.

The police were tremendously relieved that the murderer had been caught—for there could be no real doubt that this was the slayer, from the evidence he carried and the descriptions that he matched. Everyone was grateful to the FBI and very appreciative of the profile, and some people later said that the profile caught the killer. That, of course, was not true. It's *never* true. Profiles don't catch killers, cops on the beat do, often through dogged persistence and with the help of ordinary citizens, and certainly with the aid of a little bit of luck. My profile was an investigative tool, one that in this instance markedly narrowed the search for a dangerous killer. Did my work help catch Chase? You bet, and I'm proud of it. Did I catch him myself? No.

The fact that Chase so precisely fit the profile that I had drawn up in conjunction with Russ Vorpagel was gratifying to me on two counts. First and foremost, because it helped in the apprehension of a violent killer who would undoubtedly have continued his homicides if not caught immediately. Second, because when the murderer matched the profile, that gave us at the BSU more information on how to evaluate subsequent crime scenes and identify the characteristic signs that murderers leave behind; in short, it helped us to refine further the art (and I do mean the *art*, because it had not yet approached the status of being a science) of profiling.

In the days and months after Chase's apprehension, I closely followed the information coming to light about this strange young man. Almost immediately after his arrest, he was connected to an unsolved murder that had taken place in December not far from the site of the two other events. It turned out that I had been wrong about Terry Wallin being the first victim; she was actually the second. A Mr. Ambrose Griffin and his wife had returned home from the supermarket on December 28, 1977, and were taking groceries into their house from their car. Chase had driven by in his truck and had fired two shots; one hit Griffin in the chest and killed him. Ballistic research on Chase's .22 caliber gun, taken from him after the other two murders, showed that it had also discharged the bullet that killed Griffin.

Chase also fit the description of the unknown assailant responsible for some earlier fetish burglaries in the neighborhood, and was pinpointed as the probable abductor of many dogs and cats. Several dog collars and leashes found in his apartment matched up with those taken from missing dogs and puppies from the surrounding area. These dogs and cats were most likely killed for his strange purposes; he may even have drunk their blood, though we could never be certain of that.

Computer searches also came up with an incident in mid-1977 in the Lake Tahoe area, when an Indian agent on a reservation stopped and arrested a man whose clothes were soaked with blood and whose truck had guns in it, as well as a bucket of blood; it was Chase. He had gotten off that time because the blood was bovine. He had paid a fine and explained away the blood on his clothes by saying that he'd been hunting rabbits that had bled on his shirt.

As reporters and court officers interviewed people who had known Chase and unearthed records about him, the whole sorry history emerged. Born in 1950, Chase was the male child of a moderate-income family, thought of as a sweet and cooperative son. At age eight, he was a bed wetter, but this behavior soon ceased. His problems really seemed to have begun at age twelve or so, at the time when his parents began to fight at home. His mother accused his father of infidelity, of poisoning her, and of using drugs. The father, when interviewed, said that these accusations and other loud arguments had to have been overheard by Chase. A later evaluation by a group of psychologists and psychiatrists who interviewed the family labeled Mrs. Chase as the classic mother of a schizophrenic, "highly aggressive . . . hostile . . . provocative." The arguments between father and mother continued for nearly ten years, after which the couple was divorced and the father remarried.

Chase was of just about normal intelligence—IQ around 95— and an ordinary student in high school in the mid-1960s. He had girlfriends, but his relationships with them were broken off when they got to the point that he attempted intercourse but was unable to sustain an erection. He had no close friends, no long-standing relationships with anyone but his family. Psychiatrists and psychologists who examined him later were of the opinion that Chase's mental condition began to deteriorate in his second year of high school, when he became "rebellious and defiant, had no ambition and his room was always in a state of disarray. He was smoking marijuana and drinking heavily." One of the girlfriends who had been close to him said that he started hanging out with the "acid-head" crowd. He was arrested in 1965 for possession of marijuana, and was sentenced to community cleanup work.

As these sort of details were published in the newspapers, reporters and many in the public saw evidence for attributing Chase's murders to the influence of drugs. I disagreed. Although drugs may have contributed to Chase's slide into serious mental illness, they were not a real factor in the murders; we have found that drugs, while present in many cases, are seldom the precipitating factor in serial murders; the true causes lie much deeper and are more complex.

Despite his deterioration, Chase managed to graduate from high school and held a job for several months in 1969; it was the only job that he ever managed to keep for more than a day or two. He attended a junior college but could not keep up with the work or, friends remembered, with the social pressures of college life. In 1972, he was arrested in Utah for drunk driving. This seemed to have hit him hard, for after it, he later recalled, he had stopped drinking altogether. But he was on a downward curve. In 1973, he was picked up for carrying a gun without a license and resisting arrest. He had been at an apartment where a party of young people was in full swing, and had attempted to grab a girl's breast; he'd been ejected from the party, and when he returned, the men jumped him and held him for the police; as they did so, a .22 pistol fell from his waistband. Charges were reduced to a misdemeanor, he paid a fifty-dollar fine, and walked away. He couldn't hold a job, and went between his father's and mother's homes and was supported by them.

In 1976, after Chase tried to inject rabbit's blood into his veins, he was sent to a nursing home. Conservators were appointed by the court to take charge of his affairs, thereby relieving his parents of that responsibility; taking care of Chase was getting beyond the capabilities of any individuals even then. Conservatorship is also a way of having the state pick up the tab for caring for a mentally disturbed person; paying the bills privately can otherwise bankrupt any but the very wealthiest families. On the grounds of the nursing home, according to some of the nurses later interviewed, Chase was a "frightening" patient. He bit the heads off birds he had captured in the bushes, and was several times found with blood on his face and shirt. In a diary, he described the killing of small animals and the taste of blood. Two nurse's aides quit because of his presence at the institution. He became known among the staff as Dracula.

All of his bizarre actions had a reason, at least in Chase's own mind. He believed he was being poisoned, that his own blood was turning to powder, and that he needed this other blood to replenish his own and to stave off death. A male nurse was directed by the staff physicians to put Chase into a room at night with one other patient, and he refused to do so, fearing that if something happened—a distinct possibility, according to the nurse—he would lose his license. Medication seemed to control Chase to the point of stability, and a psychiatrist wanted to release him for outpatient care to make room for more seriously ill patients. The male nurse later recalled, "When we learned [Chase] was going to be released, we all raised hell about it, but it didn't do any good." An outside physician, later asked for his opinion about what had happened to allow Chase to be released, thought it had probably come about "because his medication was controlling him." (The families of the victims in the Chase murders later sued the psychiatrists who had allowed Chase out of the institution, asking for considerable damages.)

Chase was released in 1977, mostly in the care of his mother, who obtained an apartment for him—the one at which he was eventually captured. He spent some time with her, but most of the time he was alone at the apartment. Chase was an outpatient who subsisted on a disability check, and bragged to people who knew him about not having to work. Some of the bills at the apartment were paid by his father, who also tried to spend time with his son, taking him on trips for weekends, buying him presents. Old acquaintances who bumped into him during this period after his release said he seemed to dwell entirely in the past, to talk of events that had occurred when they were in high school as if they were current, and not to say anything about the intervening eight or ten years. He did, however, speak of flying saucers, UFOs, and of a Nazi party crime syndicate that he thought had been operating in high school and was still after him. When his mother complained about the disarray at his apartment, he barred her from entering it. When his father went to rescue him after the incident near Lake Tahoe, Chase dismissed it as an accident and a misunderstanding by the local police agents of a hunting mishap.

That Lake Tahoe incident was in August of 1977. Chase's actions from then until the first discovered murder provide such a clear picture of a deteriorating mind and an escalating series of criminal behaviors that we need to paint them in some detail. In September, after an argument with his mother, Chase killed her cat. Twice in October, he bought dogs from the ASPCA for about fifteen dollars each. On October 20, he stole two dollars' worth of gasoline for his truck; when an officer questioned him about it, he was calm and denied the charge, and was allowed to drive away. In mid-November, he answered an ad in the local paper for Labrador pups, showed up at the owner's home, and bargained successfully to take two home for the price of one. Later in November, he made a phone call to torment a family whose dog he had taken on the street, and who had placed an ad in the paper asking whether anyone had seen it. Police received reports of other animals missing in the neighborhood.

On December 7, Chase went to a gun shop and purchased the .22 revolver. He had to fill out a form that required him to answer whether or not he had ever been a patient in a mental institution, and he swore that he had not. There was a waiting period, and he would not be able to pick up the gun until December 18. During the intervening days, he did some work on reregistering his truck and other tasks that required a coherent mind. He kept articles from the newspapers about a Los Angeles strangler and circled advertisements for free dogs. His father took him to a store to pick out a Christmas present, and Chase accepted an orange parka, which he wore steadily from the moment he obtained it.

After picking up the gun from the store on December 18 and buying several boxes of ammunition for it, he began to shoot. First, he fired one shot at a windowless wall of the residence of a family named Phares. A day or so later, he fired through the kitchen window of the house of the Polenske family, parting the hair of Mrs. Polenske, who stood bent over the kitchen sink; one shot was fired. Shortly thereafter, Chase fired the two shots at Ambrose Griffin, one of which killed him. The Griffin home was located across the street from the Phares house. The shots at Mrs. Polenske and Griffin were hardly random; later analyses showed that from a traveling car one would have had to fire carefully to avoid hitting the many trees on the Griffin block and to hit the man in the chest. Mrs. Polenske was extremely lucky to be alive.

On January 5, 1978, Chase bought a copy of the *Sacramento Bee*, which had an editorial about the Griffin killing; he kept this page, with its societal condemnation of the senseless shooting. On January

10, he bought three more boxes of ammunition. On January 16, he set a fire in a garage in order to drive out of the neighborhood some people whose playing of loud music had annoyed him.

On January 23—the day he killed Terry Wallin—the police were able to trace Chase's actions moment by moment. Early in the day, he attempted to enter a home in the neighborhood, but he left after coming face-to-face with the woman occupant at the kitchen window. He then sat on her patio, motionless, for some time. She called the police, but he left before the authorities could arrive. Not too many minutes later, a homeowner caught him in the act of having illegally entered another residence. He fled, and the man ran after him down the street, lost him, and then went back to assess the damage. Chase had taken some valuable objects, defecated on a child's bed, and urinated on clothing in a drawer—the latter behaviors were signs of classic fetish burglaries. An hour later, Chase was in the parking lot of the shopping center, where he met the woman he recognized from high school—and who became suspicious of him.

He was wearing a bloodstained shirt, had a yellow crust around his mouth, and was shockingly different from the boy she had known years ago. She didn't recognize him until he asked her whether she had been on the motorcycle when her former boyfriend, a friend of Chase's, had been killed. She said no, and asked him who he was. He told her his name. She tried to edge away, and said she had to go to the bank. He waited for her, then followed her to her car and attempted to get in on the passenger side; she locked it and sped away. Minutes later, he walked across the porch of a home near the shopping center, and when the owner called out to him not to do that, he said he was just taking a shortcut. Then he left those premises and entered the almost-adjoining home of Terry Wallin.

By mid-1978, the body of the missing child had been found, also not far from Chase's last residence. In prison, he had refused to do much talking. The trial site was moved from Sacramento to Palo Alto, and there were other delays. During the next year, one psychiatrist did manage to gain Chase's confidence enough to have conversations with him, and, in one of these, elicited the following rather remarkable confessional statement in response to a question about whether Chase would have continued with his killings.

> The first person I killed was sort of an accident. My car was broken down. I wanted to leave but I had no transmission. I

had to get an apartment. Mother wouldn't let me in at Christmas. Always before she let me come in at Christmas, have dinner, and talk to her, my grandmother, and my sister. That year she wouldn't let me in and I shot from the car and killed somebody. The second time, the people had made a lot of money and I was jealous. I was being watched, and I shot this lady—got some blood out of it. I went to another house, walked in, a whole family was there. I shot the whole family. Somebody saw me there. I saw this girl. She had called the police and they had been unable to locate me. Curt Silva's girlfriend—he was killed in a motorcycle accident, as a couple of my friends were, and I had this idea that he was killed through the syndicate, that he was in the Mafia, selling drugs. His girlfriend remembered about Curt—I was trying to get information. She said she was married to somebody else and wouldn't talk to me. The whole syndicate was making money by having my mom poison me. I know who they are and I think it can be brought out in a court of law if I can pull the pieces together like I've been hoping.

The trial began in early 1979, and on May 6, 1979, *Sacramento Bee* reporter Iris Yang described Chase in the courtroom: "The defendant has a totally lusterless quality. Dull, limp brown hair, sunken opaque eyes, a sallow complexion and scarcely a spare ounce of flesh clinging to his bony frame. For the past four and a half months, Richard Trenton Chase, just a couple of weeks short of his 29th birthday, has sat hunched in his chair, toying with papers in front of him or staring vacantly at the fluorescent lights of the courtroom."

There was a trial only because the prosecution vigorously sought the death penalty under a recently enacted California state law. The defense had wanted to say that Chase was mentally ill and incompetent to stand trial, but the prosecution had argued that Chase had had enough "knowing shrewdness" at the time of his crimes to be deemed responsible for his actions and that he must be held accountable for them. He was charged with six counts of first-degree murder— Terry Wallin, the three people at the Miroth home, the dead baby, and Ambrose Griffin. The jury deliberated only a few hours before pronouncing him guilty on all counts. The judge sent him to death row at San Quentin to await the electric chair.

I did not agree with this verdict or with the disposition of the case. It occurred in the same time frame as the murders of Mayor

Mosconi and Supervisor Harvey Milk by former San Francisco City Hall employee Dan White. White claimed he had been made insane by such things as eating the junk food Twinkies, and his diminished-capacity defense was accepted and he was sent to a mental hospital and not given the death penalty. Richard Chase, who was clearly mentally ill, and who should have spent the rest of his life in a mental institution, was sentenced to die in the electric chair.

While Chase was on death row at San Quentin, in 1979, John Conway and I visited him. Conway was the FBI's prison liaison man in California, an exceptionally smooth, good-looking, and polished guy who had a knack for getting inmates quickly into a conversational mood. Going to see Chase was one of the strangest experiences I have ever had. From the moment I entered the prison to the moment I sat down in the room where we would conduct the interview, it was a series of doors slamming behind us, an oppressive and frightening experience. I'd been in many prisons before, but this was the most grisly; I felt I was going beyond a point of no return. Conway was much more nonchalant about it than I.

We went up through several elevators, and the final one disgorged us on death row. I heard weird noises, groans, and other almost-inhuman sounds coming from the cells. We sat in a room awaiting Chase, and heard him coming down the hall. He was in leg irons and clanked as he walked, and I thought immediately of Marley's Ghost in Dickens's *A Christmas Carol*. In addition to the leg irons, he was handcuffed and had one of those security belts with a loop through which the handcuffs were attached. He could do nothing but barely shuffle along.

His appearance was another shock. Here was this skinny, odd-looking young man with long black hair; but it was his eyes that really got me. I'll never forget them. They were like those of the shark in the movie *Jaws*. No pupils, just black spots. These were evil eyes that stayed with me long after the interview. I almost got the impression that he couldn't really see me, that he was seeing through me, just staring. He showed no signs of being aggressive, and simply sat, passive. He carried in his hands a plastic cup, which he didn't talk about at first.

Since he had already been convicted and was on death row, I didn't have to go through the sort of romancing that usually characterizes my first interview with a murderer. Ordinarily, I have to work hard to show the interviewee that I am worthy of his trust and that he can talk easily with me. Chase and I talked with relative ease, considering his mental state. He admitted his murders, but said he had done them in order to preserve his own life. He told me that he was fashioning an appeal, and that it would be based on the notion that he had been dying and had taken lives in order to obtain the blood he needed to live. The threat to his life was soap-dish poisoning.

When I told him that I wasn't aware of the nature of soap-dish poisoning, he enlightened me. Everyone has a soap dish, he said. If you lift up the soap and the part underneath the soap is dry, you're all right, but if it's gooey, that means you have soap-dish poisoning. I asked him what the poison did to him, and he responded that it turns one's blood to powder, essentially pulverizes the blood; the powder then eats at one's body and energies and reduces one's capacities.

Readers may find Chase's explanation laughable or impossibly weird. In this situation, when I was confronted with it, however, I had to react properly. I could not appear appalled or shocked, and had to take the explanation for what it was worth—an illustration of the reasoning of a murderer. The rule is, you stay out of commenting on the fantasy, and, by your comments, urge him to continue. So I couldn't say about soap-dish poisoning, "There isn't any such thing," because that wouldn't have helped. Neither could I say, "Oh, yes, I know people who've had soap-dish poisoning." I merely accepted his explanation and didn't debate him about it.

The same principle applied when he began to tell me that he had been born Jewish—I knew that to be untrue—and that he had been persecuted all his life by the Nazis because he had a Star of David on his forehead, which he proceeded to show me. To this announcement, I could have said, "That's baloney!" or gone in the other direction and answered, "Gee, what a beauty, I wish I had one like it." Neither answer would have helped much in the conversation. I saw no Star of David, but I thought his mention of it might be a trap that Chase was setting for me, or a test of how far I was willing to go along with his explanation. He might be tricking me, telling me it was on his forehead when it was really on his arm or his chest, and he wanted to see how much I knew about him. In this instance, I merely told Chase that I hadn't brought my glasses along, and that the lighting was dim and I couldn't see the birthmark, but that I accepted his word that it was there. He said that the Nazis had been connected to the UFOs that constantly hover over the earth and that had commanded him by telepathy to kill in order to replenish his blood. He summed up his explanation by saying to me, "So you see, Mr. Ressler, you see very clearly that the killings were in self-defense."

Perhaps the most important information that I obtained from this interview came from a question as to how Chase had chosen his particular victims. It was a point that had eluded many other of Chase's interviewers, but I had gained his confidence enough that he was comfortable telling me. He had been hearing voices that told him to take a life, and he just went down the street, rattling doors. If a door was locked, he wouldn't go in. If it was open, however, he went in. I asked him why he hadn't simply broken down a door if he wanted to go inside. "Oh," he said, "if the door is locked, that means you're not welcome." How slim the line between those who escaped being the victims of a heinous crime and those who died awful deaths at the hands of Chase!

At last, I asked him about the little cup that he carried. He said it was evidence that the prison was attempting to poison him. He shoved it forward, and it contained some gooey yellow mess that I later identified as the remains of a packaged macaroni and cheese dinner. He wanted me to take it and have the FBI lab at Quantico analyze it for him. It was a gift I felt I could not refuse.

The information I gleaned from this interview was helpful in verifying the portrait we at the BSU were already putting together of the "disorganized" killer, a portrait that is in sharp contrast to that of the "organized" killer. Chase not only fit the disorganized pattern, he embodied it more than any other individual that I or others in law enforcement had encountered. In that regard, his was a classic case.

While at San Quentin, the other inmates taunted Chase. They threatened that if he came near enough, they'd kill him, and told him he ought to commit suicide. Prison psychologists and psychiatrists who examined Chase in those days waited for the brouhaha over the death penalty to calm down, and then suggested that since Chase was "psychotic, insane, and incompetent, and chronically so," he ought to be transferred to the prison at Vacaville, California, known as the California Medical Facility of the prison system, the place that houses the criminally insane. I certainly concurred in that judgment. By this time, and following up on the notion that the FBI was going to analyze what the prison was feeding him, Chase was writing letters to Conway and to me, conveying to us that he needed to come to Washington, D.C., to perfect his appeal. He was certain that the FBI would want to know that the UFOs were now connected to airplane crashes, and to antiaircraft weapons of the sort that were being used against the United States by the Iranians. "The FBI could easily detect the UFO's by radar," he wrote to me, "and find they follow me and are stars in the sky at night that light up through some type of controlled fusion reaction machines.''

It was the last I heard from Chase. Just after Christmas in 1980, Chase was found dead in his cell at Vacaville. He had saved up many antidepressant pills that had been given to him to damp down his hallucinations and make him a tractable prisoner, and had taken them all at once. Some called his death suicide; others continued to believe that it was accidental, and that Richard Trenton Chase had taken all those pills in an effort to quiet the voices that had driven him to murder and that continued to torment him until he died.

2

"WHOEVER FIGHTS MONSTERS..."

There was a monster on the loose in Chicago, and I was intrigued. It was 1946, and I was all of nine years old. My dad worked in security and maintenance for the *Chicago Tribune*, so we always had the newspaper around the house. In the *Tribune* the summer before, I had read about the killing of a middle-aged married woman in an apartment building. It was just an isolated case until the following December, when an ex-Wave was killed in an apartment hotel. The killer had written on a mirror, in the woman's lipstick, "For heaven's sake, catch me before I kill more. I cannot control myself." From evidence that was too awful to print in the newspaper (and at which I could not even guess), the police thought the killings of the two women might be connected.

The *Tribune* was in the thick of the chase for the killer, sending reporters here and there in search of clues. Shortly after the turn of the year, there was another crime that at first was not thought to be connected to the other two. A six-year-old girl, Suzanne Degnan, was taken from her room in her house and killed; her body was found scattered in parts in the sewers in the Chicago-Evanston area. All of Chicago was aghast at this grisly murder; many parents were worried for the safety of their children. I wondered, What kind of person would kill and cut up a little girl? A monster? A human being? As a nine-year-old boy, I couldn't imagine what sort of person would commit such a heinous crime, but I could fantasize about catching Suzanne's killer. I suppose I was somewhat afraid, and the fantasy was my way of coping with that fear—but I think I was actually more fascinated than afraid.

At the movie houses on Saturdays, I had seen a model I wanted to reproduce. Either in "Our Gang" or "The Little Rascals"—by now I've forgotten which—there was a detective agency; in the summer of 1946, I formed one with three of my friends. The RKPK Agency had an office in a garage and a "war wagon," a wooden structure on wheels that we called the RKPK Express. When we weren't conducting an investigation, we'd use the Express to haul groceries, a quarter a delivery. That delivery business was only a subsidiary that we kept going in order to meet our overhead costs. Like most fictional movie detectives, we weren't getting enough cases to pay the rent. Our main activity that summer of '46 was to put on "detective" clothes—hats and long coats—and to lurk around the bus stop waiting for a suspect to trail. We were trying to look like FBI men, who were heroes to the country, back then, or maybe like Sam Spade. When one of the fathers or elder brothers in the neighborhood would get off the bus with his lunch pail or briefcase, we'd assume that this was a suspect in the killing of Suzanne Degnan and follow him home, then stake out positions around his house until it was time to change shifts and compare notes. The men would wonder what these goofy kids dressed up in long coats were doing; they never did figure it out.

William Heirens was caught that summer, and I found it amazing that he had killed the little girl as well as the two women in the apartments; the reason he gave was that they had surprised him in the course of committing burglaries that were described as sexual in nature. According to the mores of the time, no further details were given, and since I didn't know very much about sex at age nine, I shrugged off that part of the description. Years later, I would learn far more than the average person gets to know about what were, in effect, fetish burglaries. At the time, the most intriguing fact about Heirens, to me, was that he wasn't that much older than I—just seventeen, a student at the University of Chicago. It later turned out that he had been sane enough after each murderous event to go back to his dormitory room and act calmly enough to avoid detection. His arrest came almost as an accident, when an off-duty policemen was called to stop Heirens as he was trying to make a getaway after an unsuccessful burglary. There was quite a scuffle, and the policeman had been extremely fortunate that Heirens's gun misfired twice before another officer arrived and was able to smash Heirens's skull with a handy flowerpot. In his dormitory room, the authorities found souvenirs from his fetish burglaries and the murders. *Time* magazine called the Heirens case "the crime story of the century," and marveled at how many reporters flocked to Chicago from all over the country to learn about it and to observe the trial. Once Heirens had been caught, we nine-year-olds watched the bus stop, waiting for Heirens the dangerous killer, and we played that we were following him to his lair.

The fantasy game and our detective agency faded that summer, but in a way I continued even at that age to follow and be fascinated by Heirens himself and many criminals like him, and, as I grew up, to fall naturally into what became an important part of my life's work, catching and understanding criminals.

An average student in high school, I wasn't particularly interested in any one subject, and that attitude carried over into two years of ho-hum attendance at a community college in Chicago. Then I joined the Army, got married, and was sent to Okinawa. While overseas, I still received the *Chicago Tribune*, and in one Sunday supplement read about a school of criminology and police administration at Michigan State. It sounded good. I applied, was accepted, and began a bachelor's program after I finished my two years in the army. Law enforcement interested me greatly, and, as a consequence, my grades steadily improved. After completing the undergraduate program, I was accepted for graduate work. I finished only one semester of that, though, before I went back into the Army—this time as an officer, having been in ROTC while at Michigan State University.

I had attempted to get a job on the Chicago police force, only to be told that the force wasn't interested in recruits with too much schooling, because they "might make too much trouble." The chairman of our school had some influence, but the best Chicago would offer, my Chicago patrolman brother-in-law, Frank Graszer, told me privately, was a patrolman's job, which I could have obtained with only a high school education. Frank continued to encourage my interest in law enforcement. The Army, however, offered me a position as a lieutenant in the MPs, and a post in Germany. That intrigued me, because both my wife and I were of German extraction, and we leapt at the chance to go to the land of our forefathers.

I was fortunate enough to receive a choice assignment, that of provost marshal of a platoon of MPs in Aschaffenburg. The town had a population of about 45,000, and our garrison held about 8,000, so I became, in effect, the chief of police for a small town; there were homicides, burglaries, arson cases, the whole gamut of problems that a police chief would see. After four years, when I was ready to get out of the army again, I was offered another plum assignment, as commander of a Criminal Investigation Division (CID) unit based at Fort Sheridan, just outside of Chicago, a plainclothes investigations unit responsible for operations in military jurisdictions in five surrounding states. I supervised men in and around Chicago, Detroit, Milwaukee, Minneapolis–St. Paul, and so on. Contrary to what the general public often thinks about the military—that inside such an organization, talent and drive get lost—the Army has developed ways of trying to intrigue and retain good people by watching them closely and offering them good assignments; I had twice already been the beneficiary of their interest.

As I discovered later, the assignment at Fort Sheridan was similar to running one of the FBI's field offices: All my agents wore civilian clothes, carried credentials, a badge, and a .38. In fact, we frequently worked with the local police and the FBI. In Aschaffenburg, as a lieutenant, I had replaced a senior captain; at Fort Sheridan, as a first lieutenant (still quite a junior officer), I replaced a major.

One of our largest cases involved my bringing in some agents of the Federal Bureau of Narcotics (later known as the Drug Enforcement Agency) to Fort Sheridan to penetrate a narcotics ring. The agents posed as troublemaking enlisted men who had been posted to Fort Sheridan while they awaited dishonorable discharges. The ring was infiltrated, but not without some danger—the undercover men were on the verge of being set up to be ripped off and murdered when we learned of the proposed hit. The finale of the affair was right out of the movies. As all units at the fort were mustered in the company streets for a final inspection before everyone was to get a three-day pass, my units and those of the FBN and the FBI surrounded the area with cars, trucks, and machine guns; the undercover men stepped out of ranks, pinned on their badges, and accompanied the commanding officer through the ranks, fingering the dope dealers, who were then led away to the brig.

The whole affair left me feeling as if I would like to continue this sort of work for the government, but as a civilian with the FBI. As commander of the CID unit, I frequently was the host at liaison parties for the various policing agencies with whom we routinely interacted, including the FBI.

There were lots of FBI–type cases in those days, the mid-1960s. On college campuses, there were the beginnings of riots and other antiestablishment activities, some of which spread to young people the same age as college students who were on nearby military bases. My CID agents worked their way into groups that were planning disruptive activities, and reported back with what they had seen, not just to me but also to the FBI. Lest the reader think that this was much ado about nothing, I should point out that one of these groups had stolen explosives from Fort Sheridan and was interrupted while planning to bomb some military targets. Several years later, after I had joined the FBI, I had occasion to do research into these old cases, and learned that the Bureau people in the Chicago field office of the FBI had taken credit for the work of my CID investigators. That was a first and a somewhat rude insight into how the FBI sometimes went about its business. There was what FBI insiders called a one-way street in operation: The FBI took from other law-enforcement agencies but gave back nothing—ever.

I was due to be discharged from the Army and was looking for a way to go further in law enforcement when my status was frozen as a result of the escalation of the war in Vietnam. No one of my rank in my part of the armed services was allowed to leave just then. The Army came to me with an interesting proposition: Someone higher up in the service had looked over my records and had seen that I had completed a semester of graduate work; the Army now offered to pay for me to complete my master's in police administration and to continue my salary while I studied—in exchange for signing up for an additional two-year hitch after I finished the master's program.

This time, at Michigan State, I had a wife and two children along, and, in addition to my studies, a secret assignment from the Army: undercover work within the groups that were actively resisting the Vietnam War. I grew my hair long, and went to SDS and various New Left meetings, including marches and so on. Painting myself as a disgruntled veteran, I attended organizational get-togethers and other meetings. There's even a picture of me in a campus newspaper some-where, long-haired, and with my infant daughter perched on my shoul-der for additional cover. We were protesting CIA recruiting on campus; I wonder whether that picture of me ended up in the CIA files.

I thought these "radical" protesters didn't know what they were talking about; they hadn't been in the military, didn't know what the military was doing, but were determined that the military was their enemy. Often, they seemed to want to disrupt things just for the joy of making a mess. One assistant professor of psychology was hanging around these same meetings, trying to motivate students to protest the war, even suggesting to them that they massively enroll in ROTC in an attempt to disrupt the system. He counseled that while in classes they should make things difficult for the instructors by asking dumb questions, and that at the time they were supposed to graduate, they refuse to take commissions in the armed forces. The assistant professor was soon advised to get a job somewhere else.

The classes went quickly and well. Among my cohorts in the graduate program was Ken Joseph, then the senior resident agent of the Lansing, Michigan, FBI office; Ken stayed on to finish his doctorate while I went back into the army to fulfill my obligation.

After finishing my degree, I served for a year as a provost marshal in Thailand, and another year as deputy provost marshal at Fort Sheridan. By now, I was a major, and seriously had to consider continuing on in the military as a career, but my friends in the FBI convinced me to reinstate the application I had made earlier, just before my position in the military had been frozen, and to come into the Bureau. The alternative didn't seem as attractive in 1970, when I was thirty-two, as it had been in 1967, but I certainly liked the sort of investigations I knew the FBI to be conducting, so I applied in earnest and was accepted. Several of my commanders in the army tried to talk me out of leaving, and touted my prospects for advancement with the CID, but I was enthralled by the prospect of becoming a special agent of the FBI, and was no longer listening to reason.

I was in trouble in the FBI from the first half hour of my tenure. I had received a letter telling me to report to a room in the Old Post Office building at eight on a Monday morning in February 1970, and arrived there at 7:50 A.M., bright and eager, only to find a note posted announcing that the class had been transferred to a room at the Department of Justice building, some blocks away. Hustling there, I was met in the halls by agent counselors, who, upon learning my name, told me that everything was about to hit the fan, and that I should be worried. In the classroom, an instructor was droning on about Bureau insurance and retirement matters, and he halted the class to tell me that I was late; I stood my ground, saying that I had been ten minutes early and had had no prior notice that the location had been changed. He couldn't deal with that, and sent me to a high Bureau official.

J. Edgar Hoover was still alive and firmly in charge at that time, and Joe Casper, Deputy Assistant Director of the Training Division, was an old Hoover hand. Although Casper was nicknamed "the Ghost" (for the cartoon character Casper the Friendly Ghost), he was anything but friendly. I reiterated my argument to him: that I had been on time, but that the location had been changed. The Ghost tried to tell me that everyone had been sent a letter advising them of the room change, and I replied that all I had was the letter telling me to go to the Old Post Office building. He wanted me to admit that I was wrong and had disobeyed orders, and I wasn't going to do that; I informed the official that I'd been in the army for quite some time and knew all about orders, both giving and receiving them. I thought steam was going to come out of the Ghost's ears as he threatened me with being kicked out of the FBI that very minute. I responded by saying that perhaps that would be best for everyone, if the FBI was such a nit-picking outfit that it didn't know how to treat new agents who had been so actively recruited. The army would take me back in a minute, no questions asked.

"Raise your goddamn right hand," Casper said to me, and proceeded to swear me in, to advise me to shut my mouth, and to warn me that "we'll be watching you" from that moment on. It was a typical attempt to intimidate a new agent, but I was a little older, a little wiser, and a little more used to the ways of a military or quasimilitary bureaucracy than the average recruit, and so stood it reasonably well. This experience left me, however, with a bad taste in my mouth for the "do it by the book" stodginess and inflexibility of the Bureau, an attitude I would continue to fight from that day until my retirement twenty years later.

New Agents Class 70–2 was counseled by two experienced agents in their mid-forties who aspired to higher management in the Bureau, and who, as part of "getting their tickets punched," had to manage a class of new agents successfully through sixteen weeks of training. As I learned, theirs was a "high risk for high gain" proposition, for if the new agents didn't pan out, the counselors could be headed for oblivion rather than for desk jobs at headquarters. Joe "O.C. Joe" O'Connell was known for his work against organized crime figures; a multimillion-dollar lawsuit was pending against him for bugging mob members. (The lawsuit was ultimately dismissed.) He didn't seem worried about that, but he did have a bee in his bonnet about the "white shirts," his nonaffectionate name for headquarters supervisors. These supervisors would come to lecture about various violations of the laws that FBI agents were to administer, and after one had come and gone, O.C. Joe would tell us to throw away the notes we had just taken, and that he would help us prepare for the test on that particular law. He also told anyone that needed extra help to see him in the hall. Today, I look back and recognize that those agents who did regularly see O.C. Joe in the hall for additional guidance—

because they truly needed help—were nevertheless the ones who progressed well up the management ladder, while many smarter agents
toiled in the field for years and never made supervisor.

The other counselor was Bud Abbott, nicknamed "Shakey"
because of his nervousness. What he was nervous about was the antiestablishment attitude of O.C. Joe. Because the two men shared this
particular class, their fates were tied one to another, and Shakey, a
rather standard bureaucrat, was worried that O.C. Joe's antics would
sabotage his own attempts to land a headquarters job. Eventually, both
men went on to higher management, so I guess we must have done
well enough to satisfy the powers above.

After training, I put in several years of fieldwork as a Special
Agent based at the FBI offices in Chicago, New Orleans, and Cleveland. During those years of the early 1970s, the Bureau had opened
the new FBI Academy at Quantico, Virginia, the last positive legacy
of J. Edgar Hoover, who had championed the building of what was to
be the world's finest training facility for law-enforcement personnel.
Ken Joseph had been tapped to come to headquarters and help in the
setting up of the Quantico programs, and in 1974, he pulled me in
from Cleveland. At the FBI National Academy (FBINA), I began as
a baby-sitter for the visiting policemen; each instructor handled about
fifty students, shepherding them through the several-month program.
By June of 1974, I was convinced that I should make a stay at Quantico
part of my FBI resume; the academic environment was attractive, as
was the beautiful Virginia countryside, and I also thought that a stint
at Quantico was imperative if I was to go up the ladder into higher FBI
management. Another factor luring me to Quantico was the fledgling
Behavioral Sciences Unit, then consisting mainly of two senior men,
Howard Teten and Pat Mullany, a Mutt and Jeff team. They always
taught together, and were quite a pair, with Teten the six-seven, thin
straight man and Mullany the five-ten, slightly chubby comic. Teten,
quiet, low-key, and methodical, and Mullany, quick and energetic,
devoted most of their time to teaching, but now and then analyzed a
violent crime and "profiled" the appearance and behavior of likely
suspects. They were my mentors in profiling, and within a few years,
when they retired, I took up the mantle of chief profiler.

Learning to profile was an ongoing process, part of trying to
understand the violent criminal mind, something I was also pursuing
personally in another way in my lectures at Quantico about abnormal
and criminal psychology. The people who commit crimes against other
people, crimes that have nothing to do with money, are a different

breed from the ordinary criminals whose motivation is profit. Murderers, rapists, and child molesters aren't seeking monetary profit from their crimes; in a perverse though sometimes understandable way, they are seeking emotional satisfaction. That makes them different, and, to me, that makes them interesting.

At Quantico, I taught subjects ranging from abnormal psych to interviewing techniques; and I discovered that I was a pretty good teacher. I also learned that I liked being an instructor. We got to go on the road for our training sessions, both nationally and sometimes internationally, and while travel can be wearing, we did journey to some interesting places overseas and met a great many law-enforcement personnel.

It was at one of these international sessions that I coined the term *serial killer*, now much in use. At that time, killings such as those of "Son of Sam" killer David Berkowitz in New York were invariably labeled "stranger killings." This term didn't seem appropriate to me, however, for sometimes killers do know their victims. Various other terms had also been used, but none hit the nail on the head. I'd been invited to participate in a week of lectures at Bramshill, the British police academy, and while there, I took the opportunity to attend the other seminars and lectures. In one of them, a man was discussing what the Brits called crimes in series—a series of rapes, burglaries, arsons, murders. That seemed a highly appropriate way of characterizing the killings of those who do one murder, then another and another in a fairly repetitive way, and so in my classes at Quantico and elsewhere I began referring to "serial killers." The nomenclature didn't seem to be a big deal at the time; it was part of our overall effort in trying to get a handle on these monstrous crimes, of seeking ways of comprehending them so we could move more quickly toward apprehending the next serial killer.

Now that I look back on that naming event, I think that what was also in my mind were the serial adventures we used to see on Saturday at the movies (the one I liked best was the Phantom). Each week, you'd be lured back to see another episode, because at the end of each one there was a cliff-hanger. In dramatic terms, this wasn't a satisfactory ending, because it increased, not lessened the tension. The same dissatisfaction occurs in the minds of serial killers. The very act of killing leaves the murderer hanging, because it isn't as perfect as his fantasy. When the Phantom is left sinking in the quicksand, the viewer has to come back next week to see how the hero gets out of difficulty. After a murder, the serial murderer thinks of how the crime could have been bettered. "Good heavens, I killed her too quickly. I didn't take time to have enough fun, to torture her properly. I should have approached her a new way, thought up a different way of sexually assaulting her." When he follows this sort of train of thought, his mind jumps ahead to how he can kill more nearly perfectly the next time; there's an improvement continuum.

That's not how the public imagines serial killers, however. Most people conceive of the murderer as being a kind of Jekyll and Hyde: One day he's normal and on the next a physiological drive is taking hold—his hair is growing, his fangs are lengthening—so that when the moon is full, he'll have to seize another victim. Serial killers are not like that. They are obsessed with a fantasy, and they have what we must call nonfulfilled experiences that become part of the fantasy and push them on toward the next killing. That's the real meaning behind the term *serial killer*.

Between 1975 and 1977, I became involved in teaching hostage negotiation techniques. The Bureau had been quite a bit behind the New York City police department, the leader in understanding and dealing with hostage situations. However, it had succeeded in extracting a good deal of information about such situations from the New York City experts, Capt. Frank Bolz and Det. Harvey Schlossberg. We expanded and taught the techniques to law-enforcement agencies throughout the country. As an army reserve officer, I also taught such techniques to MP and CID contingents, and I estimate that over the past fifteen years I have actually instructed about 90 percent of those in the U. S. Army throughout the world who are trained in hostage negotiations.

It was an interesting time in law enforcement. In the late 1960s and early 1970s, a large number of men came out of the military— ex–Green Berets and other men schooled in the jungles of Vietnam— and went into police forces. Their skill and expertise with weaponry and assault tactics became the basis of SWAT teams, an entirely new concept in American law enforcement. A SWAT team is essentially a paramilitary force, and we'd never had such forces before. Even in the FBI, where agents were trained in the use of rifles and machine guns as well as pistols, until these years there had been little attention paid to the paramilitary aspects of making a raid. SWAT teams were sexy, however, and drew media attention. SWAT teams used snipers to kill criminals, and such heavy weaponry as assault rifles and grenade launchers in their attempts to storm hideouts or to rescue hostages. The problem was that these tactics were producing a lot of carnage. Mostly, criminals were being killed, but police officers were also going down in record numbers, and there were a fair number of hostages hurt, as well. The NYPD had started its hostage negotiation team in an effort to avoid the carnage, and the FBI quickly embraced the idea of advocating a softer approach to hostage situations.

I liked this approach because it emphasized the need to understand the criminal mind, which was my own hobbyhorse, and, of course, was the basis for profiling. At that time, law-enforcement people were unprepared for an understanding approach. Most police lacked any real training in psychology, and were more prone to think in terms of using force than using persuasion. However, as the FBI took over the teaching of hostage negotiation techniques and added its own spin, the whole trend of using SWAT teams turned around, and so did the number of deaths in hostage situations. It became accepted practice to talk first, and to avoid using weaponry whenever possible. This approach was also midwifed into existence by some lawsuits against various police jurisdictions for undue use of force, lawsuits that cost cities millions of dollars. These soon translated into mandates to exhaust all nonviolent avenues before resorting to SWAT team assaults.

Within a decade, the behavioral approach to crime would go far beyond hostage negotiation and profiling, into the establishment of the FBI's National Center for the Analysis of Violent Crime, and the Violent Criminal Apprehension Program; I was at the forefront of nurturing into existence both the NCAVC and VICAP—but I'm getting ahead of my story, and so will leave those developments for a later chapter.

While I was in Cleveland, as instructor of a traveling school—a road show, as we called it—I became involved in a hostage negotiation crisis. A black gunman held a police captain and a seventeen-year-old girl hostage inside the Warrensville Heights police station, and we were trying to talk everyone out and avoid bloodshed. Somehow, the gunman's demands had been made public. Among them were that he wanted all white people immediately to leave the face of the earth, and he wanted to speak with President Jimmy Carter about this. Since these particular demands were clearly not rational, I made no attempt to meet them. At the command site, I was handed a telephone and told that someone important wanted to speak to me. It was Jody Powell, the President's press secretary, who informed me that the White House had learned of the situation and that President Carter was ready to

speak to "the terrorist." Dumbfounded, I told Powell that we had no
terrorists in Cleveland. Trying to be polite, yet incredulous that the
White House would even think to intervene in such a delicate situation,
I lied to Powell and told him that we were unable to raise the gunman
on the phone just then; if we had need of the President, I said, we'd
call back. The situation was resolved without bloodshed and without
presidential intervention.

I was in charge of the FBI's hostage training for just two years,
but continued to be involved in the area for many years after 1977—
mostly, as the chief resident terrorist. At a remote desert atomic facility
in 1978, at Lake Placid in the early 1980s, and at other sites throughout
that decade, major law-enforcement agencies of our government and
of some foreign countries participated in full-scale, week-long simulations of terrorist attacks and subsequent hostage negotiations. On several of these exercises, I played the part of the head terrorist. We would
hijack a busload of volunteers who played important people—scientists
or visiting dignitaries, for example—and take them to an isolated farm
or ski lodge, where we would hold them hostage. Real guns, grenades,
dynamite, and other weapons were used, and when I demanded an
airliner to fly us out of the country, one was commandeered and
delivered to the nearest airstrip. Once the exercise had begun, we were
in earnest about it, and stayed in character. At Lake Placid, I was
"10," while an FBI machine-gun expert was "20," and the parts of
"30," "40," "50," and "60" were taken by men from the CIA, the
Secret Service, the army's Delta Force and from the British counterpart
of that Delta Force, the SAS. These simulations were so realistic that
some hostages became subject to the "Stockholm syndrome," in which
the hostage so identifies with the hostage-takers that he or she is willing
to act with them in order to survive. The men on the other side of the
telephone from me, negotiating for the FBI, were former students of
mine who sometimes complained that I was too tough an adversary
because I knew and countered all of their tricks. In each exercise,
however, the "good guys" did manage to retake the hostages and the
terrorists, though not always without—simulated—bloodshed.

That I had gotten into teaching hostage negotiating techniques
at all, in the mid-1970s, was a sign of restlessness on my part. Not
entirely comfortable with repeating the same lessons in classes all the
time, I thirsted for new challenges. Many of my fellow instructors at
Quantico were not interested in looking for something new to do;
innovation is discouraged in most bureaucracies, and the FBI is no
exception, though management claimed they always encouraged in-

structors to improve their techniques and presentation. A lot of guys were perfectly content to teach "canned" cases, the majority of which they had inherited from an earlier generation of instructors. My colleague John Minderman called such instructors "oil slicks," because they covered a lot of territory but only at a depth of a millimeter or so. Minderman, a former San Francisco motorcycle policeman, taught me a good deal about how to relate to the police officers who made up the bulk of our classes.

Most of the cases I expounded upon in my criminology lectures were not canned, but widely known cases where the basic information came from sources available to the public. Books and articles about Charles Manson, Sirhan Sirhan, David Berkowitz, the Texas Tower killer Charles Whitman, and so on, formed the basis of our arsenal. Studying these cases intently, I began to see that our classes were not presenting original or unique information on these killers, principally because none was readily available. The books on Manson had been written from the point of view of the prosecuting attorney, or from a gleaning of media coverage and interviews with ancillary members of Manson's entourage. Where was the unique understanding of the mind of Manson that a police officer would want to gain from having attended a course on criminal psychology at the world's leading facility for the teaching of law enforcement? Most people, viewing the Manson cases from the outside, had long ago decided that Manson was "crazy" and that nothing further could be gained from studying what he had done. What if he wasn't precisely "crazy"? Would that mean there was new understanding to be gotten from the Manson-inspired murders? Unfortunately, that question couldn't be answered, because all we had to go on was what everyone else had. On Richard Speck, killer of eight nurses in Chicago, the material was somewhat better, a book written by a psychiatrist who had done extensive interviews with him. Even these interviews were inadequate, though, because the man who had conducted them did not have the background in dealing with criminals, or the need to understand matters from a law-enforcement perspective, that would be necessary for our students. I wanted to better understand the mind of the violent criminal, first of all to satisfy my own curiosity, but also in order to become a better teacher, so that our classes at the FBI Academy would be more highly prized by the police personnel who attended them.

At the time that I came to this conclusion, the FBI was almost completely uninterested in murderers, rapists, child molesters, and other criminals who prey on their fellowmen. Most of these violent-behavior cases fell entirely within the jurisdiction of local law-enforcement agencies and were not violations of the federal laws that the FBI was charged with enforcing. At the Academy, we did teach criminology to visiting police officers, so the study of the criminal mind was a relevant exercise for me—but, in the eyes of most of my colleagues and superiors, it was only barely relevant. They wanted no part of it. Conversely, I became deeply intrigued by it.

I was encouraged in pursuing my interests by people I met at the conferences and conventions I was beginning to attend, gatherings of professionals in mental health and related fields. My curiosity brought me into the American Psychiatric Association, the American Academy of Forensic Sciences, the American Academy of Psychiatry and the Law, among others. None of my colleagues at the FBI saw any value in associations like these, and the Bureau did not consider them particularly worthwhile, either; for many years, I paid all my dues as a member of these and other organizations myself, although the Bureau occasionally did reimburse me for attendance at professional conferences. The Bureau's avoidance of mental-health professionals was of a piece with the Bureau's belief that if there was something worth knowing about criminals, the Bureau already knew it.

I had a different view, a sense that there was a great deal to be learned, and that many experts outside of law enforcement could teach us things we didn't know. Certainly my outlook and horizons expanded when I attended professional conferences and, later, was invited to speak at them and share my work with people other than police officials. Meeting psychiatrists, psychologists, people active in caring for victims of violent crime, and other mental-health professionals gave me the impetus to look further into doing the sort of research that I was uniquely positioned to do.

As I traveled around the country doing road schools, I began to drop in at local police departments and ask them for copies of case files on particularly violent offenders—rapists, child molesters, murderers. Because of my years of liaison work with policing agencies, I was able to talk rather easily with the various authorities, and to obtain such information. If I was interested in a case, when an officer from the jurisdiction involved in that case showed up for training at Quantico, I'd assign them the task of assembling their department's files on the case for their own miniresearch report, and would gratefully accept a copy of the materials for my own private burgeoning file cabinets of data. People were so cooperative, so interested in the area of trying to systematize what we knew and didn't know about violent criminals, that they sent me reams of stuff. In a way, their cooperation was a recognition of our great need for information and for understanding in this area.

At around this time, I came across a quotation from Nietzsche that stuck with me. It seemed to pinpoint both the fascination I had with this research and the dangers it posed. Thereafter, I put it on a slide that I always showed during my lectures and presentations. Here it is:

Whoever fights monsters should see to it that in the process he does not become a monster. And when you look into an abyss, the abyss also looks into you.

It was important for me to keep such sobering thoughts in mind as I proceeded to muck about in the depths of human criminality. As a result of my inquiries and requests for information, I soon had far more factual files on violent criminals than were available to the news media or any local police department, and I had more of them than anyone else—perhaps because very few people were asking for them. As the quotation suggests, dealing with monsters entails problems. Then, too, other seekers encountered a procedural difficulty: Academics couldn't obtain police files as easily as an FBI man could, and they had often been discouraged from trying. So I was in a privileged position from which to undertake this research.

In the office and at home, I pored over this material, gaining occasional new insights from it, systematically analyzing it, and began to get a feeling for the possibilities of doing in-depth research that would lead to a greater understanding of violent offenders. At last, I came to the point where I wanted very much to talk to the people about whom I'd been lecturing, the killers themselves. I discussed this idea with John Minderman, and we decided we'd have a go at it. We wanted to learn more about what factors in the killer's environment, childhood, and background made him want to commit such crimes. And we also wanted to know many more details about the crimes themselves—what happened during the assault, what went on immediately after the killer was certain that the victim had died, how had he chosen the site for disposal of the body. If we got enough information from enough interviewees, we'd be able to compile useful lists: So many took souvenirs; so many read or viewed pornographic materials. Then, too, there were some old chestnuts in regard to murder that we wanted to test; for instance, whether killers really did return to the scenes of their crimes.

Grace Hopper, a naval admiral and computer expert, had come to Quantico to give a lecture, and she was especially eloquent in describing her strategies for dealing with the bureaucracy of the Navy when she wanted to get something innovative accomplished. She said that the basis of her success in neutralizing the bureaucracy was the axiom "It is better to ask forgiveness than to ask permission." Once something was out on paper in a request format, Hopper said, if it was then denied, the project was dead. But if it's *not* on paper . . . well, you get the idea. To avoid being stopped before I got started, I thought that I'd better go ahead with my pet project to interview some killers, and not tell anyone in a supervisory capacity about it.

In early 1978, I was to go to northern California to teach at a road school, and I saw a window of opportunity. Agent John Conway, who had been in one of my classes at Quantico, was stationed in San Rafael and was the Bureau's liaison officer to the California prison system. I asked Conway to locate certain offenders in the California prisons, and when I arrived for my week of teaching, he had all the information ready for me. As Bureau agents, we could enter any prison in the country just by showing our badges to the prison authorities, and once inside, we didn't have to explain why we wished to interview any particular offender. So, on a Friday, after four days of teaching, Conway and I took off on a whirlwind tour of prisons and inmates that lasted through the weekend and into the next week. In one swoop, we interviewed seven of the most dangerous and notorious murderers ever apprehended in the United States: Sirhan Sirhan, Charles Manson, Tex Watson (a Manson associate), Juan Corona (killer of many migrant workers), Herbert Mullin (who had killed fourteen people), John Frazier (who had killed six), and Edmund Kemper. Interviewing convicted killers in this way had never been done before and was a breakthrough of rare proportions.

My first interview was with Sirhan Sirhan, in Soledad. The prison authorities put Conway and me in a fairly large room, one that appeared to be used for staff meetings. It was not really intimate enough for my purposes, but we made do. Sirhan entered the room with his eyes wild, frightened, and apprehensive. He stood against the wall, with his fist clenched, and refused to shake hands. He demanded to know what we wanted from him; he believed that if we were really FBI agents, we were probably consorting with the Secret Service, who regularly conducted interviews with assassins. The Secret Service's interviews were conducted for reasons unrelated to ours. At the time of his conviction for the assassination of Senator Robert F. Kennedy, Sirhan had been diagnosed as exhibiting all the signs of paranoid schizophrenia. Now we were seeing why. He didn't want to let us use a tape recorder, and wanted to talk to a lawyer. I told him this was all informal and preliminary, and that we were just there to talk.

To coax Sirhan out of his fright, I asked him about the prison system itself, and that got his motor going. He was annoyed at a former cellmate who had ''betrayed'' him by speaking to an interviewer from *Playboy*. Slowly, he began to relax his fist, to edge closer to the table where Conway and I sat, and, eventually, to sit down and be somewhat more at ease.

He told me, for instance, that he had heard voices that told him to assassinate the senator, and that once, when he had been looking into a mirror, he had felt his face cracking and falling in pieces to the floor; both of these were consistent with a diagnosis of paranoid schizophrenia. When he got rolling, Sirhan always referred to himself in the third person: Sirhan did this, Sirhan felt that. He said that he was in protective custody not because the prison authorities feared for his life—which was the actual case—but because the authorities were treating him with more respect than they accorded common thieves and child molesters.

Sirhan is an Arab who grew up in a war zone, and his motivations and orientation had much to do with those facts. Out of the blue, for instance, he asked me whether Mark Felt was a Jew. Felt was a high-ranking, high-profile assistant director of the FBI; the question from Sirhan reflected his beliefs about the world. Sirhan said that he had learned that Senator Kennedy supported the selling of more jet fighter planes to Israel, and that by assassinating Kennedy, Sirhan had prevented the elevation to the presidency of a man who would continue to befriend Israel—and therefore he, Sirhan, had changed world history and helped the Arab countries. He believed that the parole board was afraid to put him back on the streets because they feared his personal magnetism. He preferred, if released, to go back to Jordan, where, he was certain, people would pick him up on their shoulders and parade him through the streets as a hero. He saw himself as having done something that was not correctly understood at the time but that would become clear only in historical perspective.

Sirhan had studied political science in college, and told me he had wanted to be a diplomat, to work in our State Department and eventually become an ambassador. He admired the Kennedys—but he shot one of the clan. The psychotic desire to fuse oneself through assassination with a notable figure is common among men such as Sirhan, John Hinckley, Mark Chapman, and Arthur Bremer. Sirhan knew that ten years in prison was about the average that one spent for such a crime in the United States, and therefore he felt that now, in 1978, he should be released; he believed he had good potential for being rehabilitated unless he remained in jail too long.

At the end of the interview, he stood at the door, sucking in his stomach, flexing his muscles, giving me a profile of his magnificence. He had done quite a bit of weight lifting and was somewhat sculpted. He said, "Well, Mr. Ressler, what do you think of Sirhan now?"

I didn't answer the question, and Sirhan was then taken away. Obviously, he felt that to know Sirhan was to love him: the schizoid aspects of his behavior had diminished in prison, but not the paranoia. Sirhan refused any further interviews with us for the program.

Frazier, Mullin, and Corona all fell quite completely into the "disorganized" category of killers, and were nearly so mentally strange that I hardly got anywhere with them at all. Corona was entirely uncommunicative, and Frazier was a prisoner of his delusions. Mullin was docile and polite but really had nothing to say.

I had better luck with Charles Manson, Tex Watson, and the others, who could most definitely be placed in the category of "organized" killers, though Manson and his associates had taken pains to make their murders appear as if some disorganized personality had committed them.

Before going to see any of these killers, I had, of course, done a great deal of research into them and their crimes, and as a result had obtained rather deep knowledge of each man; this stood me especially well in regard to Manson. He wanted to know, as he entered the interview area, what the FBI wanted with him and why he should talk to us. Once I had convinced him that I was interested in him as a human being, I got a very good response, for Manson is a great talker and his favorite subject is himself. I discovered him to have a complex, wonderfully manipulative personality, and learned a great deal about how he perceived himself in relation to the world and how he had manipulated those who killed for him. Far from insane, he had keen insight into his crimes and into the personalities and rationales of those who had been fatally attracted to his charismatic presence. The information gleaned from this preliminary interview with Manson was more than I'd hoped for, and certified to me that doing such interviews in depth would result in whole new insights into the behavior of such killers. There was nothing in the literature to compare with what I was getting from the killer himself. Formerly, I and everyone else looking into these matters had been on the outside of a killer's mind, looking in; now I was gaining a unique perspective, from the inside of that mind, looking out.

I'll tell the story of the interview with Manson and subsequent interviews with killers in detail in the next chapters, but for the present, I want to bring forward the narrative of how the interviewing of murderers was brought into the rather rigid structure of the FBI.

About halfway through the week of interviewing, and perhaps as a consequence of dealing with these strange, driven men, I began to become a bit paranoid myself, thinking that I had no sanction from the Bureau to be conducting these interviews and therefore needed a way to cut the Bureau in on them. I should have had prior permission to go and see such well-known inmates as Manson or Sirhan, but I didn't. I figured I was just doing preliminary interviews, not even taking notes, and was just requesting permission from these men to come back later with a tape recorder—but, nonetheless, I should have had something on paper. I had violated a cardinal principle of the Bureau, and had done something without authorization. Actually, agents in the Bureau are divided into two camps by the way they go about their business. There are the majority who ask permission for everything they do because they don't want to get in trouble with the hierarchy. To my way of thinking, such agents are basically insecure. The second group, a much smaller bunch, consists of those who never ask permission to do anything because they want to get things accomplished. I was firmly in the second camp and was getting prepared to pay the consequences for my brash actions. Following Admiral Hopper's rule, I hoped that if and when I was called on the carpet, I'd devise a strategy for dealing with that eventuality.

When I got back to Quantico, however, I was so excited by the new information that I decided to make another run before putting things down on paper, at which point my ''project'' could very likely be deep-sixed forever. It was the spring of 1978. Not too far away from Quantico was the women's reformatory at Alderson, West Virginia. Two of Manson's ''girls,'' Squeaky Fromme and Sandra Good, were incarcerated there, as well as Sarah Jane Moore, who had tried to assassinate President Gerald Ford. I could interview them all in a day. Minderman was going through a divorce, and decided to return to his home in San Francisco as an FBI squad supervisor. I needed a backup to replace him, and I chose John Douglas, a young, flamboyant agent whom I had earlier championed into the BSU after he had completed a stint at Quantico as a visiting counselor.

I decided to tell my immediate superior, Larry Monroe, what I was going to do. Larry was upset. "You talked to *who* in California? You're going to interview *who* in West Virginia?" I told him not to worry, that after I came back I'd put the whole thing on paper, and Larry made a typical middle-management response. He agreed to let us go to West Virginia on the condition that if, as a result, anything bad happened bureaucratically, he would be able to claim that he had known nothing about it and that it was all my fault. Since it certainly was my fault all the way, I had no problem with this condition.

We talked to all three women, and got some good information. Basically, Fromme and Good bolstered the ideas I had been forming about Manson and his influence, which had been based on my preliminary interviews with Manson and with Tex Watson.

When I got back to Quantico, my own actions could be called "serial"—I now hoped to perfect my crimes by doing still more interviews before I had to face the paper hangman. This strategy was cut short by an accidental leak, however. One of my friends, to whom I had bragged a bit about my exploits, happened to be gossiping about them to someone else in the lunchroom, and didn't realize that Ken Joseph was within earshot. Ken was by now the director of the FBI Academy, and even though he was my mentor, he was the chief administrator, a fan of the late Director Hoover, and of his belief that the hierarchy had to be kept informed at all times of what was going on in the ranks; now he had to act as a high official was obliged by this heritage to do in the face of what was clearly unauthorized behavior by one former Michigan State pal Robert Ressler.

Larry Monroe and I were called onto the carpet in Ken's office and asked why he had not been advised of this Ressler initiative. Fortunately for me, a month or two earlier Joseph had put out a memo that for the first time encouraged instructors to do research, and I told him that my project—a preliminary project, I stressed—had been in response to that memo. Now this wasn't entirely true, and I think all three of us knew that, but we went on without acknowledging that fact. Ken bored in, pointing out that interviewing "significant" people such as Sirhan and Manson could incur liabilities for the Bureau. I replied that I had put my intentions in a memo and circulated that before I'd gone off to California. Ken said he'd never seen that memo, and I blithely suggested that I'd have to see whether a copy could be located in the files somewhere, so I could show it to him. Larry Monroe kept an appropriately straight face through all of this, and so did Ken Joseph, and you can be sure that no smile creased my visage, either. We were engaged in a bureaucratic tap dance well known to the people who toil in government offices. When we left Joseph's carpet, I knew I must now write and backdate that memo, double quick. I wrote an appropriate memo suggesting that I was going to do some "pilot work" in preparation for a major program of interviewing serial killers. Going to the prisons of California was merely to test the waters, to learn whether these convicted killers would be willing to participate in the research.

I then crumpled up the memo, stepped on it a few times, Xeroxed that, then Xeroxed the copy, stuck it in the files, then retrieved it and took it up to Ken Joseph, saying that it must have previously been misfiled and had now luckily been located. That, of course, was not hard for Joseph to believe, since things get misfiled all the time. Moreover, since Joseph was basically in agreement on my idea to interview the inmates, he was willing to play the game properly.

Now that we had "justified" the pilot project, Ken wanted me to write up a complete memo that laid out the true dynamics and dimensions of the actual interviewing project, replete with ground rules for conducting the interviews, liaisons with outside professionals and academic institutions, and so on. I was pleased to do that, and drafts of the proposal went back and forth between me, Larry Monroe, and Ken Joseph until we had a first-class proposal that identified the long-term objectives, the targets to be interviewed, the ways in which both the Bureau and the inmates would be protected, and so on. There was a seven-step approval process before an interview would be conducted; for instance, we would have to certify that anyone whom we were about to interview was not currently going through an appeal. For another instance, we would confine our interviews to the subjects of crimes for which the inmate had previously been judged guilty. We said we wouldn't spend any Bureau money on the interviews, for they would be done as adjuncts to the road schools we regularly conducted. This memo went out in late 1978 over Ken's signature to John McDermott at Bureau headquarters in Washington, an official who was in the top ranks of men just under Director Clarence Kelley.

McDermott was known throughout the Bureau as "the Radish," because he was beet red above the starched white collar, probably due to high blood pressure, which itself had to have been in reaction to the difficulty of serving under Hoover for so long. The Radish looked at what we had styled the Criminal Personality Research Project (which included the information that the "pilot" had been going on for the previous eighteen months)—and turned it down flat.

In the first place, he wrote, the whole idea was ridiculous. The FBI's job was to catch criminals, get them to court, and incarcerate them. Our job was not to do something that a social worker could and should do; we weren't sociologists and shouldn't be; if criminals were to be sympathetically interviewed, that could be done by academics. There was no Bureau tradition of doing something so outrageous as interviewing killers, and, besides that, due to the adversarial relationship we had always enjoyed with the criminal fraternity, the Radish was dead certain that the criminals wouldn't talk to us, anyway.

The Radish's response was completely characteristic, and in keeping with the Bureau attitude of the 1940s, when he had come up under Hoover. The fact that I had managed to interview a dozen convicted killers, that they had talked freely to me, and that the Bureau had thereby gained some insight into criminal behavior was totally ignored. Tradition held no precedent for this sort of action, and if there was no precedent, the action could not possibly be any good. One of my objectives in the memo had been to involve outside authorities on criminal behavior and abnormal psychology, and the Radish didn't like that, either, because it went against the old Bureau attitude that no outsider could ever teach us anything of value. That posture was absurd, as was the Radish's whole response—but once he had said no to the memo, the project was dead. Grace Hopper's rule had come home with a vengeance. I couldn't do any more prisoner interviews.

So I simply waited until the Radish had retired and Clarence Kelley had been replaced by the forward-looking William Webster. By this point, Ken Joseph himself had also retired, but our new administrative head, James McKenzie, was enthusiastic about the project. McKenzie was the youngest man ever to reach the level of assistant director, and his rise toward the top was an indication of his abilities and his understanding of the bureaucracy. What McKenzie did was resubmit the memo to Webster, with very few changes. The new director had been given a mandate to take the FBI in a new direction, and he had talked about collaborating with outside experts and about breaking into previously uncharted areas. His initial response to the memo was to want to hear more, and he invited me, McKenzie, and Monroe to a "working lunch" in his office.

The lunch was held in a midsized conference room adjacent to the director's office, one of those bland places beloved of people who plan the newer government buildings. A number of bureaucratic hangers-on from Quantico had attached themselves to the project from above, so we had a good-sized crowd, but this was my baby, so I made the presentation. The others ate their lunches and didn't say much. I had a sandwich in front of me but couldn't really eat it because I was very busy talking. Director Webster was a cool and collected man, skilled in not revealing his emotions, and during my pitch, I received no sign that he either liked or disliked the idea. He was so hard to read that I despaired of trying. At last, however, I made the point that this project had been previously rejected by the Radish, and that got his attention, because Webster had been brought in to move the Bureau in new directions.

Now the director went from passive to active, and—in an action that was somewhat amazing in the light of usual bureaucratic procedure—we got a go-ahead at the same lunch meeting in which we presented. He endorsed the project, but only if it was done correctly. He didn't want it conducted on a haphazard basis; the phrase he used to deprecate the ordinary way of doing it was "shoe-box research." He insisted that we collaborate with first-class universities and hospitals, and was pleased that the major collaborators I had chosen came from Boston University and Boston City Hospital, and that others included in the project were among the country's recognized academic experts in psychiatry, psychology, and the study of criminal behavior. They were all people I had met at conferences and had been talking to for years. Shortly, the project was approved all up and down the hierarchical ladder of the FBI.

Later I was amused to learn that the session with Webster had truly been a working lunch, for I got a memo asking for seven dollars for the sandwich I had not eaten because I was too busy talking. But we had a "go," and that was what was really important. In the ensuing months, too, we obtained funding for some of the research from the Department of Justice. Now we'd even be able to spend an entire week interviewing inmates and not have to piggyback that research onto a road school.

Before the Criminal Personality Research Project was funded, but when I knew that approval and funding were solidly in the works, I decided to go and see William Heirens, the killer in whom I had been so interested when I was nine years old. An associate and I were—as usual—at a road school, this one in St. Louis, when we drove to a southern Illinois correctional facility to see Heirens. Heirens had been in prison for more than thirty years, and was now a man in his late forties. I explained to him that I'd been intrigued by his crimes since childhood, and that in a sense we had grown up together in Chicago. He'd been seventeen when I was nine, and now the age difference of eight years seemed even less a barrier than it had then.

In the interim between the 1940s and the 1970s, I'd learned a lot about Heirens, about the sexual content of his murders, about the string of fetish burglaries that had preceded them, about the many unsolved attempted murders and slashings to which he had been tentatively connected, and about his ability to conceal his crimes from family and friends. His initial defense had been as extraordinary as his crimes: He claimed that the crimes had been done by another person, George Murman, who had lived with him. Heirens had even taken investigators to the sites of the three murders and had been able to retrace his actions during those murders, which gave the lie to his pinning them on George Murman. Only under close questioning had he admitted that George Murman lived inside his head.

Heirens was not really a multiple personality, but his problems had begun and become evident when he was quite young. They blossomed to visible proportions as a young teenager: He had sexual fantasies and in the secrecy of his room pasted pictures of Nazi leaders into a scrapbook and stared at them while trying on women's undergarments. After the thirteen-year-old was discovered to have an arsenal of pistols and rifles in addition to the secret photos, and admitted to several burglaries and fire-settings, he'd been sent to a Catholic boarding school as an alternative to incarceration. In a few years, he had completed his studies at the boarding school and his behavior was deemed appropriate to reentering society, especially since he had done so well academically that he was going to be allowed to skip most of his freshman year work at the University of Chicago and take some advanced studies. His murders began shortly after he was let out of the boarding school, and in retrospect could be seen as a continuation of the burglaries and other crimes he had committed earlier in his teenage years. In fact, in between the murders, Heirens committed many more burglaries.

Heirens had never actually gone to trial. In pretrial work, psychiatrists had advised his counsel that although Heirens might be able to claim that he was subject to becoming George Murman (Murder-man?) and not really responsible for his actions at certain times, no jury would understand or believe that, and if tried, he would undoubtedly be given a death sentence. The evidence against him, consisting of fingerprints, handwriting, "souvenirs" found in his rooms, and his confession, was overwhelming. The alternative to a trial was to plead guilty, and for the psychiatrists to recommend a prison sentence and treatment. Heirens took the bargain, pleaded guilty, and was sentenced to life. After his conviction, his parents divorced, changed their names, and started accusing each other of having been responsible for their son's crimes. As for Heirens, since his conviction, he had been a model prisoner, the first prisoner in the state to complete his bachelor's degree while incarcerated, and had even gone on to postgraduate work.

I was really primed for my interview with this man whose life I had been following since childhood, but the interview didn't go as well as I'd hoped. He did respond to my knowing a lot about him, but he no longer wished to admit to the crimes to which he had once pleaded guilty. He had decided he'd been framed, and so would no longer acknowledge—as he had done in the 1940s, after his arrest— that he had killed two adult women who surprised him while he was in the midst of masturbating in their homes, or that he had strangled and dismembered a six-year-old girl. I remembered particularly that he had overpowered Suzanne Degnan in her bed, and when her mother had called out to see whether the child was all right, he had forced Suzanne to say that she was, and then had waited until the mother must have concluded that the child was asleep. Only after that did he kill the little girl, roll her in a blanket, take her to a basement for his sexual assaults and dismembering, and then cooly dispose of the body and return to his dormitory room. Here was a monster, now denying his culpability.

Heirens did acknowledge having had some sexual problems and having committed the break-ins that he now deprecated as adolescent pranks; he said he'd never been a danger to society and that his years as a model prisoner qualified him to spend the remainder of his life out of prison.

A disappointment. The larger issue, however, the attempt to learn from carefully conducted interviews with convicted serial killers some information that would be helpful to law enforcement, was now on track, part of an established program within the Bureau and the Department of Justice. In time, I would personally interview more than a hundred of the most dangerous violent criminals in the prisons of the United States, and train others to continue this task, and with the information so gained add significantly to our understanding of many murderous patterns and how to apprehend the people in whose minds those patterns were born. In his youth, Bill Heirens had written on a mirror, in lipstick, "Stop me before I kill more." I would interview serial murderers in an attempt to learn how to do just that.

3

INTERVIEWS WITH MURDERERS

I was nearing the end of my third interview with Edmund Kemper, an enormous man, six feet nine inches in height and weighing nearly three hundred pounds, a man of extremely high intelligence who in his youth had killed his grandparents, spent four years in youth facilities, then had emerged, only to kill seven more people, including his mother. Kemper was serving seven consecutive life terms. Twice before, I had ventured into the Vacaville prison in California to see and talk with him, the first time accompanied by John Conway, the second time by Conway and by my Quantico associate John Douglas, whom I was breaking in. During those sessions, we had gone quite deeply into his past, his motivations for murder, and the fantasies that were intertwined with those crimes. This was a man of great intellectual complexity, whose murders had included the beheading and dismembering of his victims. No one had ever succeeded in talking to him in the ways and at the depths we had achieved. I was so pleased at the rapport I had reached with Kemper that I was emboldened to attempt a third session with him alone. It took place in a cell just off death row, the sort of place used for giving a last benediction to a man about to die in the gas chamber. Although Kemper was in the general population, rather than isolated from it, this was the place that the prison authorities had chosen for our interview. After conversing with Kemper in this claustrophobic locked cell for four hours, dealing with matters that entail behavior at the extreme edge of depravity, I felt that we had reached the end of what there was to discuss, and I pushed the buzzer to summon the guard to come and let me out of the cell.

No guard immediately appeared, so I continued on with the conversation. Most serial murderers are pretty much loners; even so, they look forward to anything that eases the boredom of their confinement, and that includes visits such as mine. They have a lot on their minds and, properly approached, they are inclined to talk. Conversations with them are rather readily prolonged. Kemper and I had now talked ourselves out, though. After another few minutes had passed, I pressed the buzzer a second time, but still got no response. Fifteen minutes after my first call, I made a third buzz, yet no guard came.

A look of apprehension must have come over my face despite my attempts to keep calm and cool, and Kemper, keenly sensitive to other people's psyches (as most killers are), picked up on this.

"Relax. They're changing the shift, feeding the guys in the secure areas." He smiled and got up from his chair, making more apparent his huge size. "Might be fifteen, twenty minutes before they come and get you," he said to me.

Though I felt I was maintaining a cool and collected posture, I'm sure I reacted to this information with somewhat more overt indications of panic, and Kemper responded to these.

"If I went apeshit in here, you'd be in a lot of trouble, wouldn't you? I could screw your head off and place it on the table to greet the guard."

My mind raced. I envisioned him reaching for me with his large arms, pinning me to a wall in a stranglehold, and then jerking my head around until my neck was broken. It wouldn't take long, and the size difference between us would almost certainly ensure that I wouldn't be able to fight him off very long before succumbing. He was correct: He could kill me before I or anyone else could stop him. So I told Kemper that if he messed with me, he'd be in deep trouble himself.

"What would they do—cut off my TV privileges?" he scoffed.

I retorted that he would certainly end up "in the hole"— solitary confinement—for an extremely long period of time. Both he and I knew that many inmates put in the hole are forced by such isolation into at least temporary insanity.

Kemper shrugged this off by telling me that he was an old hand at being in prisons, that he could withstand the pain of solitary and that it wouldn't last forever. Eventually, he would be returned to a more normal confinement status, and his "trouble" would pale before the prestige he would have gained among the prisoners by "offing" an FBI agent.

My pulse did the hundred-yard dash as I tried to think of

something to say or do to prevent Kemper from killing me. I was fairly sure that he wouldn't do it, but I couldn't be completely certain, for this was an extremely violent and dangerous man with, as he implied, very little left to lose. How had I been dumb enough to come in here alone?

Suddenly, I knew how I had embroiled myself in such a situation. Of all people who should have known better, I had succumbed to what students of hostage-taking events know as "Stockholm syndrome"—I had identified with my captor and transferred my trust to him. Although I had been the chief instructor in hostage negotiation techniques for the FBI, I had forgotten this essential fact! Next time, I wouldn't be so arrogant about the rapport I believed I had achieved with a murderer. Next time.

"Ed," I said, "surely you don't think I'd come in here without some method of defending myself, do you?"

"Don't shit me, Ressler. They wouldn't let you up here with any weapons on you."

Kemper's observation, of course, was quite true, because inside a prison, visitors are not allowed to carry weapons, lest these be seized by inmates and used to threaten the guards or otherwise aid an escape. I nevertheless indicated that FBI agents were accorded special privileges that ordinary guards, police, or other people who entered a prison did not share.

"What've you got, then?"

"I'm not going to give away what I might have or where I might have it on me."

"Come on, come on; what is it—a poison pen?"

"Maybe. But those aren't the only weapons one could have."

"Martial arts, then," Kemper mused. "Karate? Got your black belt? Think you can take me?"

With this, I felt that the tide had shifted a bit, if not turned. There was a hint of kidding in his voice—I hoped. But I wasn't sure, and he understood that I wasn't sure, and he decided he'd continue to try and rattle me. By this time, however, I had regained some composure, and thought back to my hostage negotiation techniques, the most fundamental of which is to keep talking and talking and talking, because stalling always seems to defuse the situation. We discussed martial arts, which many inmates studied as a way to defend themselves in the very tough place that is prison, until, at last, a guard appeared and unlocked the cell door.

The procedure is for the interviewer to remain in the room while the guard takes the inmate back to his own cell. As Kemper get ready to walk off down the hall with the guard, he put his hand on my shoulder.

"You know I was just kidding, don't you?"

"Sure," I said, and let out a deep breath.

I resolved never to put myself or any other FBI interviewer in a similar position again. From then on, it became our policy never to interview a convicted killer or rapist or child molester alone; we'd do that in pairs.

The Criminal Personality Research Project was my baby, and as it got going in the late 1970s, I threw myself into it, taking opportunities when I was out of town at road schools to interview men (and a few women) in various prisons around the country. Before I stopped doing all the interviewing myself, and turned the task over to associates, I had interviewed more than a hundred convicted violent criminals, more than any other man alive. (My efforts were eventually recognized within the FBI, and by associated institutions, when I twice won the Jefferson Award, announced annually by the University of Virginia, for which the FBI's Quantico campus functions as an extension school.) The information collected from these interviews was systematized and analyzed for the CPRP, and eventually my research associates and I were able to discern and document certain patterns in the backgrounds and behaviors of these murderers. The patterns of their childhoods and adolescences, their precrime stresses, and the ways in which they acted during their crimes forms the basis of several later chapters in this book. Before going into those conclusions, however, I want to concentrate on the art of interviewing convicted murderers, and on a few of the highlights of the time I spent in small rooms inside various prisons, speaking with these intense people who had committed the crime held by society to be the most serious of all offenses.

Interviewing violent criminals is only valuable insofar as it can provide insight into their actions and personalities that can be of importance to law enforcement. To extract such information, the interviewer needs to be taken seriously by the inmate, and to achieve a level of trust so that the inmate will talk freely. And to do that, you have to earn the inmate's respect.

Establishing respect requires a good deal of masking your personal feelings about the heinous crimes these people have committed. If, while a murderer was describing the way he had mutilated a body, I had conveyed my disgust by body language or facial grimace, that would have ended the discussion. On the other end of the spectrum, if I said something in response such as, "Oh, you cut her head off. No big deal, I know a lot of guys who did that," the murderer wouldn't be inclined to give me much further detail, either. Humoring violent criminals is not the way to deal with them. These people may be crazy, but they're not stupid—nor entirely insensitive to the nuances of interpersonal behavior.

Most interrogators move in too quickly to ask the difficult questions. Then the mental barriers go up and the interview is effectively terminated. These inmates have all the time in the world, and if they don't feel comfortable, you'll come out of the interview with nothing; therefore, it's imperative to spend time allowing them to feel good about revealing intimate details of their lives to you. I proceed slowly, stroking, probing gently, and moving closer and closer until I feel the moment is right to ask the hard questions; sometimes it takes many hours, or multiple visits.

A number of men and women who worked in the Behavioral Sciences Unit were not up to the formidable task of interviewing convicted violent criminals for one reason or another. One colleague of mine had to interview a man who had molested and murdered several children. The interviewer had children of his own, disliked the killer because of it, and the interview session became hopelessly compromised. When the inmate objected to cigarette smoke in the room and wanted to open a window, the agent responded that he should sit down and answer the questions without objection. When the interview subject was asked one of our standard questions—what he might rather have done if he had not entered into criminal pursuits—the convicted man said he would have liked to have been an astronaut.

"Yeah, and you'd have liked to have a little boy there in the cabin with you," the agent said in an aside to an FBI colleague in the room.

That was unnecessarily hostile behavior on the agent's part, antagonistic questioning that defeated the purpose of the interview. The agent had fallen victim to the stress of the situation. Shortly thereafter, this agent came to me—for I was the one who had sent him to interview the child molester—and admitted that he wasn't cut out for interviewing. "I can't work with these animals," he told me. I admired his courage in facing up to his shortcomings. He took up another specialty; in short order, he became one of our stars in the area of police stress and psychological counseling of law-enforcement personnel. There had been no flies on his talent and potential to do good work; but he wasn't suited to the difficult task of interviewing convicted child molesters and trying to extract from the interviews something of help to law enforcement.

Lots of people wanted in on the Criminal Personality Research Project, but most of them didn't want to do the hard work. They'd be all too glad to traipse along on interviews of high-profile murderers such as Manson or Berkowitz, but they didn't want to put in the time and effort necessary to properly interview a criminal who was less well known but whose crimes were equally heinous. Many hours of preparation were necessary before going into a prison. Then, prior to conducting the interview, there were prison records to be combed over and part of our lengthy "protocol" to complete. Interviews with inmates regularly lasted three and four hours, and immediately afterward you had to debrief yourself in order to complete the rest of the protocol, as well as other administrative tasks.

Nearly everyone in our unit fell victim to its situational stress. One woman profiler bailed out after a few years because the work was giving her nightmares. She found herself unable to deal rationally with cases in which someone broke into a house and raped a woman; she, too, went on to other work for the FBI. Several of our people developed bleeding ulcers and three had anxiety attacks that were so severe that they were initially misperceived as heart attacks. Four of us, myself included, had periods of rapid and unexplained weight loss, some twenty to forty pounds in six-month periods. We went for batteries of tests, including the standard gastrointestinal series, and no purely physical reasons for the weight loss were discovered; it was all stress-related. Another male agent fell under the spell of one mass murderer so completely that he would misrepresent the man's antagonism toward me in order that only he would have access to this murderer; the agent even passed to the murderer a good deal of Bureau-developed information, from which the murderer hoped to fashion a successful appeal of his death sentence. The bizarre behavior on the part of the agent occurred because the murderer was a masterful manipulator— and because the novice was unprepared for the amount of control the murderer was able to exert on those who crossed his path. The agent even managed to entangle in his exploits a Bureau paper shuffler. Soon, the supervisor wanted to go along with the agent to interview the murderer; the supervisor, too, had dreams of later boasting how close he had been to a glamorous and evil figure. When the murderer was finally executed, the agent was ashen and disoriented, as stricken as if he had just lost a close friend or relative—a startling example of the dangers of his having peered far too deeply into "the abyss."

Stability in one's life enables one to keep some helpful distance from the work of interviewing violent criminals, but even when the agents involved are basically stable, as I am, the stress is considerable. Of course, I didn't know the extent of the stress I would encounter when I began doing these prison interviews in 1978.

A word about the circumstances of the interviews. Most outsiders visiting a prison are allowed only limited access to prisoners, even if the visitor is family or legal counsel. You speak through a hole in a glass, or on a telephone, or in some other way are at a distance from the prisoner. I was usually permitted to conduct the interviews in an attorney's room or a guard captain's quarters, so I could sit in relative comfort with the convict. Occasionally, prisoners would be brought to the room handcuffed; invariably, I'd ask that these cuffs be removed—it was part of trying to reach rapport with the person being interviewed. When I began an interview, the inmate would naturally be curious about what the FBI wanted with him, and so I'd begin by talking about him, demonstrating the depth of my knowledge, and saying that I wasn't here to seek information on a particular crime but, rather, just to research certain categories of offenders. I didn't say that it was sexual murderers; to do so would have been a mistake. I told the inmate I wanted to know about his childhood, his entire life, and that anything they told me would not be passed on to the prison authorities. This last "rule" was quite important, because that was the inmates' largest fear, that some of the intimate details they might divulge to me would become known to the prison apparatus and that the authorities would somehow use it against them. For some reason (perhaps it was my earnest assurances), they believed me, and I've kept my promises. I also warned the inmates not to speak of any crimes that had not been adjudicated—for instance, an admission that they'd really killed two dozen people, not a dozen—because if they did so, I would have to read them their rights, and the information might lead to an investigation, and so on.

Nearly everyone wants to talk to Charles Manson, primarily in order to be able to say they've done so, not really because they have a need to hear what Manson has to say. Manson and some of the others have been interviewed repeatedly by journalists and sensation seekers of one sort of another, and are sick of such treatment. I recall an interview that television and radio host Tom Snyder did with Manson a few years ago in which Snyder asked Manson what it felt like to slice off an ear. That was just the sort of question that could have been calculated to turn off Manson, to make him ease into glibness and evasion and hostility toward the interviewer. I could tell from watching the interview that at that point Manson's respect for Snyder declined to nil. ''This guy's a dummy,'' I could almost hear Manson saying in his mind. ''He's playing games, so I'll play games, too.'' That was the end, as far as extracting any serious information was concerned. Snyder might profitably have asked Manson what reason he had for slicing off an ear, and might have obtained an interesting answer, one that would probably have to do with the relevance of that bizarre act to Manson's fantasy. Snyder went in a different direction, however, and ended up with nothing of value to anyone, except perhaps in terms of titillating the audience.

In talking to these spectacular criminal personalities, I found it was imperative to be extremely well prepared, so that they understood I wasn't there to waste their time. I had to impress on them that I was worthy of being talked to. Being well prepared about their lives and cases was one aspect of my presentation of self that convinced them I might be deserving of trust. For instance, when the inmate was in the midst of a story, it always helped if I knew the names and other antecedents to which he referred. ''Now Bobby would take me along to meet some drug dealers,'' Manson began a story, and before he could continue, I butted in.

''Bobby Beausoleil?''

''Yeah,'' he responded, and then he went on, secure in the knowledge that his questioner had done enough homework to be familiar with every known fact in his life story, that I understood all the references. I had made the interjection to demonstrate just that, to tell him that I knew what he was talking about and considered it important. In reaction, he raised the level of his candor. Talking with Tom Snyder, Manson had to go slowly and explain everything, and as a consequence said nothing of importance. To an interviewer who approached him with respect, as I did, Manson could clip along, rattle out matters he'd thought about, portions of his story that no law-enforcement person had ever heard before, confident that I knew enough of the background to be able to follow what he was saying.

Another aid to my interviews was my consistent attempt to find and discuss something positive in the lives of these killers. Tex Watson had been born again; we could start with that. Heirens had been an exemplary prisoner. It was more difficult to find something positive

with a man such as Manson, of course, but at least I could zero in on
something that he might consider positive in his world, even if the rest
of humanity might not consider it in the same way: In Manson's case,
it was the way in which people related to him.

Manson wanted to inform me—once we got past what I later
came to label as the courtship phase of a conversation—that he really
didn't know why he was in prison this time, because he had not been
present when the murders were committed; more deeply, he wanted to
impress on me that he was not truly guilty. If you hold up a photographic negative, Manson maintained, you see a version of the world
that is reversed; Manson said he was that sort of negative of society,
a reflection of society that showed all of its bad aspects.

Key to deciphering the enigma of Charlie Manson is the fact
that, indeed, he had had a rotten early life. By the time he was thirty-
two, he had been in prison or juvenile institutions twenty years,
from his teenage years up until the day when he emerged from the
Terminal Island facility in California with the determination to remain
out of prison for the rest of his life. (Many men who were criminals
in their teens and twenties mature out of their antisocial behavior in
the early thirties and do manage to sustain noncriminal lives after
getting out.) A small man, physically unprepossessing at five-six and
130 pounds, Manson was perceptive emotionally. In prison, he had
learned to play the guitar, and even wrote some music. He planned to
be a musician and earn his living that way. When he got out of
prison, it was the middle 1960s, and he was able to slip right into the
counterculture life that was then becoming prevalent among young
people on the West Coast. He locked into the youth movement and
rode it.

"I could see the kind of people the kids were shining up to,"
Manson told me, "so I became that." He understood perhaps better
than the youngsters what and who they respected: people with long
hair, people who wore sandals on their feet, people somewhat out of
the ordinary who spoke in metaphysical terms, played guitars, and
wrote songs that few could comprehend. Manson found that he could
walk up and down the Haight-Ashbury district of San Francisco—the
heart of the acid (LSD) culture—and that because he was older than
the hippies by a dozen years, because he appeared in certain garb and
behaved in a certain way, the kids would flock to him. "I looked at
what they wanted to see, and I became that."

Soon he was getting "free meals, free lodging, free sex, free
dope" and had set himself up as a sort of guru. "I became a negative,"

he told me, "a reflection of these kids." Manson explained this image by saying that when you hold up a mirror, you don't actually see the mirror but, rather, what is reflected in its shiny surface. "They were looking for themselves," Manson avowed. "Hey, I'm not a real big guy. I can't go kicking ass, I have to get things by using my brain." The staring, hypnotic eyes served him well; he found he could control some youngsters better than others, and that these would do whatever he asked. In the desert near Death Valley, he ran what amounted to a summer camp for aberrant, wayward kids. Older than they were, more experienced in the methods of manipulation learned in twenty years of being a convict, he broke down the kids' defenses and began to require more and more of them, until they went beyond marginal incursions into illegality and committed serious crimes.

Manson had concluded that because he had done nothing more than mirror what his disciples wished to become, he was not really responsible for their murderous actions; that was the reason he "didn't know why" he was in prison. This explanation was baldly ingenuous, of course, because Manson refused to take into account his own lifelong psychopathic personality and his bent toward achieving power; but still, in our discussion, he expounded in an unmistakable way on the techniques by which he had dominated the young people around him. An understanding of his manipulative genius is key to decoding the murders that he and his disciples committed. He didn't point-blank order the murders—as prosecutor Bugliosi charged—but, rather, he created the climate in which his disciples knew what they had to do to please him, and they wished to do so. At that moment in the La Bianca home when the murders themselves were about to be committed, Manson told his kids that he was leaving the house to go outside, because as a former convict he ought not to be present when the actual crime went down, because it would violate the terms of his parole. His disciples believed this explanation.

Once, during our interview, Manson became a bit wild, jumping on the table to demonstrate the ways in which guards controlled prisoners in the institutions. I would have let him rant and rave some more, but John Conway told him flatly, "Charlie, get off the table, sit down, and behave yourself." In this instance, Conway's unwillingness to indulge Manson's theatrics was the appropriate response, for after the table-hopping, Manson did sit down, and was more forthcoming about his techniques of mental control.

Near the end of the interview, Manson begged me to give him

something that he could take back to his cell; he wanted a souvenir so that he could say he'd "ripped off" an FBI agent. Otherwise, he suggested, no one would believe he'd spent all this time talking to us; he'd have a lot of explaining to do, and that might lower his status among the inmates. He grabbed my FBI badge and held it up to his shirt, then acted as if he was issuing orders to guards and other inmates. I told him he couldn't have that. Manson admired a pair of old aviator sunglasses I'd brought with me, and I decided they were certainly a gift I was prepared to donate. He took them and put them in his breast pocket, but cautioned that the guards would probably accuse him of stealing them; sure enough, that's precisely what happened. Manson was brought back in to me by the guards, straining and protesting all the way about the perversity of anyone believing him capable of pilfering. With a straight face, I attested that I'd given the sunglasses to him. The guards looked at me as if I was a jerk. Then, with his best strut, and with the glasses incongruously perched on his face—hiding those fearsome eyes—Charlie Manson strode down the hall. I have no doubts that once back in the population, he bragged about having put one over on the FBI. It was a shining example of Manson's manipulative tricks. For me, the glasses and the momentary loss of dignity were a small price to pay for unique insight into the mind of a murderer.

On my initial trip through the prisons, I proceeded from Manson's prison down the California coast to the San Luis Obispo prison to interview Charles "Tex" Watson. Watson claimed to have found Jesus in prison; he had been saved and born again, and had actually become a rather renowned preacher; people would come from surrounding communities, as well as from the prison population, to hear him on Sundays. Frankly, he seemed to have the penal authorities snookered; he walked around as if he owned the place. The administrators there thought of him as doing good work, that he was a shining example of rehabilitation. To my mind, there was no question that he was doing good work and helping people; whether his proselytizing was completely genuine, or a line that he pursued in the belief that it would eventually assure his parole, I could not be certain.

Watson was a rather normal-appearing man—certainly so to me, just then, after having visited Sirhan Sirhan, Charles Manson, and Ed Kemper. He readily admitted that at the time of the Tate–La Bianca murders, he had been out of his mind on drugs and under the total influence of Manson; had justice been served then, he said, he would have been executed right after the trial. But he was spared, Satan had left him, and he had been taken into the hand of the Lord and was truly a different man than the one who had committed the crimes.

In the book *Will You Die for Me?*—written with the prison chaplain, Ray Hoekstra—Watson placed all the blame on Manson, saying that Manson ordered his disciples to kill. Just before the Tate murders, Manson had taken care of a bad situation for Watson— by stabbing a drug dealer they had ripped off—and told Watson to reciprocate and kill some "pigs" for him. In his conversations with me, Watson admitted that Manson had not given him direct and explicit orders to commit murder, but that there had been no question that Manson understood what Watson and the others were going to do, did not stop it, and that Manson later reveled in the knowledge that it had been done for him.

Watson had grown up in a small Texas town, and had been the all-American boy—"honor student, track star (my record in high hurdles still stands), Yell Leader, the boy next door with the crew cut and the prizewinning calf," he described himself in his book. Graduating from college in the late 1960s, he drifted to California, he told me, yearning to experience the beach, the sun, the girls, the mind-bending drugs, the easy life. He fell in with Manson by chance, began to hang around him, and then gave up everything else in his life to be near Manson. Now, after having been in prison for some time, Watson understood Manson: Charlie had acted like an old convict, he told me, wrapping a new one around his finger. Manson hadn't turned him into a homosexual as he had done to others, Watson told me, but Manson had made him into a slave.

"When I started taking acid," Watson wrote, "Charlie was not an important figure in my life." However, one friend was an evangelist for the "gospel according to Charlie," and the "Family girls" echoed the philosophy constantly.

> They said that each one of us has an ego, a desire to assert ourselves and our existence as something separate and cut off from the rest of life around us. We hang on to that ego, thinking that independent self is the only thing that lets us survive, thinking without it we'd perish. But . . . True freedom means giving up ourselves, letting that old ego die so we can be free of the self that keeps us from one another, keeps us from life itself. "Cease to exist," Charlie sang in one of the songs he'd written. "Cease to exist, come say you

love me." The girls repeated it, over and over—*cease to exist, kill your ego, die*—so that once you cease to be, you can be free to totally love, totally come together.

Manson broke down the personalities of those around him by means of mind-altering drugs, by verbal assaults on his disciples' personalities, by embroiling them in orgies. Every night after dinner, Manson would climb up on a mound in back of their ranch and spout his philosophy to an adoring audience stoned on drugs. The past, he preached, must be put behind them and ridiculed, especially their birth families and middle-class roots. All that mattered was the new family, the Family. Manson was in his early thirties, and the Family was urged to think of him as the new Christ, who had also been in his mid-thirties when crucified. Like Christ, Manson was going to change the world. Manson, too, spoke in apocalyptic phrases and derided the teachings of the fathers and preached love. To symbolize the new personality of each acolyte after he was exposed to Manson's truth, Manson gave them new names. Watson became Tex, not only because of his origins and the twang in his speaking voice but also because there could be only one Charlie in the Manson Family. Actually, the rivalry between Manson and Watson, which I learned about from both men, was a definite factor in the dynamics of the murders.

The key was the sermons from the mound, though. Manson would say that the old world was about to come to an end, that he would lead his flock into a secret entrance in the desert where they would wait out the apocalypse and then emerge to repopulate the earth. To provoke actions that would hurry up the coming destruction of the present world, Manson said, there ought to be some bloody murders. Charlie repeated a litany from his hill: He had been cheated out of childhood, he had never had a birthday party or a life, he had been "screwed" since the day he was born. To balance what had been done to him, Manson preached, some "pigs" had to be killed. He defined pigs as middle-class, advantaged people, who he thought should be rousted out of their comfortable lives by being confronted with torture and bloody murder.

"As bizarre as Charlie's teachings might sound to an outsider," Watson wrote, "it was compelling to us. The more acid we took and the more we listened, the more obvious and inevitable it all seemed." Manson would talk to them while they were in the throes of LSD, and paint compelling word pictures of killing and torture. Then, "We'd all follow Charlie's lead and imagine the butchery and the terror, and even though it was all just a game, the images stayed locked in our brains after the game was over.''

One night, after some of this role playing, Watson gathered up a few of the girls and told them and Manson they were sallying forth to do the devil's work. He, Watson, would be the ringleader and take the responsibility for the actual killings; the women—trained by Manson in the need to devote their lives to serving men—would be his accomplices. Watson claims that he told Manson, ''We're doing this for you, Charlie,'' and that Manson responded, ''Yeah, Tex, do it and do it right.'' Manson told me that he had merely advised Watson, ''Do what you have to do.''

I believe their two stories essentially coincide and are not contradictory: if Manson did not directly order the murders, he nonetheless made it eminently clear that he condoned them and would not stop his disciples from killing. Though the murders were Charlie's fantasy, conveyed to his kids often in verbal descriptions that were overtly violent, they (not he) would make that fantasy into a gruesome reality, and thereby hasten the end of the ''bad vibrations'' world that had to end before Charlie's peace and love would start a new one. Since on the basis of Manson's instructions all of his disciples had earlier committed burglaries and stolen cars and money, and the women had slept with men at his direction and generally obeyed his every whim, when Manson did not overtly prevent Watson and the women from going out to murder, he more than blessed the action.

That wasn't the whole story, however. In his own interview with me, Manson had confided that the dumbest thing he'd ever done was to ''let that SOB Watson have too much power in the Family.'' And Watson casually acknowledged to me that he certainly had been attempting to elevate himself in the Family power structure, to get the girls to look to him for authority. By committing murder, Watson sought to become, if not the leader of the Family, then Manson's chief lieutenant, a man who all must respect because of the enormity of his crimes and his familiarity with violence. So the Tate–La Bianca murders were not carefully planned, masterminded executions, but, rather, snowballing events in which a bunch of screwed-up, runaway kids, their personalities burned out of them, and caught in a ''familial'' power struggle, took part in disasters that snuffed out a half-dozen lives.

I had wanted to speak with other members of the Manson Family in the California prisons, principally Susan Atkins, who had assisted in the murders, but could not manage that on my initial trip.

At the Alderson Federal Women's Penitentiary in West Virginia, however, I did see Lynette "Squeaky" Fromme and Sandra Good. Neither one had been present at the actual murders, but they had been around Manson for a considerable amount of time. When these two "girls" came into the interview room, it was like something out of a movie. Squeaky wore a red outfit and a matching red bandana around her head, and Sandra wore a green outfit and a green bandana as a headband. They approached in the posture of nuns, walking together, moving in unison. In their conversation, they called each other Red and Green, and proclaimed they were sisters in the church of Charles Manson.

Squeaky Fromme had come from a normal family, well-educated participants in the space program. Sandra Good had a master's degree. Both were intelligent, but had yielded up their lives to Manson. Squeaky was convicted of having pulled a .45 pistol on President Gerald Ford and squeezing the trigger; the gun did not go off because a Secret Service agent had put his hand between the hammer and the firing pin (and had been injured in the process). Sandra had been convicted of attempting to extort through the mails; she had written letters to directors of large corporations, telling them that unless they ceased polluting the earth, Manson Family members (who were all over the place, in hiding) would start killing the directors and their families. In prison, the "girls"—who were now women in their thirties—kept the faith. One day, they believed, Charlie would emerge from prison and restart the movement that would be the only hope for earth's future, and they would join him in the endeavor. They told me that even if I had brought with me presidential commutations for them both, they would not leave prison until Manson also had been released. I didn't get much more from them than that, and verification of the willingness of inadequate personalities to submit their lives and destinies to a psychotic man who led them very far astray. Sandra Good was released from prison in late 1991 and moved to a town twenty-five miles from Manson's prison.

Richard Speck was not really a serial killer, but what I call a "spree killer." One terrible night in Chicago during the late 1960s, he had entered a house with the intent of robbing it, and found student nurses there. Others returned during the course of the evening. He tied them up—some of the American nurses told the others to go along with this, because they were convinced if they did so he wouldn't harm them, though the Filipino nurses objected. One by one, he took them into another room, assaulted them, and then killed eight of them, mainly so they could not identify him. A ninth student had rolled under the bed, and lived through the experience of having Speck assault and kill one of her friends directly above her. Speck must have lost count, because after the eighth murder, he left the house. The ninth nurse came out and provided the police with a good description, including that of a tattoo on Speck that read, "Born to Lose." That description had been sent to hospital emergency rooms on the odd chance that this violent man might injure himself. Sending such descriptions around is a usual police technique, which in this instance paid off. A few days later, when Speck showed up in a hospital with a wound in his elbow, the tattoo was recognized and Speck was arrested. (One of my questions to Speck was going to be about that apparently self-inflicted wound in his inner elbow.) The surviving nurse positively identified Speck, as did some fingerprints left at the scene of the murders, and he was convicted and sent to prison for life.

I wanted to interview Speck because he was a well-known murderer, but he wasn't very intelligent and seemed to have no insight into his crimes. According to the prison counselors, he was a bully whose assaultive and violent behavior was well known, in the prison system and out. Prior to going to Chicago, he had been a fugitive from Texas, where he was wanted for the attempted murder of his father-in-law. In the months just before the murders, Speck's idea of having a good night on the town was to get drunk, take some pills, then go to a bar and pick on another patron until he got into a fight. If he beat up his opponent badly, that was a successful evening; if not, he'd look for a hooker and beat her badly before falling asleep. In prison, a guard told me, Speck had captured a sparrow and made a pet of it, tied a string around its leg and wore it on his shoulder. One of the guards told him to get rid of it, as pets were not allowed in prisons. Speck did not. After several go-around's, the guard told Speck that if he didn't get rid of the sparrow, he would be put into solitary. At that, Speck walked over to a rotating fan and threw the bird in. It was demolished. The surprised guard said, "What did you do that for? I thought you liked the sparrow." "I did," Speck was reported as saying, "but if it ain't mine, it ain't nobody's."

Speck didn't want to talk to us, and was surly and posturing when he was brought in to see us. One of the prison guards began talking to him, though, and eventually told Speck that he had been a single man in Chicago at the time of Speck's murders and was a bit annoyed that Speck had taken eight eligible young women away from the prowling bachelors of the city. Speck started to chuckle, and then loosened up a bit.

I was uneasy, because I always make it a point in my interviews not to get into the gutter with the murderer, and—just as important— never to make light of the victims. To me, there's no excuse for deprecating those who have suffered, simply to get on the good side of a murderer. Nonetheless, we tried to use the opening that the guard had made to talk to Speck.

As I quickly discovered, he didn't have much to say, and little insight into his own condition. Speck displayed a callousness for human life, admitting that he had killed his victims so they couldn't testify against him. Frustrated by his low intelligence and bad attitude, I tried to get something out of the interview, and inquired as to how he had ended up in the hospital, where his tattoo had been recognized. Though several doctors believed that the cut to the artery in his elbow had been the result of a botched suicide attempt made in the flophouse where he lived after the murders, Speck denied this, saying that he'd been in a fight in a bar and had been cut by a broken whiskey bottle. Ten years after the crime, he was still trying to be the macho man.

On the other end of the scale from Richard Speck was Ted Bundy, who became the most celebrated killer of his time, perhaps because he was so photogenic and so articulate that many people concluded he could not have committed the crimes for which he'd been convicted. A handsome, intelligent young man who seemed to some people to have considerable sex appeal, Bundy was painted by the media as a smooth guy, respected, clean, a former law student, a Mr. Nice Guy, almost a benign killer, a good lover who would kill his victims quickly.

Far from being the Rudolph Valentino of the serial killer world, Ted Bundy was a brutal, sadistic, perverted man. His last victim was a twelve-year-old girl whom he suffocated by shoving her face in the mud during his sexual assault. By his verbal skills, Bundy would habitually lure girls and young women into a position of vulnerability, then bludgeon them with a short crowbar that he had concealed in a cast on his arm, or hidden under the seat of his car. He would then commit gross sexual acts with the unconscious or semiconscious women, his favorite practice being anal assaults. After that, he'd kill them by strangulation, then transport the bodies, often several hundred miles. Before leaving them, he would mutilate and dismember them, and sometimes commit necrophilic acts. After several days, he often returned to the body of a recent victim and sexually attacked the severed body parts—for instance, ejaculating into the mouth of a disembodied head. This guy was an animal, and it amazed me that the media seemed unable to understand that. Following Bundy's execution, at a seminar run by the FBI at Quantico, the police officers from all over the country who had been trying to question him estimated that he had murdered between thirty-five and sixty young women in a dozen states.

Bundy had begun his career in Seattle, and after eleven homicides had brought the authorities very close to him, he moved southeast, leaving a trail of bodies behind him, until he reached the ski resorts of Colorado, where he settled for a while. He was apprehended in Colorado but escaped, was recaptured, and escaped a second time, after which he again proceeded southeast, committing more homicides on his way to Florida.

I had briefly and tangentially been involved in his case when he became a fugitive from Colorado. I worked with chief profiler Howard Teten on an assessment that became part of a Wanted poster. We alerted people to the killer's MO: He would go to locations where young people congregated—beaches, ski resorts, discos, colleges—and look for young, attractive, outdoors-type women who parted their long hair in the middle.

After Bundy's conviction and the exhaustion of most of the appeals, I wanted to interview Bundy for our research project, because he was articulate and intelligent, and I hoped he would add to our base of knowledge. On my first visit to his prison in Starke, Florida, I wasted several days trying to see him, was delayed because of certain pending appeals, and eventually had to leave the interviewing task to associates because I was due to teach at a road school. A few years later, we at the BSU were surprised to receive a letter from Bundy, asking to see our records and crime-scene photographs on the thirty-six incarcerated killers included in the research project I had initiated; Bundy said that he wanted to assist us by becoming a consultant to the BSU. This prompted my second visit to his Florida prison.

Bundy stuck out his hand even before I'd put mine forward. I started to introduce myself, and he said, "Oh, Mr. Ressler, I know who you are; I've been reading your stuff for years." He had many of the BSU's published reports in his cell, and he wondered why I hadn't come to see him earlier. I reminded him that I had done so but had been unable to wait out the appeal. Bundy regretted his earlier unavailability and said he was eager to talk, because "I like to talk to somebody I can relate to, who understands what I'm saying." It was a clear attempt on his part to control me, and I was glad to understand that as we sat down to chat.

Bundy continued to try to flatter me by saying that the various college professors, newsmen, and local police officers who had interviewed him had all been amateurs, but now he was talking with a professional. He had written his letter in an attempt to obtain our research and use it for his appeals, to stave off his death sentence. Believe it or not, one of my superiors in the FBI wanted to give that research to this convicted killer; I refused to do so. I told Bundy that the only crimes we were interested in talking about were his own. Bundy wouldn't look me in the eye. He said he'd win on appeal, anyway, and would never be executed.

After further fencing, he agreed to discuss some of the murders on a hypothetical basis. One of the cases, the one that had gotten him charged in Colorado, involved the abduction of a woman from a hotel bar when she was with her boyfriend. I asked him how this could have been accomplished. Using the third person, Bundy told me that "it could have happened this way." The killer might have had the woman under surveillance, and perhaps approached her in the hall, posing as a security guard or an official in the hotel—someone with a bit of authority in this place—and, by a ruse or a trick, lured her to a specific room where he could disable her quickly.

It was most likely that Bundy was telling me precisely how he had committed this particular crime, but he wouldn't say so directly. After three or four hours of this sort of dancing around the issues, I realized that Bundy would never talk, that he would attempt to con people (as he had done so successfully) until executed, and I went home.

Just three or four days prior to his execution, some months later, Bundy said that he would tell all, and a dozen officers from around the country came to interview him, each one allotted a few hours. The first to speak with him was Robert Keppel from Seattle, who had meticulously tracked Bundy's first eleven murders. Bundy spent the hours allotted to Keppel verbally sparring around the first murder, and never got to the other murders. He informed the officer that this task was going to take longer than he had thought it would, and that if the policemen got together and petitioned so that Bundy would be allowed another six to eight months of life, they'd be able to get to the bottom of many things. This didn't wash. He'd had ten years in jail in which to reveal the details, and it was clear that he would never do so. Bundy was executed several days later.

When all of those police officers came from Florida to Quantico for our seminar, I learned a disturbing fact. Bundy had managed one last con job. He had previously convinced someone else in the Bureau to obtain from me an autographed copy of my textbook on serial murder, and had it in his cell at the time he went to the electric chair. He even quoted from it in his last videotaped interview with Dr. James Dobson.

David Berkowitz, the Son of Sam killer, sat with me and my associates three times in mid-1979. In the space of a single year in New York, Berkowitz had killed a half-dozen people, mostly in cars parked in lover's lanes, and seriously injured a half-dozen more. He had left notes for the police at the scenes of his crimes, and communicated with newspaper columnists during a reign of terror that had many New Yorkers staying home at nights. At the time of our interviews, Berkowitz was in Attica prison, isolated from the rest of the population.

Berkowitz was as he had appeared in court at the time of his trial, pudgy, pasty, extremely shy, reserved, polite, low-key. He accepted my handshake readily—always a good predictor of how well the interview will go, I had discovered; then he sat down and spoke only when spoken to. I took handwritten notes, as he indicated he did not want a tape recorder running.

Since Berkowitz's crimes were committed in New York City, there had been even more than the usual media interest in the crimes and in him; that had provided a lot of material to read through as I prepared to meet Berkowitz. As I soon noted, it was also the basis for a complex interreaction between Berkowitz and the New York newspapers. Among other matters, I learned that Berkowitz had a scrapbook in which he had pasted the newspaper stories about his crimes; many criminals compile these memento books prior to their arrest, but Berkowitz had been allowed to keep his scrapbook in his cell, and, he told me, he used it to keep his fantasies alive.

What I really wanted to talk to Berkowitz about was the sexual content of his crimes. At first, he didn't want to discuss it, saying that he had had a normal sex life, with girlfriends, and that the murders were just shootings. So I asked him about his early life. He had been adopted when very young and had had problems with the adopted family. He had always wanted to locate his birth mother, especially after his adoptive mother died when he was fourteen. On graduating from high school, he wanted to go into the Army and to Vietnam; he envisioned himself becoming a hero, receiving medals, being recognized as an important individual and thereby fashioning an identity for himself. Instead, the Army sent him to Korea, where he had an undistinguished year of service. He went to a prostitute to gain sexual experience, and was deeply disappointed when he contracted a case of venereal disease. Later, he would tell interviewers that this was his sole consummated sexual experience with a woman.

Returning home, Berkowitz managed to locate his birth mother. He met with her and with his half sister, who was living with the birth mother, but this, too, was a disappointing experience. He wanted the birth mother to take him in and make him part of the family, and things didn't work out that way.

Before committing his murders, Berkowitz had set at least 1,488 fires in New York. That's an amazing number, and we know it only because he kept a diary of them; he had also pulled several hundred false alarms. He had a desire to be a fireman but never took the qualifying test; he did participate in some fireman-type rescues in the course of his duties as a security guard for a private trucking firm in Queens.

At the point in our interview where he came to describe the murders, Berkowitz started to say, as he had to psychiatrists who had examined him for the court, that his neighbor Sam Carr's dog, possessed by a three-thousand-year-old demon, had barked orders at him, instructing him to kill.

I told Berkowitz that I thought this explanation was nonsense and that I didn't accept it. Stunned, Berkowitz continued to advance the demon-dog story. I reiterated that if this was the extent of his being honest with us—to attribute the motive of his crimes to a talking dog—the interview was over. I shut my notebook and started to leave the room.

Berkowitz stopped me, protesting that the psychiatrists had accepted his story as the reason for his crimes, and if it was good enough for them, it should be good enough for the FBI.

"That's not the story we're looking for, David," I said. "We want the factual basis for these crimes, and if we're not going to talk about that, then we'll leave."

Berkowitz sighed, settled down, and began to talk about the real stuff. The Son of Sam business, and the assertion about the talking dog, he indicated, had been his way of signaling the authorities that he was insane. In other words, it was a construct made for the purpose of attempting to avoid proper prosecution for his crimes. He had been sane enough to know what he was doing. By the time I interviewed him, Berkowitz also had done enough talking with psychiatrists and other counselors in prison to be somewhat comfortable conversing about the true basis for his crimes. He admitted that his real reason for shooting women was out of resentment toward his own mother, and because of his inability to establish good relationships with women.

His first attempt at murder had been a stabbing. He had sliced a knife through a woman on the street, then had run away. He'd looked through the newspapers after the crime but saw no notice of it, and so he concluded that she had lived. He then decided to improve his MO. The knife, he reasoned, had been a mistake; it had resulted in too much blood on him and on his clothes, and he didn't like that. So, with the precise intention of finding a weapon with which to kill, he had traveled to Texas and bought a Charter Arms .44 pistol and some bullets. He was afraid to buy the bullets in New York, thinking that somehow if he did so and the bullet shells were found, the authorities would be able to trace them to his New York residence. After committing several of the murders, Berkowitz even went back to Texas in order to purchase additional bullets.

His MO was to look for women alone in cars, or necking with men in parked cars. Then he'd walk up and shoot the women and sometimes the men with them. He told me that in the process of stalking and shooting women, he would become sexually excited, and that after the shootings, he would masturbate.

Now we were getting toward the heart of the matter. Under my gentle probing, Berkowitz said something that hadn't been widely known—that stalking for victims was a nightly occupation. It didn't depend on phases of the moon, particular days of the week, or any other matter that had been advanced as a theory by those who tried to solve the case. He was out looking every night but would strike only when he felt the circumstances were ideal. This amount of premeditation alone cuts the ground from under any instant analysis of Berkowitz as an insane killer.

Berkowitz told me that on the nights when he couldn't find a proper victim or proper circumstances, he would drive back to the scenes of earlier murders he had committed and revel in the experience of being where he had formerly accomplished a shooting. It was an erotic experience for him to see the remains of bloodstains on the ground, a police chalkmark or two: Seated in his car, he would often contemplate these grisly mementos and masturbate. (No wonder that he kept his scrapbook in his cell.)

In this single moment of revelation, almost casually given, Berkowitz told us something extremely important for law enforcement, and at the same time provided new understanding to a staple of detective stories. Yes, murderers did indeed return to the scene of their crimes, and we could try to catch future murderers on that basis. Equally as important, the world could now understand that this return to the scene of the crime arose not out of guilt, which had been the usual explanation accepted by psychiatrists and mental-health professionals, but because of the sexual nature of the murder. Returning to the murder site took on a connotation that Sherlock Holmes, Hercule Poirot, or even Sam Spade had never dared to suggest.

For me, the revelation also had another reverberation. I had long argued that the aberrant behavior of killers is in some ways only an extension of normal behavior. Every parent of an adolescent girl has observed that teenage boys will repeatedly walk or ride their bikes or drive their cars by a girl's house, or hang around as close to her as they are allowed, and engage in impetuous, spontaneous behavior. Hanging around the scene of the crime, then, is an an instance of arrested, inadequate personality development, an extension of something normal into abnormal behavior.

Berkowitz had felt a great urge to go to the funerals of his victims. Many killers do so. He didn't, fearful that police would be watching the ceremonies (as, indeed, they were). Berkowitz had learned from television shows and detective magazines that such events were watched by police. He did take off from work on the days of funerals, and often hung around diners near police stations to try and overhear cops talking about his crimes. He heard nothing. Although he didn't go to the funerals, he would go so far as to try and locate the graves of his victims, which he was also unable to do. Berkowitz was incredibly ineffectual at anything other than setting fires and murdering people.

He liked the idea of becoming notorious, and that was why he communicated with the police and, later, directly with the newspapers. The power that he held over the city, and over the sale of newspapers, was stupendous, and very exciting for him. Having read about the idea of communicating with the police from a book on Jack the Ripper, he slipped a note into the seat of the car in which his first victim lay dying, a note in crude letters that read, "Bang-bang. . . . I'll be back," and was signed with the appellation "Mr. Monster." At that point, Berkowitz was not the Son of Sam. That phrase was a minor part of a letter that he sent to the newspapers. Only after the press started calling him Son of Sam did he adopt the moniker as his own, and even fashioned a logo for it. Publicity spurred his creativity.

In my view, such people as newspaper columnist Jimmy Breslin baited Berkowitz and irresponsibly contributed to the continuation of his murders. Breslin wrote columns about the Son of Sam, and the killer sent him letters directly. After the initial murders, when the city was gripped by fear, Berkowitz came to be directed by the media. For instance, the papers would draw maps to indicate that the killer had struck in several of the boroughs of the city, and would wonder in print whether he was going to hit them all in turn. Berkowitz hadn't really considered doing so, but after the map and articles appeared, he decided he'd try. The story was kept alive even when there was nothing new to report, because it sold newspapers. It was clear to everyone, even the most doltish of newspapermen, that Berkowitz wished to be famous (or infamous) and was murdering in order to impress and shock society and thereby gain attention and identity. Feeding that ego by consistently printing and televising stories about the murders was assuring that there would be more murders. Perhaps, since this was New York, there was no hope of controlling media attention to the case or keeping it at a low enough level not to hamper police or incite the killer, but it has always been clear to me that David Berkowitz kept on killing so he would continue to be the focus of columnists such as Jimmy Breslin.

In his adolescent years, Berkowitz admitted to me, he had started developing these fantasies that involved sex but also violent acts, disruptive and homicidal themes mingling with normal erotic ones. Even earlier in his life, at six or seven, he remembered pouring ammonia into his adoptive mother's fish tank to kill her fish, and spearing them with a pin. He also killed her pet bird with rat poison— he got a thrill out of watching the bird die slowly, and from his mother's anguish at being unable to reverse the illness. He tortured small animals such as mice and moths. All of these were control fantasies, involving power over living things. Berkowitz also confided to me his fantasies about wishing to cause fiery air crashes. He had actually never interfered with an airplane, but arson was a logical extension of this fantasy. Most arsonists like the feeling that they are responsible for the excitement and violence of a fire. With the simple act of lighting matches, they control events in society that are not normally controlled; they orchestrate the fire, the screaming arrival and deployment of the fire trucks and fire fighters, the gathering crowds, the destruction of property and sometimes of people. Berkowitz loved to watch bodies being carried out of burning buildings. These fires were all a prelude to his moving into the arena in which he could exercise the ultimate in control, homicide. Here was a man who obtained his biggest thrills in life from sitting at home and watching the news on television as it reported his latest killing and the fear that he caused to grip the city.

What about his courtroom antics? The suggestion that he had been demonically possessed? All nonsense, he told me, brought to the fore in hopes of mounting an insanity defense. He believed he had been caught just in time, he said, because his fantasy had been growing to the point where he envisioned going out in a blaze of glory. He imagined going to a disco where lots of couples were dancing, and just shooting up the place until the police came and there was a Hollywood-style gun battle in which he and many others would be killed.

Berkowitz's final fantasy was a remarkably vivid display of his envy of normal people involved in normal heterosexual relationships. He recognized that envy, and told me earnestly that if, before he got into the bizarre murders, he had been able to have a relationship with a good woman who would accept him, fulfill his fantasies, and marry him, he would not have begun the killings.

It was a nice note on which to end the interview, but I didn't believe Berkowitz then and don't now. A good woman would not have solved his problems or prevented murders. The reality is that he had tremendous inadequacies, that his problems went far deeper than rejection by women, and stemmed from fantasies that began to surface at the age when most males are entering into their first important personal relationships with members of the opposite sex. It was these fantasies, and the behaviors that embodied them, that prevented his having a mature relationship with a woman. As with so many of the criminals that I interviewed, he had grown up to murder.

4

CHILDHOODS
OF VIOLENCE

"Where do we come from? Who are we? Where are we going?" These three great questions from Gauguin's triptych were the real subject of the prison interviews of murderers I had started on my own in the late 1970s. I wanted to know what made these people tick, to understand better the mind of the murderer. Shortly, my curiosity became systematized and the interviews brought under the umbrella of the Bureau; they became the core of the Criminal Personality Research Project, partially funded by the Justice Department, and involving Dr. Ann Burgess of Boston University, and other academics, with myself as principal investigator. Using a research protocol of some fifty-seven pages, we interviewed thirty-six individual incarcerated murderers, concentrating on their histories, their motives and fantasies, their specific actions. Eventually, we were able to discern important patterns in their lives and learn something about their developing motivation to murder.

In the opinion of a number of experts, our study was the largest, most rigorous, and most complete investigation of multiple murderers ever undertaken, one that included the greatest percentage of the living, incarcerated multiple murderers. In a 1986 article, forensic psychiatrists Drs. Katie Bush and James L. Cavanaugh, Jr., of Chicago's Isaac Ray Center called the research "exemplary" because of its breadth, and said that "its conclusions warrant evaluation in great detail."

Before going into the details of who these murderers are and how they became murderers, let me state unequivocally that there is no such thing as the person who at age thirty-five suddenly changes from being perfectly normal and erupts into totally evil, disruptive, murderous behavior. The behaviors that are precursors to murder have been present and developing in that person's life for a long, long time—since childhood.

A common myth is that murderers come from broken, impoverished homes. Our sample showed that this wasn't really true. Many of the murderers started life in a family that was not desperately poor, where family income was stable. More than half lived initially in a family that appeared to be intact, where the mother and father lived together with their son. These were, on the whole, intelligent children. Though seven of the thirty-six had IQ scores below 90, most were in the normal range, and eleven had scores in the superior range, above 120.

Nonetheless, though the homes seemed to outward appearances to be normal, they were in fact dysfunctional. Half of our subjects had mental illness in their immediate family. Half had parents who had been involved in criminal activities. Nearly 70 percent had a familial history of alcohol or drug abuse. All the murderers—every single one—were subjected to serious *emotional* abuse during their childhoods. And all of them developed into what psychiatrists label as sexually dysfunctional adults, unable to sustain a mature, consensual relationship with another adult.

From birth to age six or seven, studies have shown, the most important adult figure in a child's life is the mother, and it is in this time period that the child learns what love is. Relationships between our subjects and their mothers were uniformly cool, distant, unloving, neglectful. There was very little touching, emotional warmth, or training in the ways in which normal human beings cherish one another and demonstrate their affection and interdependence. These children were deprived of something more important than money—love. They ended up paying for that deprivation during the remainder of their lives, and society suffered, too, because their crimes removed many people from the world and their assaultive behavior left alive equally as many victims who remain permanently scarred.

The abuse that the children endured was both physical and mental. Society has understood somewhat that physical abuse is a precursor to violence, but the emotional component may be as important. One woman propped her infant son in a cardboard box in front of the television set, and left for work; later, she'd put him in a playpen, toss in some food, and let the TV set be the baby-sitter until she came home again. A second man reported to us that he had been confined to his room during his childhood evenings; when he wandered into the living room at such times, he was shooed away and told that evening was the time when his mother and father wanted to be alone together; he grew up believing he was an unwanted boarder in his own home.

These children grew up in an environment in which their own actions were ignored, and in which there were no limits set on their behavior. It is part of the task of parenting to teach children what is right and wrong; these were the children who managed to grow up without being taught that poking something into a puppy's eye is harmful and should not be done, or that destroying property is against the rules. The task of the first half-dozen years of life is socialization, of teaching children to understand that they live in a world that encompasses other people as well as themselves, and that proper interaction with other people is essential. The children who grow up to murder never truly comprehend the world in other than egocentric terms, because their teachers—principally their mothers—do not train them properly in this important matter.

Richard Chase, the "vampire killer" discussed in the first chapter of this book, killed a half-dozen people before he was apprehended. According to psychiatric interviews conducted in conjuction with Chase's sentencing, Chase's mother was a schizophrenic, emotionally unable to concentrate on the task of socializing her son or to care for him in a loving way. The mothers of nine more subjects of the study also had major psychiatric problems. Even those mothers whose problems did not reach the level where they came to the attention of a mental-health professional could be considered dysfunctional in other ways; for instance, many were alcoholic. Neglect has many faces. Ted Bundy summed it up when he reminded an interviewer that he had not come from a "Leave It to Beaver" home. He had been brought up by a woman who he thought was his sister but was actually his mother, and although there was no neglect or abuse pinpointed in that relationship, there were strong indications that Bundy was physically and sexually abused by other members of his family.

Sometimes the mother, even when nurturing, cannot balance out or offset the destructive behavior of the father. One murderer came from a family in which the father was in the Navy, was often away on assignments, and was present only occasionally; the children went into a panic when he did come home, because he would then beat up his wife and the children, and sexually abuse the son, who later became a murderer. Over 40 percent of the murderers reported being physically beaten and abused in their childhoods. More than 70 percent said they had witnessed or been part of sexually stressful events when young—

a percentage many times greater than that usually found in the general population. "I slept with my mother as a young child," said one; "I was abused by my father from age fourteen," said another; "My stepmother tried to rape me," reported a third; "I got picked up downtown one night by some guy when I was around seven or eight," said a fourth man.

The quality of a child's attachments to others in the family is considered the most important factor in how he or she eventually relates to and values nonfamily members of society. Relationships with siblings and other family members, which might make up for a parent's coolness in these situations, were similarly deficient in the murderers' families. These children, nurtured on inadequate relationships in their earliest years, had no one to whom they could easily turn, were unable to form attachments to those closest to them, and grew up increasingly lonely and isolated.

It is true that most children who come from dysfunctional early childhoods don't go on to murder or to commit other violent antisocial acts. As far as we could see, the reason for this is that the majority are rescued by strong hands in the next phase of childhood, that of preadolescence—but our subjects were definitely not saved from drowning; they were pushed further under in this phase of their lives. From the ages of eight to twelve, all the negative tendencies present in their early childhoods were exacerbated and reinforced. In this period, a male child really needs a father, and it was in just this time period that the fathers of half the subjects disappeared in one way or another. Some fathers died, some were incarcerated, most just left through divorce or abandonment; other fathers, while physically present, drifted away emotionally. John Gacy killed thirty-three young men and buried them beneath his home before he was caught. In Gacy's youth, his father used to come home, go down into the basement, sit in a stuffed chair, and drink; when anyone approached, the father would chase them away; later, drunk, he'd come up for dinner and pick fights and beat his wife and children.

John Joubert killed three boys before he was caught. John's mother and father divorced when he was a preadolescent, and when John wanted to see his father, his natural mother refused to take him to the father's residence or provide money for his trip. That's abuse, too, in a manner psychologists call passive-aggressive. Now, divorce in the United States is a very common occurrence, and hundreds of thousands of children grow up in single-parent homes. Only a handful of them go on to commit murder. I'm not impugning single-parent homes; rather, I am recognizing the fact that the preponderance of murderers in our study came from dysfunctional settings, many of which were rendered dysfunctional by divorce.

Monte Ralph Rissell raped a dozen women, and killed five of them, before he was nineteen. His parents had divorced when he was seven, after which his mother moved with her three children from Virginia to California. Monte was the youngest, and he cried all the way across the country in the car. When I interviewed him in prison, years later, Monte told me that if he had been allowed to go with his father instead of his mother at the time of the divorce, he would have been in law school now, not in a penitentiary for life. His conclusion is debatable, though the sentiment is real. In any event, he'd had quite a childhood.

Monte began life as an Rh baby who required a complete blood transfusion, but was afterward healthy, though always small for his age. His parents fought for several years before they divorced. He claims he was exposed to marijuana and alcohol by his older siblings before he was seven. His first recorded antisocial behavior came at age nine, when he and several other boys were caught by the school principal while writing obscene words on the sidewalk. There were problems in the home, as well. His mother and new stepfather were spending a lot of time by themselves, leaving the children to supervise one another, and then arbitrarily punishing them if something went wrong. In our interview, Monte repeatedly claimed that his stepfather didn't know how to raise children, having been away in the military for much of his adult life. He would buy things for his new stepchildren, attempting to purchase their love, but did not know how to relate to them in other ways. Monte was still just nine years old when he took out his early anger on a cousin, shooting at him with a BB gun that his stepfather had bought for him. After the incident, his stepfather smashed the gun and then beat Monte with the barrel. Monte felt he and his sister were responsible for the breakup of his mother's second marriage, which came when he was twelve. That year, back in Virginia, he broke into an apartment and stole some property; at age thirteen, he was charged by the police with driving without a license; and at fourteen, with burglary, larceny, car theft, and two rapes. Monte Rissell was quite advanced in his deviant behavior by his early teens, but the escalation of this behavior replicates the development of many murderers.

Another murderer of women had antisocial tendencies that surfaced early. Premature at birth, the man was the last of four children of a Mobile, Alabama, family that was both poor and abusive. The story of his having been in an incubator for nine days became a family legend, as did the tale of an apparent seizure a few months later, during which the man believed he "died and was revived." During his first six years, he slept in the same bed with his mother, and for twelve years after that, he slept in the same room with his mother, in a separate bed. This was done, the mother later claimed, to protect her from the advances of the alcoholic father. She treated her son as if he was quite special—but also abused him. She was strict with her four children, at times hitting them with an electrical cord; additionally, she left them daily in the care of her mother, who beat the children if they disobeyed. The man's two older brothers quickly left the family when they graduated from high school, and after they were gone, the mother, the grandmother, and the sister used the man to ward off the drunken father, encouraging the boy to hit the father to keep him away from the mother.

In school, the boy's performance was spotty, and a principal wrote in a report that he was often "lost in fantasy," a description seconded by his sister. At puberty, he gained and then lost thirty pounds, and was openly vitriolic toward his mother. She reports that he would become violent because he wanted two hot dogs instead of one, or because he was unable to have chocolate syrup on his ice cream. He stole female underwear, and spied on his sister in the bathroom. In a later autobiographical statement, the murderer wrote, "I was a freak in others' eyes. . . . I chose to swallow the insults. . . . I was a dog who got petted when I used the paper." At age thirteen, he started to snatch purses and became involved in gang fights. His family continued to protect him, however. At age sixteen, he was charged with snatching the purse of an elderly blind woman and attempting to assault and rape her fourteen-year-old niece. During the time that these charges were being investigated, another elderly woman in the community who talked to the boy about his "wrongdoing" was shot in the head and killed. The physical evidence pointed to this boy, but the father lied about his whereabouts at the time of the murder and the mother hired a lawyer, and he got all the charges dismissed. (Many years later, after conviction on other murder charges, the killer admitted that he had shot the woman.)

Two years after these incidents, the killer completed high school and enlisted in the military, in effect leaving parental supervision and intervention behind him. Within a month of his induction, he was charged with the attempted murder of a young woman, convicted, and sentenced to twenty years in military prison. While in that system, he again received support from his mother, who instigated appeals to congressmen and attempts to reverse the conviction on technical grounds. After serving seven years, and over the objection of some mental-health professionals who had tried to treat him and were rebuffed, he was paroled in the care of his mother.

He soon married a divorced woman with several children, who reported that relations between them were somewhat normal at first, though marred by strange incidents. When she said she was depressed over the actions of her ex-husband and wanted to commit suicide, the new husband said he would kill her and started to suffocate her with a pillow. At other times, especially when he had been drinking, he would threaten to crush her skull if she did not leave him alone. She also noted, with horror, that he had killed a pet rabbit by bashing it against a post, covering himself with blood. The turning point in their relationship was the birth of a daughter, after which his behavior became erratic and he isolated himself from his wife and their child. Shortly thereafter, and within two years of having been paroled, he began a series of rapes, murders, and mutilations of several women, choosing those who were clerks in convenience stores. Caught in connection with the third one, he confessed to the others.

Potential murderers became solidified in their loneliness first during the age period of eight to twelve; such isolation is considered the single most important aspect of their psychological makeup. Many factors go into fashioning this isolation. Among the most important is the absence of a father. When there's no father or father figure present for an eight- or ten- or twelve-year-old boy, this is embarrassing for the child in front of his peers. He begins to avoid friends, to avoid situations in which father-and-son teams are usually present, such as Little League or the Boy Scouts. His preadolescent sexual activity, rather than being connected to other human beings, starts as autoerotic. More than three-quarters of the murderers we investigated began autoerotic sexual practices as preadolescents; half reported rape fantasies occurring between the ages of twelve and fourteen; more than 80 percent admitted to using pornography, and to tendencies toward fetishism and voyeurism. Again, we must realize that many boys grow up in homes without a father and do not turn into sociopaths; but for the ones who do become sociopaths, the eight-to-twelve period is critical. Investigation often leads back to just this time, and the set of circumstances in which the father figure is absent, as the period when bizarre behavior began.

When Ed Kemper was ten, after his parents' divorce, he returned home one day to find that his mother and older sisters had taken his belongings from his second-floor room and moved them into the basement. His mother, Clarnell Strandberg, was greatly respected at the university, where she worked as an administrator, for her concern for the students; at home, she was a terror, continually belittling Kemper, telling him he was responsible for all the shortcomings in her life. She told him that she had banished him to the basement because he was so large that he was making his adolescent sisters uncomfortable. Shortly afterward, Kemper, a big hulk brooding alone in a windowless room, began to have murderous fantasies.

As the psychologically damaged boys get closer to adolescence, they find that they are unable to develop the social skills that are precursors to sexual skills and that are the coin of positive emotional relationships. Loneliness and isolation do not always mean that the potential killers are introverted and shy; some are but others are gregarious with other men, and good talkers. The outward orientation of the latter masks their inner isolation. By the time a normal youngster is dancing, going to parties, participating in kissing games, the loner is turning in on himself and developing fantasies that are deviant. The fantasies are substitutes for more positive human encounters, and as the adolescent becomes more dependent on them, he loses touch with acceptable social values.

Jerome Brudos, at twelve and thirteen, began to abduct girls his own age or younger at knife point and take them into the barn on the family farm. There, he would tell them to disrobe, and then he would photograph them but do nothing else, since he was not sexually aware enough to go further. Then he'd lock them in a corncrib and go away. Minutes later, he would reappear in the barn with his clothes changed and his hair combed differently, unlock the corncrib, and announce to the girl that he was Ed, Jerry's twin brother. He would profess horror that Jerry had locked her in there, and say, "He didn't hurt you, did he?" The girl would explain that Jerry had taken pictures, and "Ed" would locate the camera and destroy the film in it, then say, "Jerry's been in therapy; we have him in psychological counseling. This is going to set him back a lot. Please don't tell my parents or anyone about this." The girl would acquiesce. Later in life, Brudos put advertisements in campus newspapers asking for women to come and model shoes and hose for him. When they arrived for appointments in his motel room, he would abduct and murder some of them, then hang them in his garage and photograph them, either nude or in various outfits (and especially shoes) that he had put on the dead bodies.

The key to these murderers, if there is one, lies in the unremit-

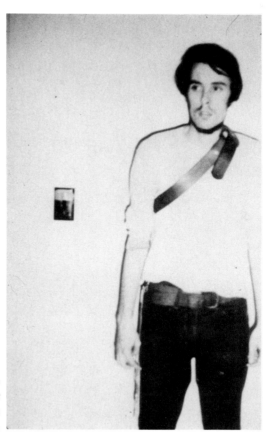

Richard Trenton Chase, the Sacramento "Vampire Killer," at the time of his arrest for seven murders.

One of two blenders used by Chase to prepare human blood and organs for ingesting to "stop his blood from turning to powder."

Above: *Statement written on the wall of sex murder victim of William Heirens, indicating his apparent guilt and compulsive motivation.* Right: *A tormented William Heirens at the time of his arrest for the murder of Suzanne Degnan.*

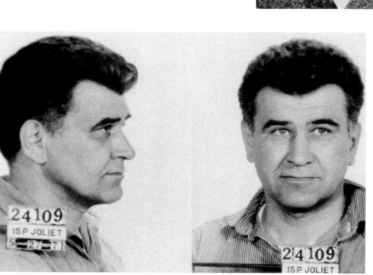

A 1971 prison photograph of William Heirens, incarcerated at Statesville Prison in Joliet, Illinois.

Robert Ressler, then a Supervisory Special Agent, acting out the role of a terrorist during an anti-terrorism hostage field problem in Upstate New York. The field exercise was designed to test the FBI and military response to terrorist/hostage situations. The center hostage is rigged with explosives during a mock press interview.

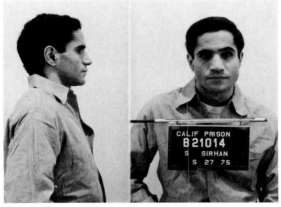

Left: *Sirhan B. Sirhan, assassin of Robert Kennedy.*

The fourteen-year-old Charles Manson.

Charles Maddox Manson, hippie cult leader, at the time of his arrest.

Manson "family" member Charles "Tex" Watson.

Manson "family" member Lynette "Squeaky" Fromme after her arrest for the attempted shooting of President Gerald Ford in Sacramento, California.

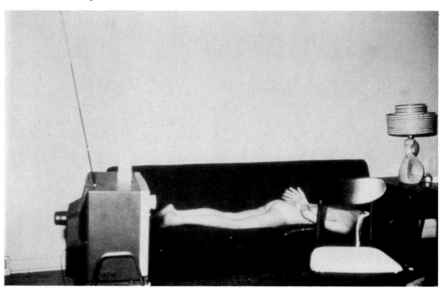

Victim of Chicago spree murderer Richard Speck.

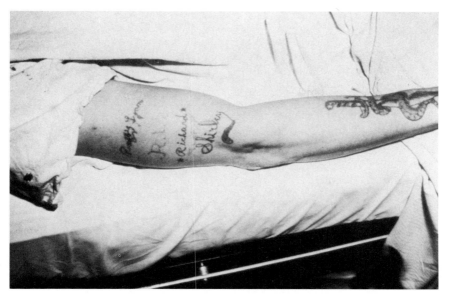

Tattoos on the arm of Richard Speck, which led to his arrest in the murders of eight women in Chicago in 1966.

Chicago Tribune newspapers under the mattress of Richard Speck, featuring the news coverage of the student nurse murders, found at the time of Speck's arrest.

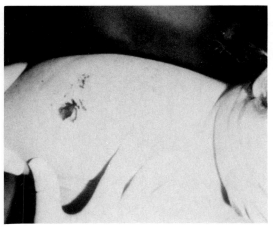

Condemned serial killer Ted Bundy within hours of his pending execution.

Photo of critical bite-mark evidence that led to the conviction of Bundy.

Body of Bundy victim near the Denver ski resort where she was abducted.

Several of the young female victims of serial killer Ted Bundy, indicating his particular preference in victims by general age and appearance.

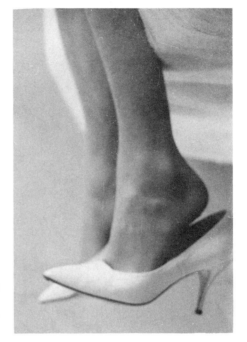

Photograph taken by serial killer Jerome Brudos that he used to enhance his murderous fantasies between the time of his actual killings.

Right: *Photograph taken of the leg of a Brudos victim. This captures the essence of his bizarre fetish fantasies— women's feet in high-heeled shoes.*

Salem, Oregon, serial killer Jerome Brudos in his cell at the Oregon State Penitentiary.

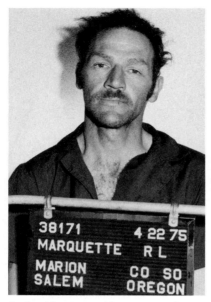

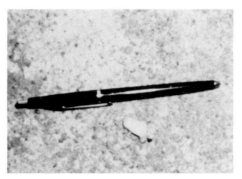

A fingernail found in the driveway of Marquette's trailer that led to the identity of his last victim.

Richard Lawrence Marquette at the time of his arrest for sexual homicide.

Above: *Victim's body dumped in a "No Dumping" zone, demonstrating the arrogance and hostility toward society of the typical serial killer.*

Serial child killer John Joubert at the time of his arrest for the murder of two boys near Omaha, Nebraska.

tingly sexual nature of their deeds. To a man, they were dysfunctional sexually; that is, they were unable to have and maintain mature, consensual sexual experiences with other adults, and they translated that inability into sexual murders. Not everyone who is unable to participate in kissing games becomes a sexually dysfunctional adult. It's also important to recognize that having a good adult sexual relationship does not imply only heterosexual activity. There is such a thing as a successful homosexual relationship that is normal when looked at from the standpoint of encompassing two people who care for each other. Those killers in our sample who were homosexual were also dysfunctional in this regard, unable to maintain long-term relationships, showing a decided preference for bondage, torture, and sadomasochism in their short-term partnerships. Nearly half the murderers reported to us that they had never had a consenting sexual experience with another adult. As important, all the murderers knew they had not had normal relationships, and they resented not having them; it was this resentment that fueled their aggressive, murderous behavior. Richard Lawrence Marquette picked up a woman in a bar; they had known one another slightly during their childhoods. At his residence, according to his later confession, he was unable to perform sexually; the woman ridiculed this inability, so he killed her and chopped her up in small pieces. Incarcerated for thirteen years for this murder, and then released, Marquette picked up two more women in similar circumstances, tried and failed to have sex with them, and killed them, too, before being apprehended and returned to prison.

Adolescence in these troubled youngsters was dominated by increasing isolation and "acting out" behavior, with lots of daydreaming, compulsive masturbation, lying, bed-wetting, and nightmares as concomitants of the isolation. There was more opportunity at this stage for antisocial behavior. Instead of being in the house or yard all the time, the youngster was now in school, on the streets, away from the home. Cruelty to animals and to other children, running away, truancy, assaults on teachers, setting fires, destroying the property of others and their own property—these overt acts began in adolescence, though the mind-set that generated them was present earlier but had been below the surface because the child had been controlled in his home environment.

Many of the murderers were intelligent, but they did not do well in school. "I failed the second grade because I was uneducable," one murderer told us. His parents wanted to take him out of school to work on their farm, "but then I skipped the third grade because I passed the second grade and went on and excelled in many areas and dropped out in others. I excelled in math but couldn't spell.'' Their spotty record in school was a pattern that carried over later in life. Most were incapable of holding jobs or living up to their intellectual potential. They were not successful employees, and were fired often, involved in disputes at the workplace, and had continual problems with authority. They had the intellect necessary for skilled jobs, but most of them were employed in menial capacities. When they went into the military, as about 40 percent did, most of them received less than honorable discharges.

Just as there had been very little love in the family environment, there was also a lack of stimulation or encouragement to achieve within the family (and the school). Their energy became directed to negative outlets. In school, they were either chronically disruptive or subdued and withdrawn to the extent that no one paid them any attention.

"I felt guilty of having those thoughts [toward family]," Rissell told me—after years of listening to psychologists and picking up their jargon—"and submerged them and built up lots of hostility, and then it gets off into fantasy. . . . They should have noticed it at school, so excessive was my daydreaming that it was always in my report cards. . . . I was dreaming about wiping out the whole school."

School systems as well as families fail these children. Too often, confronted with a problem child, a school system does not get him to counseling, or, if counseling is done, it does not address the significant issues in his life, especially including those pertaining to the dysfunctional home. If a teacher says, "You ought to look at Joe, he has problems," the school system is unable to properly examine Joe's life, unable to get at the root of those problems in the home, unable to move other bureaucracies, such as the social services system, to the point where these could interrupt the downward spiral to salvage the child. Moreover, since the damage to the child is emotional, it is not easy to reach. These above-average-intelligence children find ways to disguise and conceal their mental wounds until they are covered over with thick scar tissue.

Many people survive enormous difficulties in childhood and don't grow up to murder. However, when the problems of childhood are reinforced by added neglect in the school, the social services system, and the neighborhood, they steadily worsen. In a situation where you find a distant mother, an absent or abusive father and siblings, a nonintervening school system, an ineffective social services system, and an inability of the person to relate sexually in a normal way to others, you have almost a formula for producing a deviant personality.

I am often asked why I don't discuss female serial killers. Only one female has been arrested and accused as a serial killer—Aileen Wuornos in Florida. Although there may be others, my extensive research has not come across them. Women do commit multiple murders, of course, but they tend to do so in a spree, and not sequentially, as is the pattern with the men I am discussing. Do the psychological impairments that characterize the men also describe the personalities of violent women? Frankly, I don't know; such research remains to be conducted. Serial killers are mostly male, white, and in their twenties or thirties at the time of their murders.

The ability to initiate, maintain, and develop good interpersonal relationships begins in childhood and is reinforced in the preteen years. But if it isn't there at the beginning and is not positively reinforced in those preteen years, by the time a boy reaches adolescence, it's almost too late. Although the "acting out" behavior may not be murder or rape, it will be some other sort of demonstration of dysfunction. People whose childhoods have been deeply impaired do not go on to wholly normal lives; they become the alcoholic mothers or the abusive fathers who create home environments that perpetuate the cycle of abuse and make it highly likely that their children will become offenders. Dysfunctional adults produce a hothouse environment in which criminal fantasies and behavior are nurtured, to the detriment of their children and of society.

There are always points of intervention, ways to retard the offending behavior of the potentially dangerous child who has had a bad life up to, say, twelve years of age. A new and loving stepfather or a teacher or a Big Brother might enter the picture and exert a good influence. Psychological counseling might get at the heart of the problem and move the child away from the path leading to deviant behavior.

An important aspect to note here: Where there's some intervention at this stage, the child who has been rescued may go on to disappoint the family, be truant, not respond overtly to the better environment; but as an adult, he might never offend, at least not to the extent of committing abductions, rapes, and murders. Someone on the track toward antisocial behavior can be retracked only so far; the chances are that he will become a largely dysfunctional adult. For him to be reshaped and return completely to normal behavior is unlikely.

That means that when these murderers are caught and incarcerated, the prognosis for their rehabilitation is extremely poor—because, after all, their problems have been developing since their childhoods.

These are men who have never known how to relate properly to other human beings; it is not likely that such a fundamental interpersonal skill can be taught in prison. They have to be reeducated in how to be human beings who care for other human beings as individuals. To turn angry, resentful, aggressive men into sensitive people who can fit well into society is almost an impossible task.

Recently, one man who was in prison for repeated child molestation described quite graphically just this inability to change his behavior. In his fantasies for years, he had had sex with underage boys, he said; in prison, despite attempts by the authorities to turn his mental affections toward adults—even toward male homosexual adults—his daydreams and autoerotic play always centered on boys, and he knew it would stay centered on them forever, whether in prison or out.

Most previous researchers into the mind of the murderer thought that the roots of violent behavior were in childhood trauma—a boy who had been assaulted at age six would grow up to rape women. But not all of the rapists or murderers we interviewed had been assaulted during their childhoods. My research convinced me that the key was not the early trauma but the development of perverse thought patterns. These men were motivated to murder by their fantasies.

"I knew long before I started killing that I was going to be killing, that it was going to end up like that," one multiple murderer told us. "The fantasies were too strong. They were going on for too long, and were too elaborate." After the murders actually began, the fantasies continued. "It is a development," the killer reported, "Getting tired of a certain level of fantasy and then going even further and even more bizarre . . . it got off in such deep ends that I'm still not exposed to the worst of the fantasies that I have."

All the murderers that we interviewed had compelling fantasies; they murdered to make happen in the real world what they had seen over and over again in their minds since childhood and adolescence. As adolescents, instead of developing normal peer-related interests and activities, where they couldn't completely control what went on, the murderers retreated into sexually violent fantasies, where they could, in effect, control their world. These adolescents overcompensated for the aggression in their early lives by repeating the abuse in fantasy—but, this time, with themselves as the aggressors. As one murderer told me, "Nobody bothered to find out what my problem was, and nobody knew about the fantasy world."

It is because these murderers deal in fantasy that we characterize serial murders as sexual homicides, even when physical penetration or other sexual acts do not appear to have been perpetrated on the victim. Sexual maladjustment is at the heart of all the fantasies, and the fantasies emotionally drive the murders.

Fantasy is defined as a happenstance unattainable in normal life. A normal male fantasy might be to have sex with a perfectly beautiful movie star. Carnally possessing a sex goddess is not a perverse thought, merely the mental expression of a wish that is, for most people, beyond what can be attained. An abnormal fantasy might be to immobilize and slash such a movie star during sex. The normal guy accepts the fact that he's never going to have access to Madonna or Cher or Jane Fonda or whoever he thinks is really cool or sexy; he finds a substitute. Normal people learn to accept social control and moderation as limits on their behavior. The deviant person, having had very few true restraints on his behavior since childhood, believes he can act out his fantasy and that nobody will be able to stop him. Many young men had a crush on Jodie Foster, but only John Hinckley felt he was entitled to stalk her in New Haven, send her notes, and tape-record their conversations, while planning to assassinate President Reagan.

Similarly, we all know that many children play with pets and are fascinated by wild animals. They generally don't engage in deliberate torture, however. One deviant felt entitled to slit a dog's stomach to see how far it could run before falling into death spasms; another attached cherry bombs to cats' legs and made many cats in his neighborhood three-legged. A third strangled a cat without compunction but was outraged and deeply hurt when someone fed ground glass to his own dog.

The offenders' greater commitment to their fantasies deepens as they become loners in adolescence, subject to the onset of puberty and sexual arousal. Aggressive, and with a feeling of having been cheated by society, they channel their hostility into fantasy. Several murderers reported early attachments to high-heeled women's shoes, female underwear, rope for strangulation and asphyxiation, the last not only for others but for themselves, principally for sexual stimulation. Twelve-year-old Edmund Kemper played "gas chamber" with his sister, a game in which the sister was required to tie him in a chair and click an imaginary switch that released the gas, so he could keel over in the chair and "die," a joyless, hostile, repetitive game that mingled sexual and death themes. A second adolescent male masturbated openly into his sisters' undergarments—often in front of his sisters—and then wondered why the family was angry at him. A third, at age fifteen, dragged younger males into the bathroom of his treatment facility to force them to have anal and oral sex with him, recapitulating the way he had been victimized at age ten. A fourth boy had been discovered at age three with his penis tied to a bureau drawer, strangling and stimulating it; at age thirteen, he was found by his parents in the bathtub, trying to tie up his penis and his neck to a bar above the faucets; by age seventeen, the young man turned his aggressive instincts from himself to a young female, whom he abducted and kept all night at gunpoint.

The fantasies are characterized by strong visual components, and by themes of dominance, revenge, molestation, and control. Whereas the normal person fantasizes in terms of sexual adventures, the deviant links sexual and destructive acts. Normal fantasies of interpersonal adventure are fused with abnormal attempts to degrade, humiliate, and dominate others. Most normal fantasies have at their center the idea that the partner will have as much fun as the dreamer. With these deviant men, the more fantasy fun they are having, the more danger their fantasy partner is in.

Therein lies the key: In these sorts of fantasies, the other person is depersonalized, made into an object. "I'm sorry to sound so cold about this," Ed Kemper apologized to me, "but what I needed to have was a particular experience with a person, and to possess them in the way I wanted to; I had to evict them from their human bodies." Once evicted from a body, however, a person cannot reenter it. In other words, Kemper was saying that in order to have his sexual fantasies fulfilled, he had to kill his partner.

Fantasies about sex are not discussed in families, even intact and functional families. Adolescent males are not routinely advised that now that they've reached puberty it's okay to think about girls and nude bodies and doing things to females in bed. A child in a normal family, however, observes appropriate behavior between his parents, Mom and Dad hugging and kissing and holding hands; he accepts that his parents have a love relationship and expects that he, too, will have a similar one. Our murderers grew up without observing this sort of parental closeness, and without feeling any affection directed toward them, either. Normal people relate to sexual activity as part of loving. Deviants feel the sexual urge without having learned that it has anything to do with affection. And so they become boys who think about going out and "getting it," or "getting laid," without reference to the potential partner as an individual or even as a human being. Most deviants don't even know what they're going to do with a female when they "get" her.

What psychologists call the "cognitive mapping" process is almost complete by this time. Cognitive mapping is the development of thinking patterns that affect how the person relates to himself and to his environment; it determines how the individual gives meaning to the events that happen in his world. He moves more and more into an antisocial position, viewing the world as a hostile place. He becomes almost incapabable of interacting properly with the outside world, because his thinking patterns are all turned inward, designed only to stimulate himself in an attempt to reduce tensions, which only reinforces his isolation. A loop is developed. The lonely teenager has aberrant fantasies and tries partially to live these out by tentative antisocial acts—the lie that is not found out; the cruelty to an animal, which does not have any ill effects on his own life; the fire that burns brightly; the frightening of a younger child that is not reported. He "gets away" with such acts. The effects of these accomplishments then become incorporated into his fantasies, which are pushed to a more intensively violent level. More retreat from society follows, and, eventually, so do more experiments with actualizing the fantasies.

In my interviews, I learned that the most difficult thing for murderers to discuss was the early expression of fantasy. Ed Kemper's fantasies began quite young, yet in our interview he did not connect these with his first murders—at age fifteen, he shot and killed his grandparents. Probing, I learned that he did connect these deaths with his grandparents' previous chastizing of him for killing the birds and small animals on their farm, after which they had taken away his gun. Many children in rural areas are given guns and they use them for hunting, but the creatures Kemper killed were not game animals. Kemper was angry at not being allowed to have the gun. There was a hidden agenda at that time, however, and his grandparents did not address it. Unfortunately, all that the grandparents did was remove his gun, believing that the absence of the killing tool would stop Kemper's bad behavior. They did not ask Kemper what was going on in his head—what his fantasies were—that made him want to use the gun to kill small animals just for the "fun" of it. I couldn't get him to talk about this directly, but I guessed that part of Kemper's reason for killing his grandparents was in order to keep his murderous fantasy from their view.

What begins as fantasy ends as part of a homicidal ritual. A man who in childhood play pulled off the heads of his sister's Barbie

dolls beheaded his victims when he reached adulthood. Another man
ran around the yard as a child, chasing a friend with a hatchet; as an
adult, he used a hatchet in his murders. John Joubert at age thirteen,
while riding a bicycle, drove a pencil into the back of a young girl.
He found the act stimulating. When he was not caught or punished, he
escalated his violence; next time while on his bike, he slashed someone
with a razor blade. Going back into Joubert's life, we discovered that
just prior to this first attack, he had lost a friend. He and a younger
boy had started to develop a benign and possibly latent homosexual
relationship; then John went away for the summer and came back to
learn that his friend had moved away. Joubert's mother said she didn't
know where the friend had gone, and that John would just have to
adjust to the loss. Another mother might well have helped her son
locate a forwarding address, encouraged him to write to the friend,
said they might be able to visit during the next vacation, and so on;
Mrs. Joubert crushed the delight that her son had in this relationship,
and, soon after, John jabbed the pencil in the back of the young girl.
In doing so, he stepped over the line into actively criminal behavior.
Once John Joubert's fantasies had pushed him to attacking another
human being, very little could have prevented him from going on to
later murders. Perhaps if he had been caught, punished, and actively
counseled so that the stresses in his home environment could have
been countered, he might have been deterred from further antisocial
violence, but—and this is the sad thing—such actions were unlikely
to quell the fantasies that drove the behavior.

Though the home and social environments were nonnurturing ones,
and seriously violent fantasies developed, many potential offenders
still do not step over the line to commit violent acts. These young men
are ticking bombs waiting to go off, but their histories show that they
are not pushed over into acts of great antisocial violence unless certain
precrime stresses were present. In Joubert's case, it was the sudden
removal of his only friend that precipitated his first attack. Later in his
life, when he was in the Air Force, it was the removal by choice of
his roommate at the air base, coupled with an unexpected and expensive
repair that he had to have made to his car, that put him in the frame
of mind in which he could make terribly real his fantasy to abduct and
murder a young boy.

The escalation of Monte Rissell's crimes from rape to murder
came when he was back in high school after serving some time in
juvenile institutions, and he was actually receiving psychiatric counsel-

ing as part of his probation. Before this, he had committed rape, but had not progressed beyond that to even greater violence. His girlfriend, a year ahead of him in high school, had graduated, gone on to college, and had sent him a Dear John letter saying that she preferred to spend time with other men. Rissell drove to the college and observed the woman with her new boyfriend, but he took no immediate action. Back at home near Washington, D.C., he sat in his car in a parking lot, had a beer and smoked a joint, and thought about things until quite late at night. At around two in the morning, a woman appeared, alone in a car; she was a prostitute. There was no one around, and Rissell thought to himself that he would take from this woman—at gunpoint—what he could no longer obtain from his former girlfriend. With a .45 pistol in his hand, he approached the prostitute's car and then abducted, raped, and killed the woman. Later, he went on to kill four more women.

Richard Marquette's first murder was triggered by his inability to perform sexually with a woman he had picked up in a bar. Ted Bundy's first murder was supposedly precipitated by his loss of the financial support that had allowed him to go to law school. Some will argue that if Bundy had had no precrime stresses, had completed law school and met a woman who satisfied a lot of his needs, he might never have murdered; he might have become a viciously aggressive lawyer, someone who visited prostitutes, sought sadomasochistic relationships, and otherwise tried to get rid of his anger—his deviance might have been more socially acceptable—and he might never have stepped completely over the line. We have no way of knowing that, of course, but judging from Bundy's later behavior, it seems more likely that he would have stepped over the line at some point, no matter whether he had stayed in law school or not, and no matter whether he found a woman who would satisfy some of his sexual fantasies or not. In his mind, he had long since fused sexual desire with the need to damage and destroy. David Berkowitz's troubles reached the boiling-over point when he failed to convince his birth mother to make him part of her family; of course, his wish to be part of that family was doomed to failure, anyway. Ed Kemper, after coming out of prison for the murder of his grandparents, went back to live with his mother, at her insistence. Yet, having fought to get him out of an institution, she then berated him steadily, saying that he was responsible for her dating problems. After one particularly harrowing argument with his mother, Kemper slammed the door, got into his car, drove away, and said to himself, "The first good-looking woman I see tonight is going to die."

Then he went out searching for a likely victim, and soon found one, a woman on the college campus, to whom he offered a ride home.

Many of the precrime stresses that seem to precipitate murderous actions are the same as those that happen to lots of people every day—the loss of a job, the breakup of a relationship, money problems. Normal people cope with such problems, and do so from a scaffolding of a helpful, normal pattern of development. In potential murderers, however, the scaffolding is faulty to begin with, and so are the mental mechanisms for dealing with the stressful events. Faced with a difficult happenstance such as the loss of a job, they turn inward and focus on their own problems to the exclusion of all else, and on fantasies as the solution to the problems. A breakup with a girlfriend causes the man to be less attentive on the job, resulting in his getting fired; now, without income and without solace, he encounters other problems, matters that earlier he might have handled in spite of pressures but that now seem overwhelming. The precrime stress is the straw that breaks the camel's back.

Crossing-the-line behavior is fundamentally self-destructive and socially destructive. It entails the offender doing things that he actually knows are wrong, and that will bring him untold grief if he is caught. Yet he is impelled to cross the line by everything that has previously occurred in his life. Only later, after many such acts, will he come to believe that he is invincible and will never be caught. Just before he edges to the line, the young man isn't so certain.

Things have been building up to a point where the potential murderer is ready to commit his violent act—and then a possible victim appears, one who is in a particularly vulnerable position—and the potential murderer becomes an actual murderer.

The deed is done. The threshold has been crossed, and there is no return possible. He's frightened and he's thrilled. He has experienced a state of heightened arousal during the crime, and liked it. He waits for several days, expecting arrest and punishment, but nothing happens. Perhaps the deed makes him feel badly, and he seeks to control his impulses. Bill Heirens reported that he locked himself in a bathroom when he began to sense that he wanted to go out and commit a new crime, thereby hoping to prevent the feeling from overwhelming him. However, he managed to get out the bathroom window in a bathrobe and do something heinous, anyway. More usually, after the first murder, the man starts to feel more egocentric than ever and becomes convinced that he can do it again, with impunity. He incorporates details of the first murder into his fantasies and begins to construct future crimes. What if I toyed with her more before I strangled her? What if I dismembered the body so that the police wouldn't be able to identify the victim? What if I made the boy say and do certain things before I assaulted him physically? What if I took a ring from her so I could use it later in my fantasy replay of the crime? What if I looked for a victim in the next town, rather than five blocks from my home? What if I prepared some restraints and took them with me, so I wouldn't have to improvise at the scene? Used a gun to control the victim next time, instead of a knife?

Now that the first murder has occurred, in subsequent crimes the life stresses that preceded the first one may not need to be present. Now that he's over the line, the murderer usually and more conspicuously plans his future crimes. The first one may have had some of the earmarks of spontaneity. The next victim will in all likelihood be more carefully sought out, the murder more expertly done and displaying more violence to the victim than was evident in the first crime. And the lonely boy from the nonnurturing home has become a serial killer.

5

DEATH OF A NEWSBOY

In the fall of 1983, I was on my way to my alma mater, Michigan State University, to teach at an annual homicide seminar. It was a warm September day at Michigan State, the leaves were turning color, and the campus looked beautiful. When I walked into my hotel, I was handed a message to phone the office immediately. Anytime I get a message like that, a chill goes through me, because I know something rotten has happened; bad news travels fast, especially if you're a law-enforcement officer. I called in and my immediate superior told me that a young newsboy named Danny Joe Eberle had been abducted and murdered in Bellevue, Nebraska, near Omaha, and that I should go to Omaha and see what I could do to help find the killer. I leapt at the chance.

My mind flashed to two similar cases. Almost precisely a year earlier, in Des Moines, a young newsboy had vanished under eerily parallel circumstances—on a Sunday morning, while delivering his papers. Newsboy Johnny Gosch had never been found. The FBI had been slow to get into the Gosch case, and Mrs. and Mrs. Gosch had both told me personally that they were very bitter about that. Of course the abduction of their son had been done within a state's borders, and the FBI technically had no jurisdiction, but they quite legitimately felt that the nation's premier law-enforcement entity ought to have done more. Similarly and earlier in time, when young Adam Walsh had disappeared, the Florida police had asked the FBI to get involved in the case and the Bureau had declined, saying it was a local matter and unless there was some indication of interstate travel, we had no jurisdiction. Later, when Adam's head was found floating in a canal, and there was a suspect who had an out-of-state car, the FBI took an interest. John Walsh, Adam's father, rejected the Bureau's help at that time. He later told me his reasoning: The Bureau hadn't wanted to assist when the case was just a missing child, but agreed to participate only when the boy's head was found and the child's life was clearly beyond saving. The Walshes could do without that kind of help, he said. (John Walsh later went on to national prominence as the host of the syndicated television program "America's Most Wanted.") I had agreed with both the Gosches and John Walsh that the Bureau should have been involved in the searches for their sons and ought to be more aggressively and earlier involved in such cases of missing children in the future.

The problem had always been that lack of jurisdiction. When I went through the FBI academy as a student, we had learned about the various federal laws that we were to enforce. One of them, for instance, was the Migratory Bird Act, which we called the Blue Heron law. It was a federal crime to kill certain migratory birds; another federal crime was not removing the door from a refrigerator when it had been put on the street for pickup by the garbage department. (Both these laws, by the way, had been introduced after problems had been discerned: The bird law was passed to protect a species that was fast disappearing because it was one of the favorite sources for plumes on ladies' hats in the early part of the twentieth century, and the refrigerator-door law had been passed after a startling number of children had climbed into abandoned refrigerators and died because they were unable to reopen the doors.)

None of the federal laws involved serial murder, and the definition of kidnapping was such that the FBI could enter the case only if there was a ransom note or demand. The Walsh and Gosch tragedies, together with the urgings of child advocates throughout the country, had helped alter the climate of opinion in Washington and in state capitals toward missing and abducted children. In an ominbus crime bill introduced into Congress in the early 1980s, the Reagan Administration pressed to have murders, kidnappings, and other serious crimes become a part of the FBI's jurisdiction. This bill had recently become law when Danny Joe Eberle was abducted, and so there was a determination up and down the Bureau to assist in the case in whatever way possible.

As soon as Danny Joe had been reported missing, the Special Agent in Charge (SAC) of the Omaha FBI office had sent his deputy, Johnny Evans, to the nearby small town of Bellevue to see what he could do, and then sought permission for Evans to stay on it until it was solved. Evans was an upstanding guy, the very model of a good FBI agent—clean-cut, handsome, civic-minded, just the sort of man to help convey the wish of the FBI to throw the organization into a difficult case. Johnny Evans became extremely involved, determined to see the case through, and he worked closely with local, state, and military authorities in a coordinated effort that was unique at the time.

It was when the boy's body was found, two and a half days after the abduction, that I was asked to get into the case. This was one of the first times I would actually be able to go on-scene in the midst of a murder case; it was a chance to see things firsthand, and to have more give and take with local authorities than the telephone and teletype usually allowed. Out of the classroom, onto the front lines.

I certainly wanted to be involved, and my superiors wanted me to, because we both thought we might be able to render some real help; at higher levels in the FBI, I think that the decision to have the Bureau participate fully in the Eberle matter was political, to make sure that the Bureau had a presence in this first important missing-child case to arise after the new law had been passed. It was a good thing, too, because there was a crying need for the sort of services that the Bureau could render in the areas of added manpower, the VICAP system that we were still developing, our growing expertise at profiling, and our traditionally superb laboratory work.

It was snowing in Omaha, and I had no coat, having been prepared only for the balmy Michigan State weather. I shivered as I was picked up at the airport by Sarpy County Sheriff Pat Thomas, and driven to Bellevue police headquarters. The task force was already established and at work; dozens of people were collecting and trying to analyze information. Johnny Evans was glad to see me. Although a veteran agent, he had worked mostly on such things as organized crime, bank robberies, and interstate commerce problems, and had no experience with a murder, especially one as stomach-turning as the killing of this young newsboy.

Bellevue is an outlying suburb of a typically Midwestern city, a place of modest incomes, quiet and orderly, the sort of place you think of when describing the good quality of life that the United States symbolizes in this world. Before dawn on a Sunday morning, Danny Joe Eberle had awakened, dressed—all except his shoes, for he liked to travel barefoot, despite his parents' reminders—and taken his bicycle down to a local convenience store where he picked up papers to fold and deliver on a regular route. Danny was thirteen, a blondish, bright-eyed boy, five-two and weighing one hundred pounds, the son of a post office employee. His slightly older brother also had a paper route.

At seven that morning, Danny's newspaper route supervisor began getting calls from neighborhood patrons saying that their papers hadn't been delivered. He went to check, found nothing, and then roused Mr. Eberle, who also searched the area and did not find Danny. The first three papers had been delivered, but Danny's bike lay propped next to a fence near what should have been the fourth delivery site. The remaining newspapers were still in the bag, and there was no sign of a struggle. Danny had just vanished. The police were contacted, and they called the FBI's Omaha office. There was some suspicion that Danny might have accompanied his aunt and uncle on a trip out of state, where his uncle was going to look for employment; that notion was quickly disproved. A massive building-to-building search of the area was begun, and on Wednesday afternoon Danny's dead body was found in some high grass alongside a gravel road, four miles from the site where his bike had been found, and only a few miles from the Iowa state line.

I went out to see the place where the body had been found. There are lots of things you can tell from crime-scene photos, but being on-site has a distinct advantage. You are able to be completely oriented, to see relationships between details that you might otherwise never figure out. For instance, it was easy to see that the site was near to a gravel road and a dead end. What might not have been obvious from crime-scene photos (unless they had been taken of the quarter mile or so around the site of finding the body), however, was the existence of a crossroads nearby, with one of the roads leading to a river. Why hadn't the killer (or killers) put the body into the river, where it might have floated away or been more concealed? The site was the sort of area where people had outdoor parties, jettisoned beer cans, and such; there were tall weeds growing alongside the road, but the site was actually visible from the road if one happened to be looking carefully. Someone dumping the body there would have had to worry about a passing car's headlights silhouetting him, if it had been still dark, or otherwise courting discovery.

The public had been told that Danny Joe Eberle had been killed with a knife. The details were far more horrible, for the newsboy had been mutilated as well as killed. The body had lain as if he had fallen or been dumped in the weeds, facedown, hands and feet tied behind his back with rope. His hands, feet, and mouth had also been taped with surgical tape, and he was stripped to his undershorts. There were multiple stab wounds in the chest and the back. The neck had been slashed. It appeared as if a slice had been taken off the shoulder, and on the left calf there were postmortem wounds that seemed to be in a crisscross or ticktacktoe pattern. There was some facial battery, and pebble indentations all over the body.

The medical examiner's report suggested the body had been moved perhaps more than once after death—because of a pebble found in the victim's mouth, under the tape—and also suggested that Danny might have been kept alive for as much as a day after capture, and killed close to the time that the body was found. There had been no sexual assault on the body in any way, nor had the underpants been removed.

Being on the scene and talking to the various officers and witnesses and the like was quite important to my understanding of the case. Danny Joe's older brother reported having been followed by a young white man in a tan car on his own route a few times. There were other witnesses who couldn't provide many details but did believe they had seen a man in a car seemingly trailing other teenaged boys from time to time.

I took all of this information into account and wrote up a preliminary profile. In the profile, I said that Danny Joe Eberle's killer was a youthful white male, in his late teens or early twenties. As the reader now knows, most serial killers are white males, and this was a white neighborhood; any black, Hispanic, or even Asian man entering the area would most probably have been noticed. I thought the killer was young because of the tentative nature of the killing and because the body had been dumped not far off a road, indicating that this was the first time the killer had killed. Of course he couldn't be too young, because he (or his friends) had to have a driver's license, but the killer did not display the savvy of a man in his thirties. I thought it possible that the killer was someone who knew Danny on a casual basis, at least well enough so that he might have been able to approach the newsboy and induce him to voluntarily enter a vehicle, a car or possibly a van. I wasn't sure whether there was one killer or several. The violent male might have been accompanied by one or two other young white males, I reasoned; perhaps one lured the boy into the back of a van, where the other controlled him white the first drove away. Based on what I knew of the victim, I thought there was a possibility there had been an attempted sexual assault on Eberle that he had resisted, and that he had been killed while resisting—although there were no "defensive" wounds on the body. The way the body had been abandoned on the remote roadside suggested to me that the killer might have panicked after the killing and had hurriedly gotten rid of the body rather than dispose of it in a more orderly manner. "The dumping of the body just off a lightly traveled road suggests that the killer may not have possessed sufficient strength to carry the body further into a wooded area," I wrote. I believed the unknown suspect was somewhat aware of the location and had probably traversed the area many times previously. The ligatures and lack of abrasions under the ropes, together with the pathologist's report, had convinced me that the victim might have remained unbound for a while and could even have been treated well for a time before being killed.

Returning to the precise identity of the killer, I stated that he was from the local area—not a stranger or a transient who happened to be passing through—and that he was single and not educated beyond the high school level. He might be unemployed, or employed in a rather menial or unskilled capacity. The crime showed a certain level of intelligence, but not enough intelligence for every aspect of the killing to have been preplanned, and that was why I thought the killer hadn't gone beyond high school. Yet the binding and rope tying suggested that this was a person who worked well with his hands. After considering the nature of the wounds, the tape, the rope bindings, the most important fact was that there had been no actual sexual penetration. This almost always means a youngish man who has had no true sexual experience with a consenting peer, either male or female. Since that is unusual in our society, it also connotes psychological problems while growing up. Here was a killer who stripped the boy down to his underpants but did nothing more. I wrote of the killer's probable psychological orientation: "The main perpetrator would definitely have had a chronic sexual problem, indicating deviance and bizarre sexual experiences, throughout his life." Having reviewed many cases in which the killers did not penetrate their victims, but did mutilate them, I knew that behavior of the level of a mutilation murder does not happen without a lot of deviant fantasies paving the way—fantasies that would have had to surface in one way or another in earlier years. My profile continued: "He would likely be an avid reader of pornography, and may have been involved in experiments of a bizarre nature throughout his adolescence. This experimentation could involve animals and possibly forced sexual acts on younger children, both male and female." As the reader now knows from Chapter 4, this sort of earlier behavior is often associated with those who grow up to murder. There is one apparent contradiction here: I knew that the victim had not been penetrated, but I thought it possible that the killer might have earlier been involved in forced sexual acts with younger children. It was possible that he had been reluctant to penetrate because of the presence of other people in the car or van. The profile went on: ''Indications are that the killer would have been involved in recent stressful events in his life which might include breaking up with a girlfriend, losing a job, being dropped from school or trouble with his immediate family.'' As the reader also knows, such precrime stresses are usually involved in first murders—and I thought this to be a first murder. ''Further,'' I wrote, ''the individual may have been absent from his employment, if employed, for several days before and after the disappearance of Eberle.'' This last characteristic I suggested because of my interviews with murderers; many, such as Berkowitz, told me that the time right around the murder was quite important to them, so important that they had absented themselves from their usual routine before and after it.

I knew that the killer had been out at six in the morning, which indicated that he had no one to whom he was responsible, and therefore was most likely not living with a wife or with overly concerned parents. Sometimes when there is a case that occurs at this early-morning hour, it's the result of a killer who has been up all night, drinking, to raise his courage to the point where he can do the crime. If he had kept the child alive for some time, he must have had a place in which to do so. I was not certain why the victim had been found in only his underwear, because there could have been reasons other than sexual for keeping him that way—to prevent him from running away, for instance. I had the distinct impression from the gravity and incompleteness of the wounds that the killer had murdered the boy somewhat spontaneously and then after death had cut the victim on the back of the neck, thinking perhaps that he would decapitate him and dismember the body and scatter the parts—but then pulling back because this was hard to do, and just leaving the body somewhere that seemed remote. This indicated to me that he had never before dismembered a body—but suggested that he might have killed before.

There was one aspect of the body that I thought might be important, but I wasn't yet certain about it: On the leg and shoulder, there were some wounds that seemed inexplicable. Why would a killer cut away a portion of the shoulder, or the flesh on the inside of a leg? In the back of my mind, I thought it possible that these slices had been done in an attempt to obliterate bite marks on those parts of the body, but I couldn't yet prove my contention. Biting in a sexual frenzy was consistent with a killing that had a sexual basis, as I believed this one did.

Because of the killer's lack of control (as demonstrated by the crime scene), I thought it probable that he might inject himself into the investigation, trying to appear helpful but actually seeking information by hanging around the fringes of the dump area, the mortuary or grave site, or the neighborhood in which the crime was committed. Considering such a possibility likely, I suggested that any artist's conceptions of the killer that were produced on the basis of witnesses' recollections should *not* be made public but should be kept within the law-enforcement community, in case the killer showed his face any-where near the investigation. For some time, we had people watching the funeral, the grave site, the place where the body had been found, and the location where Eberle had been abducted, but with no luck.

In addition to the profile, I did what we might call a preliminary VICAP analysis. Using the computer in my head rather than the one at Quantico, I compared this case to others and concluded that it was not that similar to the Gosch case. Eberle's body had been found; Gosch's was still missing. Gosch's abductor, it seemed to me, had taken far more care than the killer of Danny Joe Eberle. The media continued to play up the fact that both victims had been newsboys, abducted on Sunday mornings; I, knowing more details and having more experience in comparing crimes, did not think the same abductor had been at work in both cases.

The rope used in the binding of Eberle was sent to our labora-tories for analysis, but it did not match any known samples. That in itself was an important clue, for the uniqueness of the rope might help in pinning the crime on someone who had other pieces of similar rope. In addition to providing laboratory work, the FBI wanted to put every asset in our arsenal at the disposal of the investigation, and so our hypnosis team from San Antonio was called in to assist. The older Eberle boy and other witnesses agreed to be hypnotized in order to recall what they had seen. Very little extra evidence was gleaned from them, but every bit added to our understanding of the probable killer. Despite my strong belief—seconded by Johnny Evans—that the person who had abducted and killed Eberle would strike again, there was nothing more that I could do on the scene, and so I returned to Quantico. The task force was doing all that could be done. The Eberle family was bearing up reasonably well, aided by their faith and the close support of their neighbors and fellow parishioners. I had a teenaged son of my own at home, and felt the family's loss keenly.

* * *

I was in Alabama, at yet another road school, in early December when I received a second call, directly from a distraught Johnny Evans. Another boy had been abducted near Omaha and found brutally murdered three days later. Our worst fears had been realized. I rushed to Omaha, once more without benefit of an overcoat, and was soon wading through the snow with Thomas Evans and many of the same people whose acquaintance I had made in September. At around 8:30 Friday morning, December 2, young Christopher Paul Walden, the son of an officer at Offutt Air Force Base, had been walking to school in Sarpy County, and was last seen getting into a car with a white male. Three days later, in the afternoon, Walden's body was found by two bird hunters in a heavily wooded area five miles from the abduction site. He, too, was wearing only his undershorts and had been stabbed, and had his throat slashed so far that he was nearly decapitated. There was no question in the minds of any of the law-enforcement people who viewed the damage done to the Walden boy that the killer was the same person who had similarly savaged and mutilated Eberle's body. The pattern of postmortem wounds on the second victim indicated that the killer was escalating his sadistic slashing of the victims. Christopher Walden had been the same height and age as young Eberle, but fifteen pounds lighter.

It was fortunate that the second victim was found just then, for a heavy snowfall had recently begun. Another few hours of snow would have completely covered the body and the tracks near it, making it highly unlikely that the body would have been located before the spring thaw. At that point, several other murders might have already occurred, and the clues to this one might have been degraded and no longer helpful.

In many cases, the scene where the abduction takes place is not the death scene, and the death scene may not be where the body is eventually found. That latter site is referred to as the crime scene, and invariably yields the most evidence. The abduction and murder sites may never be found. Victims are lured away from abduction scenes, and bodies are transported even farther in attempts to stave off discovery of the murder and any possible connection of the killer to the murdered person. Eberle had been killed somewhere else and his body dumped in the weeds near the river. This second victim was found many yards into the woods, but it seemed that the dump site was also the place where he had been murdered. Prints beside the body—almost covered by the snow—showed clearly that two sets of feet had walked to this site, and only one set had walked out. Walden's clothes were piled neatly next to him. Clearly, he had been killed here. That in itself was an important clue, for it told me there was only one killer, and that he had been relatively slight of build. He had evidently forced Walden to walk into the woods where the murder was committed.

To my mind, the killer was an obvious coward. These teenaged boys were low-risk victims for him, akin to little old ladies, vulnerable victims, too young or too scared to resist someone who might be a few years older but not that much larger than they were. On the other hand, I had to recognize and take into account that this was an offender who had improved his MO since the first murder. I tried to get into the murderer's mind and think as he had done. Let me attempt to replicate some of that thinking here:

The first one, I brought the props with me, the tape and the rope. Maybe they've sent such things to the FBI laboratory to be analyzed. I won't use them again. I don't need them, anyhow, because I've learned that I can control the victim through ruses, through mental pressure and threats. Maybe what I should do is take the kid a little farther into the wooded area. I certainly don't want the kid's clothing left in my car, where I left it the last time, so I'll have him walk in clothed, then disrobe, and then I'll kill him.

Such a level of planning on the killer's part led me to revise my estimate of the killer's age; I thought now that he must be in his twenties, not in his teens. The stripping of the child now stood out boldly as a sexual matter, not as a control action. That, combined with the lack of sexual penetration (now verified by a second instance), made me firm up my belief that the killer was asexual. I would have been surprised if he'd ever had a consenting sexual experience with a female. And if he had had a homosexual experience, it probably had occurred when he was about the same age as these victims had been. He would have difficulty associating with people in his own age group, though he might date because he was attempting to deny his homosexuality; if he did date, it would be significantly younger girls whom he could easily dominate. What we were seeing in these two murders was a killer's anger at himself, expressed as homicidal rage toward victims who in his mind mirrored the boy he had been at their age. In his everyday life, this killer didn't have a lot to say about his existence, about what happened to him and when it happened and how it happened. He might or might not be physically weak, but he was beyond doubt emotionally weak.

That was why I concluded that this second killing had been a different event from his first one; the first time, it had been an experiment; the second time, the killer had demonstrated his fascination with the taking of a human life, and had tested and proved to himself his power and control over the victim. For example, the cutting in the second murder had been more extensive than in the first.

The postmortem cutting indicated to me a growing morbid interest in sadistic activity that I thought might come to dominate the killer's behavior in his future murders.

In between the first and second murders, one clue was actually discovered *not* to be a clue. The pebble in the mouth, which at first had seemed evidence that the body had been moved from elsewhere, turned out to be a mistake. The medical examiner had originally stated that a pebble had been found in Eberle's mouth. Later, the ME retracted this statement and explained that the pebble was from another case and had nothing to do with the Eberle murder. The absence of the pebble allowed us to speculate that the first murder had taken place closer to the time that the body was found.

I revised my earlier profile. There was only one young male killer, I now wrote, a single killer with no accomplices. Thinking of his ability to carry the body, I wrote that he would not be much larger than his victims, and that he had killed on-site in order to avoid lugging the body any distance. I thought it certain that the killer lived in Bellevue, or on the air base. He was just too familiar with the area to be from anywhere else. In fact, I was leaning heavily toward believing that the killer had to be on the base. Staking a position quite far out on a limb, but commensurate with my earlier guesses about his intelligence and education, I said that the killer would most likely be a low-ranking airman, E-4 or lower. He would not be highly skilled, not someone who worked with computers, but a man who worked in administration or light maintenance, probably some sort of a mechanic. Leaning on the evidence of the wounds, which showed attempts to conceal signs of bite marks, I wrote that I felt the killer would be a reader of detective or police magazines, where the ability to identify someone through bite marks is routinely discussed. The pattern of the wounds and the ease with which the killer had abducted both victims were the items that concerned me when I stated that I felt it likely that the killer would be involved with young boys in some way—Boy Scouts, Little League, or some other kind of coaching.

I was entirely convinced that the killer would strike again, and soon, because school holidays were coming up; so was Johnny Evans. We talked over the details. Now the children would be out in their yards or on the streets and in the open playgrounds at all daylight hours, and the killer could approach one at any time. I recommended an all-out media blitz, utilizing the newspapers, television, and radio to caution children to play in groups, not alone, and to advise parents and guardians to look for suspicious cars and persons, and, when they saw anything suspicious, to write down license plates and descriptions and such, and to phone them in to the number of the task-force head-quarters, which would be heavily advertised. The task force also put together what they called a Code 17; in the event of another abduction being reported, the entire Sarpy County area could be sealed off within eleven minutes. It was hoped that this way, if there was another child snatched off the streets, the abductor could be apprehended before he took the victim into the woods to be killed. The media blitz was tremendous, and so was the cooperation from the public. Perhaps as a consequence, there were no killings for the remainder of the year. At home again for the holidays, I rested a bit easier.

During this period, the local authorities picked up many known sexual deviates and interrogated them quite thoroughly. One was a prime suspect in the murders; he even flunked a lie-detector test, and rope and surgical tape found in his residence seemed quite suspicious. He fit the profile in many regards, though he was openly and overtly homosexual. He passed the second lie-detector test and in other ways proved not to be the murderer, however. The community was surprised by the number of people whose deviant behavior was so noticeable that it had become of interest to the police, and a half-dozen of the worst offenders—such as a pedophile who used to pull young boys into his Cadillac—were arrested and convicted on various charges during the manhunt for the killer of Eberle and Walden.

In addition, a witness who had seen Walden and a young male walking together just prior to the abduction was hypnotized, and under hypnosis managed to recall that the two walkers seemed about the same size. She even came up with the first several digits on the license plate of the car toward which they had been walking. Because of the high degree of coordination among the law-enforcement authorities, this number was quickly given to the state's department of motor vehicles and a computer run made; there were nearly a thousand cars in the state that had those first several digits on the plates, but many fewer than that in the Sarpy County area. The police were about to start checking every single car on the list when, early on the morning of January 11, 1985, they got a break.

A female teacher at a church day-care center noticed a man in a car who seemed to be hanging around the center, a slight young man who matched the partial description that had been given out through the media. The car didn't match, but the driver did.

The young man saw her writing something, parked the car, and knocked on the door of the center, then pushed his way in and asked to use the telephone. She refused to let him do that. He threatened to kill her, and told her to give him a slip of paper on which she had written down the license number of his car. She managed to run past him into another church building, and to call the police. The man fled in the car. It was eight-thirty in the morning.

With the license plate number in hand, the police were quickly able to find the owner of the vehicle, a nearby Chevrolet dealership. Rushing there, they learned that the car the teacher had seen was on loan to an airman at Offutt whose own car was being repaired. The airman's own car, in the dealer's garage, matched the description provided by several witnesses, and its license plate had the same first digits as those recalled by the woman who had undergone hypnosis. Peeking in, police saw some rope and a knife. Proceeding with extreme caution, the police obtained a search warrant before entering the car. Later, it was learned that this car was the fourth one on the list of a thousand that had been spewed out by the DMV's computer, and it would most likely have been investigated anyhow within the next few days by a planned search for those vehicles.

Even before thoroughly searching the car, the police alerted the air base and, in the company of an FBI agent, a Sarpy County lieutenant, and several agents of the air force's OSI (Office of Special Investigations), went immediately to the quarters of A 1 C (E-3) John Joseph Joubert IV, a radar technician involved in maintenance work. Joubert agreed to a search of his quarters. The investigators found more rope inside a duffel bag. Also there were a hunting knife and two dozen detective magazines; one of those magazines appeared to be particularly dog-eared and well thumbed, and it contained a story about the killing of a newsboy. Baby-faced, twenty-one years old and slight—five-six and 164 pounds—Joubert fit the profile to a T, down to the fact that he was an assistant scoutmaster of a local troop.

Joubert was interrogated for many hours by several teams of officers; he denied the offenses at first, and said all the evidence was circumstantial and would never convict him. When confronted with the fact that the rope in his duffel and car appeared to match that taken from the first victim, and told that it was a very rare rope that the head scoutmaster of the troop had brought back with him from Korea, Joubert asked to talk to the scoutmaster and to one fourteen-year-old scout to whom he had been quite close. Those people did talk to him, and shortly before midnight on January 11, Joubert confessed to killing the two boys, citing details that only the true killer could have known.

I was at home, stoking a fire in my fireplace, when the phone rang. My wife answered it and told me Johnny Evans was on the line. My heart sank, thinking that his call must mean there had been another murder of a young boy in Omaha; I was glad beyond words that the killer had been caught, that Johnny Evans's own crusade to bring him in had paid off at last, and that I had been able to contribute something valuable to the stopping of this one-man murder wave. Evans was particularly amazed that I had been able to predict that police or detective magazines would be found in the killer's residence; in his confession, Joubert said that he had used the detective magazines as part of his masturbatory rituals.

Some of the unusual details Joubert revealed in this confession were that after the first murder, he had gone to a McDonald's to wash off the blood, and then had eaten breakfast there; later in the day, he had gone to a scout meeting where the abduction had been discussed, but he had not taken part in the conversation. He denied any sexual involvement with the boys, and even more vehemently denied that he had known them, stressing that he would not have done that sort of thing to any boy he knew, for instance those in the scout troop. After both murders, however, he had gone back to his quarters and relived the details and masturbated. During this initial confession, Joubert also said that he had been certain after the incident at the day-care center that he would be picked up that day, and was glad that he had been apprehended, for he was sure that he would have killed again.

The amount of interagency cooperation in this case was spectacular, and a model for the way things ought to be done in any major case involving an abduction and murder. Commendations for all the agencies involved were read into the *Congressional Record*, and congratulations were showered on the state, local, federal, and Air Force law-enforcement entities who had contributed to catching this killer. I was proud to receive, from FBI Director William Webster, a letter of commendation about the profile I had drawn of the probable killer, which, the Director wrote, "pointed toward the apprehension of an individual fitting the physical and mental characteristics you described. Your assumptions of the subject were very accurate and displayed great skill. . . . You have my profound thanks for a job well done.''

Of course I wanted to learn more about Joubert, and so I followed the progress of his case through the courts. He initially pleaded not guilty, despite having given a confession, then revised that plea and pleaded guilty; a three-judge panel gathered psychiatric and other reports, judged that he had been well aware of the nature of right and wrong at the time of the murders, and sentenced him to die in the electric chair. Various appeals resulted in a prolonged stay on death row.

Joubert's background was traced quite carefully, and while most of it seemed quite ordinary on the surface, a buildup toward murder that had begun when Joubert was extremely young was evident. He was born in Massachusetts and grew up in Portland, Maine. One of the first fantasies he remembered was at age six or seven, of coming up behind his baby-sitter, strangling her, and then eating her until she disappeared. Such a strange and violent fantasy at that age was unusual, and provocative. Joubert had remembered and improved on it from then on, all during his childhood and adolescence, and up to and through the time of his murders. His mother had been a hospital worker and his father a counterman and waiter in a restaurant. They had separated because of marital difficulties at almost the same time as this first violent fantasy occurred to Joubert. They divorced when he was ten, and Joubert and his mother moved to Maine. He later told one psychiatrist, whose report was submitted to the court, that his mother had a short temper and would blow up and break things; he'd retreat to his room until the tantrum stopped and she came in and apologized, as she usually did. He also reported that his mother had belittled him and made him feel as if he was not a worthwhile person. She continued to spank him until he was twelve, and had frequently disapproved of his open masturbation. His fantasies began with young women as their object, and then switched to young boys, adolescents in undershorts. Joubert did not know any longer whether the thoughts of strangling and stabbing these boys brought on the masturbation or whether the masturbation brought on the thoughts.

During his preteen years, Joubert became a pawn in the battle between his mother and father, as the latter tried to obtain custody of him but failed. To see his father during the summers, Joubert sometimes bicycled more than a hundred miles on his own, and had also made a similar trip to see an uncle. To avoid going to a public high school that he thought too dangerous, Joubert took on a newspaper delivery route and used his earnings from it to pay the tuition at a Catholic high school, for which his mother would not or could not pay. He was tormented at the Catholic high school, he reported, because people thought he might be a homosexual. He took a girl to the senior prom—his only date during those years—to avoid being labeled as gay. He was on the track and cross-country teams. He was an avid Boy Scout, even delayed getting his final Eagle Scout badge for some time in order to continue on in the program as long as possible. In his yearbook, he wrote, "Life is a highway with many roads branching off—don't get lost."

After graduating from high school, he had gone to a military college in Vermont, and the freedom he found there because of the lower drinking age in that state resulted in his not showing up for classes or in his sleeping through them, so his grade average was poor. When not drinking or sleeping, he played a great deal of the fantasy game Dungeons & Dragons. After a school year at this college, he returned home for a summer and then joined the Air Force. At his training school in Texas, he had made friends with one young man and they had taken assignments together and roomed together at Offutt, beginning in the summer of 1983. It was then that Joubert had begun collecting his detective magazines. After a few weeks at Offutt, the roommate told Joubert that others on the base were referring to himself and Joubert as "the girls." The allegation of homosexuality disturbed the roommate, and he abruptly moved out. This action provided a key precrime stress to Joubert. Less than a week after his friend moved out, Joubert abducted and murdered Danny Joe Eberle.

He told his psychiatric interviewers that he had not really found out what it felt like to kill, and that while he was doing the killing, he was acting as if by rote, simply acting out the fantasy he had been perfecting since the age of six and feeling very little. Back in his room, he masturbated, then fell deeply asleep and had not been troubled in his sleep. When in the grip of the fantasy, he could not restrain his impulses. He admitted to one person that he had felt very good when he first realized that his initial victim was indeed under his control. Several different mental-health professionals who interviewed him all agreed that he was intelligent (IQ 125), alert, and more than a little pleased at all the attention he was receiving. They categorized him as a 301.20 in the numbering scheme of the standard manual of psychiatric disorders; that is, suffering from a schizoid personality disorder with compulsive features.

Among the several psychiatrists who evaluated Joubert during this period was Dr. Herbert C. Modlin of the Menninger Clinic, who made the following observations about Joubert, and reported to the court:

> This man seems not to know what love and affection are, as though he has never experienced such feelings. In describing his relationship with his sister, the best he could do was say, "We didn't hate each other." It is striking that this intelligent man could not describe either parent. He seems so separated from emotional experiences as to suggest some sort of chronic dissociative process. I suspect that he is dimly aware of this defect or lack in himself, and, in part, the homicides were an attempt to experience strong emotions.

Dr. Modlin reported that he had many unanswered questions about Joubert and his crimes. Why had the victims been thirteen-year-olds? Why had they been strangers to him? Why had they been stabbed, and why had Joubert made multiple cuts? Why had he partially removed their clothes? Why had the abductions taken place in the early morning?

Many of these questions continued to bother me, although I believed I had some insight into the answers to a couple of them. There was more to be found out, however, and a tremendous leap forward in our understanding of Joubert and his crimes came through another chance happening. In the fall of 1984, I had brought back to Quantico with me slides and other documentary aids about the slayings and the killer, and was using the case as an example in an FBINA class. As I presented it, one of my students raised his hand and asked to see me during the next break. Lieutenant Dan Ross of the Portland, Maine, police force, said that the Omaha murders reminded him of an unsolved case in Portland.

I was excited because when Joubert had been arrested in Omaha, I had suggested that the authorities there check back to his previous Maine address and look for earlier crimes that might have similar characteristics. Although I had initially believed the Eberle killing to have been the suspect's first homicide, after learning more about him, I had come around to the suspicion that there could well have been earlier, preparatory crimes; his fantasy was just too strong not to have erupted in antisocial behavior at some earlier point in his life. Also, his relatively abrupt enlisting in the Air Force could have been a way to get himself out of town cleanly and without being noticed after the commission of an early crime. Omaha had been too busy with other aspects of the case, however, and an initial call to Portland by the Sarpy County authorities had drawn a blank.

The lieutenant went home to Portland for the weekend and returned with the files on the unsolved murder case. One of the other students in my class that quarter was a police officer from Sarpy County with whom I'd worked in the Joubert investigation, and the three of us sat down to go over the files.

The circumstances were very much the same—just before dawn, a lone boy as the victim, an attacker who had also been described by witnesses as young, and who clearly knew the area; a slashing death, bite marks on the victim. This terrible event had occurred in August 1982, a bit more than a year prior to the Eberle abduction, and just before John Joseph Joubert IV entered the Air Force. Ricky Stetson, eleven years old, blond and blue-eyed, had been out jogging over a regular route that took him near a highway viaduct. On a hillside close by the viaduct, he had been stabbed to death and his body mutilated, though not so severely as the later victims. The murder had occured just at daylight. The killer had attempted to pull off the victim's clothes but had been only partially successful. Examining the crime-scene photos, I learned that photographic evidence had been taken of the bite marks on the victim, and that the photos had been preserved.

We checked back through Joubert's records and learned that years prior to the time of that murder Joubert had been a paper boy with a route that was contiguous to the hillside where Stetson had been stabbed and bitten. More recently, Joubert had worked at a company whose plant was close to the site. Witnesses recalled seeing the jogging boy followed by a young man on a ten-speed bike; most of those witnesses, shown photos of Joubert, thought that the assailant had been Joubert, but, after several years of intervening time, couldn't be 100 percent sure.

With some difficulty, Dan Ross went to the Nebraska state prison and obtained bite impressions from Joubert, which were then shown to experienced forensic odontologist Dr. Lowell Levine, Director of the Forensic Sciences Unit of the New York State police. Dr. Levine was convinced that Joubert's bites closely matched those taken from the victim.

As the Portland case developed, the trail of crimes committed by Joubert eventually led back even further, as I had suspected it might. In 1980, there had been several unexplained slashings, one of a nine-year-old boy, and another of a female teacher in her mid-twenties.

Both victims had been cut rather badly, and were lucky to be alive. Back before that, in 1979, a nine-year-old girl had been stabbed in the back with a pencil by a boy on a bicycle who had sped past. There was not much use to indicting Joubert on those charges, but the Stetson murder demanded an answer. Joubert was eventually indicted and convicted for that murder in Maine. Should his sentence in Nebraska ever be commuted, he would have to be transported to Maine and imprisoned for the remainder of his life. In essence, the solving of the Stetson case in Maine was an early and informal triumph for what would become the VICAP system; in this instance, it was the fortuitous circumstance of having a man in my class who could connect two murders in different states with the same MO. Once VICAP was up and running, that sort of comparative analysis would be available to the authorities whenever a serious crime was committed.

My own interview with Joubert had to wait until the court processes in both Maine and Nebraska had been exhausted, years later. I took along Special Agent Ken Lanning, our BSU expert on child abuse, and an agent from the Omaha office. Joubert had put on some weight in prison and finally looked like a young man rather than an overage boy. I had learned from the prison authorities that he had been drawing on tissue paper in his cell on death row, and these drawings had been seized and taken from him. They were quite good, well drawn, but what they showed was chilling. One depicted a boy by the side of a road, hog-tied, and the second was of a boy on his knees as a man slid a knife into him.

Every ounce of information we can extract from a killer about his mind and methods gives us more ammunition to track the next one. Joubert didn't want to talk to us at first, but eventually my long interest in his case and the techniques I'd learned to apply in my interviews of more than a hundred murderers got him to loosen up a bit.

I asked about stresses in his past, and it was then that he recalled that before he had started to hurt anyone, he had lost a friend. This was when Joubert's mother refused to help him find the boy, and Joubert was bereft. Shortly afterward, his descent toward murder began. In our interview in prison, he rather plaintively asked me whether the FBI could help him find this lost friend. I said I'd try.

He admitted the murders, and we started talking about the details. Among the many subjects I wanted to explore, I was particularly interested in three matters—the unexplained bite marks, the detective magazines, and the way he had chosen his victims. They were all related.

He told us about the fantasy of cannibalism that had been with him since the time he was six or seven years of age. The working out of that fantasy had been the engine of his murders, and it had encompassed biting the bodies, including that of the first victim, back in Portland. Presumably, the slash marks on Eberle's leg, that ticktacktoe pattern that had puzzled us, had been his attempt to obliterate the bites he had made in that area. I asked him whether he had learned from detective magazines that the police could identify a killer through forensic odontology on such bite marks, and he agreed that he had; one of the reasons that he read such magazines was to get information on how to avoid detection. The main reason was stimulation; for him—as for many killers—detective magazines were pornography, even though they showed no depictions of nude bodies, only suggestions of dominance, torture, and the like.

I asked him when he had first started reading those magazines, and he said that it had been at about age eleven or twelve, when, in the company of his mother, he had seen them on a rack in a grocery store. He had been excited by the depictions of people being frightened and threatened, and had gotten his hands on one of the magazines and used it as a prop for masturbation and his fantasy of strangulation and stabbing. So the magazines had been associated in his mind with both sexual excitement and killing for nearly a decade prior to his murderous actions. And at the time of first equating those magazines, his fantasy, and sexual self-stimulation, Joubert had been a prepubescent boy, fair-haired and slim, with a bike and a predawn paper route.

After six or seven hours of talking, Joubert asked me a question. "I've been fair to you, Mr. Ressler, so can you do me a favor? Get me a set of the crime-scene photos. There's something that I have to work out in my mind."

This young man, then twenty-eight years old, was on death row for these crimes, and he still wanted depictions of them, probably for the purposes of masturbation. I told him I was unable to comply with his request, and left the interview having gained the sad understanding that John Joubert's terrible fantasy would most likely not die until he did. In 1992, he remains on death row.

6

ORGANIZED AND DISORGANIZED CRIMES

To most people, when confronted by evidence of violent criminality, the behavior may seem an enigma, even a unique occurrence. Very few of us are used to grisly murders, mutilations, bodies thrown into ravines—and the majority who are ignorant of such matters includes most local police, who seldom encounter crimes of this sort. Even outrageous, unspeakable criminal behavior is not unique and not incomprehensible, however. These sort of murders have occurred before, and, when properly analyzed, can be understood well enough so that we can even break them down into somewhat predictable patterns. By the late 1970s, the Behavioral Sciences Unit had accumulated a large amount of experience in assessing these sort of crimes. The usual police officer might never have seen an act of disembowelment or cannibalism during his career, but because so many police departments sent us their unusual cases for analysis, we were used to looking at such crime scenes and could get past the average person's disgust at them and discern what the evidence revealed about the probable perpetrator.

Amassing this knowledge was one thing. Communicating it to our audience—those police officers who sought our help in tracking down violent criminals—was another. To characterize the types of offenders for police and other local law-enforcement people, we needed to have a terminology that was not based in psychiatric jargon. It wouldn't do much good to say to a police officer that he was looking for a psychotic personality if that police officer had no training in psychology; we needed to speak to the police in terms that they could understand and that would assist them in their searches for killers, rapists, and other violent criminals. Instead of saying that a crime scene showed evidence of a psychopathic personality, we began to tell the police officer that such a particular crime scene was "organized," and so was the likely offender, while another and its perpetrator might be "disorganized," when mental disorder was present.

The organized versus disorganized distinction became the great divide, a fundamental way of separating two quite different types of personalities who commit multiple murders. As with most distinctions, this one is almost too simple and too perfect a dichotomy to describe every single case. Some crime scenes, and some murderers, display organized as well as disorganized characteristics, and we call those "mixed." For instance, Ed Kemper was a highly organized killer, but his mutilation of bodies after death was more typical of a disorganized one. In the following pages, I'll paint the principal characteristics of both classic organized and classic disorganized offenders. Please remember that if I say that a particular attribute is characteristic of an organized offender, it is not so 100 percent of the time, but is something that is *generally* applicable. For instance, I say that the organized offender hides the bodies of his victims; in our research interviews, and in analysis of crime scenes, we found this to be true more than three-quarters of the time. That's enough to make the generalization hold up pretty well, but not enough to make it an absolute condition for our characterization. All of the "rules" of profiling are like that. Though the distinction between organized and disorganized itself is very apparent once recognized, the list of attributes that go along with each of the categories has grown, over the years, as we have learned more details about these murderers, and it continues to be enlarged.

When trying to figure out whether the crime has been perpetrated by an organized or disorganized offender, we look at crime-scene photographs, and, if possible, we examine information from or about the victim. For instance, we try to assess whether or not this particular victim meant a low risk for the criminal. It would be a low risk if the victim was frail or weak. Where did the victim become a victim? When Monte Rissell abducted a prostitute from a deserted parking lot in the early-morning hours, he chose a victim who might not be missed for some time. Knowledge that the perpetrator would deliberately choose such a victim can be important in trying to apprehend him.

We ordinarily divide the crime into four phases. The first is the precrime stage, which takes into account the "antecedent behavior" of the offender. Often, this is the last stage about which we finally obtain knowledge, though it is the first in temporal sequence. The second phase is the actual commission of the crime; in this stage, we place victim selection as well as the criminal acts themselves, which may include far more than murder—abduction, torture, rape, as well as the killing. The third phase is the disposal of the body; whereas some murderers do not display any concern about having the victim found, others go to great lengths to avoid its discovery. The fourth and final phase is postcrime behavior, which in some cases can be quite important, as some offenders attempt to inject themselves into the investigation of the murder, or otherwise keep in touch with the crime in order to continue the fantasy that started it.

The major attribute of the organized offender is his planning of the crime. Organized crimes are premeditated, not spur of the moment. The planning derives from the offender's fantasies, which, as I've shown in earlier chapters, have usually been growing in strength for years before he erupts into overt antisocial behavior. John Joubert had his crimes in mind for years before the opportunity for a slashing murder presented itself and he crossed the line into action. Rissell, too, had had violent fantasies for years before a likely victim showed up in that parking lot after the night when, in his mind, he had been spurned by his former girlfriend.

Most victims of organized offenders are targeted strangers; that is, the offender stakes out or patrols an area, hunting someone who fits a certain type of victim that he has in mind. Age, appearance, occupation, hairstyle, and lifestyle may be elements in the choice; David Berkowitz looked for women who were alone or sitting with men in parked cars.

The organized offender often uses a ruse or con to gain control over his victim. This is a man who has good verbal skills and a high degree of intelligence, enough to lure the victim into a vulnerable area. Control is of the essence for the organized offender, and law-enforcement personnel learn to look for control as an element in every facet of the crime. An organized offender might offer a prostitute a fifty-dollar bill, give a hitchhiker a ride, assist a disabled motorist, tell a child that he's taking him to his mother. Since the crime has been planned, the offender has devoted time to figuring out how to obtain victims, and may have perfected the ruse. John Gacy promised money to young men in a homosexual transient district in Chicago if they would come home and perform sex acts with him. Ted Bundy used his charm, but also the aura of authority that some police paraphernalia gave him, to lure young women into his car. With the organized killer, the victims are personalized; the offender has enough verbal and other interchange with the victims to recognize them as individuals prior to killing them.

The disorganized killer doesn't choose victims logically, and so often takes a victim at high risk to himself, one not selected because he or she can be easily controlled; sometimes this lack of choice produces a victim who will fight back hard enough so that later their body reveals defensive wounds. Moreover, the disorganized killer has no idea of, or interest in, the personalities of his victims. He does not want to know who they are, and many times takes steps to obliterate their personalities by quickly knocking them unconscious or covering their faces or otherwise disfiguring them.

Therefore, the major attribute of the organized killer is planning, which in this sense of the word means that the killer's logic is displayed in every aspect of the crime that is capable of being planned. The disorganized offender's actions are usually devoid of normal logic; until he is caught and tells us his version of the crimes, chances are that no one can follow the twisted reasoning he uses to pick his victims or to commit his crimes.

During the criminal act, the organized offender adapts his behavior to the exigencies of the situation. After Ed Kemper shot two young women on a college campus, he had the presence of mind to drive past security officers at the gate with the two dying women in his car, without alarming the officers. Though admittedly in a state of anxiety, Kemper was not on a hysterical shooting spree. He was able to adapt his behavior to the danger of getting past the checkpoint. Other murderers, less organized, might have panicked and attempted to drive through the gates at high speed, thereby attracting attention, but Kemper behaved as if he had nothing to hide, and was "successful" in getting away with his crime that night. Adaptability and mobility are signs of the organized killer. Moreover, organized killers learn as they go on from crime to crime; they get better at what they do, and this shows in their degree of organization. If the police have a series of five homicides that demonstrate the same MO, we advise looking most closely at the earliest one, for it will most likely have "gone down" closest to the place where the killer lived or worked or hung out. As he becomes more experienced, the killer will move the bodies farther and farther away from the places where he abducts his victims. Often that first crime is not thoroughly planned, but succeeding ones will display greater forethought. When we see more planning in a later crime than in an early one, we know we're after an organized killer.

This leap forward in criminal expertise is an important clue to the nature of the offender. In the previous chapter, I've detailed how evidence of improved criminal behavior helped refine a profile that led to the capture of John Joubert. Another offender who improved his crimes, and steadily escalated them in violence, was Monte Rissell. Only after he was caught and convicted for a series of rape-murders did he confess that he had committed a half-dozen rapes earlier in his teenage years, rapes for which he was never caught. He began by attacking victims in the apartment complex in which he and his mother lived; later on, while at a youth facility, he forced a woman whom he abducted in a parking lot to drive to her residence, where the rape took place. Still later, he drove a car out of state to find a victim. Each time, he made it less and less likely that he would be identified as the rapist. It was only when he reversed this pattern that he was actually caught: Rissell's last six crimes, of which five were murders, again occurred in or near the apartment complex where he lived. Even in that last series of murders, there was some escalation: With his first three murder victims, he made the decision to kill them during the rapes; with the last two, he had consciously decided to kill them even before the actual abductions.

Further evidence of planning that sometimes becomes available to police investigators lies in the organized offender's use of restraints—handcuffs, ropes, and the like. Many murderers take what we call "rape kits" along when they hunt victims, so that they will not have any difficulty restraining those whom they wish to assault. The presence of a rape kit also allows the offender to have a submissive victim, something essential to his fantasies. We once assisted in the investigation of a bizarre sexual murder on a Bronx rooftop: We noticed that the murderer had not brought anything with him to immobilize the victim; he had taken his tools for that task from her own clothing and handbag. The absence of a rape kit helped us profile a killer who was *not* organized.

Was there a vehicle used? To whom did it belong? Someone as disorganized as Richard Trenton Chase, I had told the police when his murders were still unsolved, would most likely have walked to the scene; I was certain of this, because I had decided that the killer displayed all the signs of a disorganized offender, one too mentally ill to drive a vehicle while at the same time controlling his victims. As the reader will recall, the part of the profile that really helped the police a good deal was my insistence that the killer would reside within a locus of a half mile from the site of his latest victims. Like Chase, the disorganized killer walks to the scene or takes public transportation, whereas the organized offender drives his own car or sometimes takes the victim's car. If the disorganized offender owns a car, it will often appear unkempt and in poor condition, as will his dwelling. The organized offender's car will be in proper condition.

Taking one's own car, or a victim's car, is part of a conscious attempt to obliterate evidence of the crime. Similarly, too, the organized offender brings his own weapon to the crime and takes it away once he is finished. He knows that there are fingerprints on the weapon, or that ballistic evidence may connect him to the murder, and so he takes it away from the scene. He may wipe away fingerprints from the entire scene of the crime, wash away blood, and do many other things to prevent identification either of the victim or of himself. The longer a victim remains unidentified, of course, the greater the likelihood that the crime will not be traced back to its perpetrator. Usually the police find the victims of an organized killer to be nude; without clothing, they are less easily identified. It may seem a very large step from wiping away fingerprints on a knife to decapitating a body and burying the head in a different place from the torso, but all these actions are in the service of preventing identification of the victim and of the killer.

The disorganized killer may pick up a steak knife in the victim's home, plunge it into her chest, and leave it sticking there. Such a disorganized mind does not care about fingerprints or other evidence. If police find a body rather readily, that is a clue that the crime has been done by a disorganized offender. Organized ones transport the bodies from the place that the victims were killed, and then hide the bodies, sometimes quite well. Many of Ted Bundy's victims were never found. Bob Berdella, a Kansas City, Missouri, killer who, like John Gacy, abducted, tortured, and killed young boys, cut up their bodies into small pieces and fed them to the dogs in his yard; many that were so treated could never be identified.

A different dynamic seems to have been at work in the instance of the Hillside Strangler, who was later identified as two men. The victims were found, and the killers later turned out to have been quite organized offenders. Their desire seems to have been an egotistical one—to flaunt the bodies in front of the police rather than to conceal them in an effort to prevent tracing the killers through identification of the victim.

An organized offender may sometimes stage a crime scene or

death scene in order to confuse the authorities. Such staging takes a fair amount of planning, and bespeaks a mind that is working along logical and rational lines. No disorganized offender is capable of staging a crime scene, although the very chaos of some crime scenes later attributed to disorganized offenders may at first give rise to various contradictory theories of what has happened at the site.

When law-enforcement personnel look at a crime scene, they should be able to discern from the evidence, or lack of it, whether the crime was committed by an organized or disorganized perpetrator. A disorganized crime scene displays the confusion of the killer's mind, and has spontaneous and symbolic qualities that are commensurate with his delusions. If the victim is found, as is often the case, he or she will likely have horrendous wounds. Sometimes the depersonalization of the victim by the attacker manifests itself in an attempt to obliterate the victim's face, or in mutilation after death. Often the death scene and the crime scene are the same for the disorganized offender; he does not possess the mental clarity of mind to move the body or conceal it.

The organized offender often takes personal items belonging to his victims as trophies, or to deny the police the possibility of identifying the victim. Wallets, jewelry, class rings, articles of clothing, photograph albums—all of these, once belonging to victims, have been found in the dwelling places of organized killers after their arrests. Usually, these are not items of intrinsic value, such as expensive jewelry, but, rather, items that are used to recall the victim. These trophies are taken for incorporation in the offender's postcrime fantasies and as acknowledgment of his accomplishments. Just as the hunter looks at the head of the bear mounted on the wall and takes satisfaction in having killed it, so the organized murderer looks at a necklace hanging in his closet and keeps alive the excitement of his crime. Many take photographs of their crimes for the same purpose. Sometimes trophies of the crime, such as jewelry, are given to the killer's wife or girlfriend or mother, so that when she wears it, only the killer knows its significance. John Crutchley was convicted only of kidnapping and rape, but I believed his actions to be extremely similar to those of an organized serial killer: He had dozens of necklaces hanging on a nail in his closet. Though Monte Rissell stole money from the purses of his rape and murder victims, he also took jewelry from them and kept it in his apartment. He further extended his fantasy involvement with the victims by driving their cars for hours after he had killed them.

The disorganized murderer doesn't take trophies; rather, in his confused mental state, he may remove a body part, a lock of hair, an article of clothing, and take it with him as a souvenir whose value can not be discerned.

As I have said earlier, all these crimes are sexual in nature, even when there is no completed sexual act with the victim. The truly organized killer generally completes a sexual act with a living victim, taking full advantage of the situation to rape and torture before murdering someone. Even if they are impotent in ordinary circumstances, while they are punching, slashing, strangling, and whatever, they are able to have sex, and do. The disorganized killer often does not complete the sex act, or, if he does, completes it only with a dead or entirely inanimate victim. The disorganized killer kills quickly, with a blitz style of attack. The organized offender seeks to increase his erotic interest through keeping the victim alive and performing perverted and destructive acts on the victim. Power over the victim's life is what this type of offender seeks. John Gacy brought his victims near death several times before the actual murders, so that he could enjoy their suffering while he raped them. During rapes, the organized offender demands that the victim display submissive behavior and act fearful and/or passive. If a victim fights back, the organized offender's aggressive behavior usually becomes heightened, sometimes so much that a man who had originally planned only on raping a victim escalates his violence into murder when the victim resists.

In stages three and four, the organized offender takes steps to hide the bodies of his victims, or otherwise attempts to conceal their identity, and then keeps track of the investigation. He does so in order to elongate the time period in which his fantasy seems to be in control of events. In one particularly egregious case of postcrime fantasy, the killer was a hospital ambulance driver. He would kidnap his victims from the parking lot of a restaurant and transport them elsewhere for rape and murder. Unlike many organized offenders, he would leave the bodies in locations that were only partially concealed, and then would call the police and report seeing a body. As the police rushed to the location of that body, the offender rushed back to the hospital, so that when the call from the police came to the hospital for an ambulance to be dispatched, he would be in a position to answer that call. He derived especial satisfaction from driving the ambulance to the dump site, retrieving the body that he himself had killed, and transporting it back to the hospital.

* * *

Organized and disorganized killers have very different personalities. The ways in which those personalities develop, and the behavioral consequences of those developmental patterns, are often important to unraveling a crime.

The disorganized offender grows up in a household where the father's work is often unstable, where childhood discipline is harsh, and where the family is subject to serious strain brought on by alcohol, mental illness, and the like. By contrast, our interviewing of murderers found that the organized killer's childhood was characterized by a father who had steady and stable work but where the discipline was inconsistent, often leaving the offender with a feeling that he was entitled to everything.

The disorganized offender grows up to internalize hurt, anger, and fear. While normal people also internalize these emotions to some degree—that's necessary in order to live together in a society—the disorganized offender goes far beyond the norm in his internalization. He is unable to let off steam, and lacks the verbal and physical skills for expressing these emotions in the proper arenas. He can't be easily counseled because he can't tell the counselor very much about the emotional turmoil inside him.

Part of the reason for unexpressed anger within the disorganized offenders is that they are not normally handsome people. They don't appear attractive, as measured by others, and they have a very poor self-image. They may have physical ailments or disabilities that make them different, and they are not comfortable being different. Rather than accepting their disabilities, they believe themselves to be inadequate, and they act in an inadequate manner, thus reinforcing their hurt, anger, and isolation. Disorganized offenders tend to withdraw from society almost completely, to become loners. Whereas many organized killers tend to be reasonably attractive, outgoing, and gregarious, the disorganized ones are incapable of relating to other people at all. Therefore, the disorganized offender will most likely not be living with a member of the opposite sex, and probably not even with a roommate. If they live with anyone else, chances are it will be a parent, and probably a single parent at that. No one else will be able to stomach their strange ways, so the disorganized offender is alone, possibly a recluse. Such offenders actively reject the society that has rejected them.

Commensurate with these disorganized offenders' poor self-image is that they are underachievers. In general, they are less intelligent than the organized offenders, but most are not seriously deficient. However, they never live up to their potential, either in school or in the workplace. If they work at all, it will be at a menial job, and they are habitually disruptive because of their inability to get along with other people. They also accept that they underachieve. When the killer of the young woman on that Bronx rooftop was questioned by the police, he said he was an unemployed actor. That was wishful thinking. Actually, he was an unemployed stagehand—certainly by his own lights an underachiever in the theatrical profession.

By contrast, the organized offender, rather than internalizing hurt, anger, and fear, externalizes them. This is the boy who ''acts out'' in school, who does aggressive and sometimes senseless acts. In years past, the public has believed that all murderers have been disruptive and outwardly violent in their childhoods, but that stereotype is applicable only to the organized offender. The disorganized boy is quiet in school, maybe too quiet; often, when he is caught for a heinous crime, teachers and fellow students from his childhood hardly remember him. And when his neighbors are interviewed, they characterize him as a nice boy, never any trouble, who kept to himself and was docile and polite. On the other side of the coin, the organized offender is recalled by everyone from his childhood as the bully, the class clown, the kid who made people notice him. As opposed to being loners, organized offenders are gregarious and they like crowds. These are the guys who pick fights in bars, who drive cars irresponsibly, and who are described throughout life as troublemakers. They may land jobs that are above menial labor and commensurate with their intelligence, and then act out in such a way as to provoke a confrontation that will result in their being fired. Such stresses often lead to their first murders. A former Ohio police officer in the midst of job troubles, difficulties with the law, and woman troubles abducted a young woman and, almost by accident, murdered her. With disorganized killers, this important factor, the precrime situational stress, is often absent; their crimes are triggered by their mental illness, not by events in the outside world that impact on them.

Instead of feeling inferior to people, organized killers feel superior to nearly everyone. Gacy, Bundy, and Kemper all belittled the police who were too stupid to catch them and the psychiatrists who were too inept to understand them. They overcompensate, often believing themselves to be the smartest, most successful people to have come down the pike, even when they are only moderately so, and not particularly distinguished except by the monstrousness of their crimes. After the crime, they often follow the progress (or nonprogress) of the investigation in the news media; the disorganized offender takes little or no interest in the crime after it has been committed.

There is another area in which the organized offenders seem to be successful: in the sack. Often, they have had multiple sex partners. As good con artists, with excellent verbal skills, they are often able to convince women (or men, in some cases) to have sex with them. They may be superficially attractive, and good amateur psychologists. However, they are unable to sustain normal, long-term relationships. Their lives are characterized by having many partners, none of whom stick with them for very long. A disembowelment killer in Oregon had many affairs with women, none very deep or of long duration. Ted Bundy's main squeeze before his incarceration said that he was an unexciting sex partner. Most if not all of the organized killers have tremendous anger toward women, often expressed in the belief that a certain female is not "woman enough" to "turn him on." The ranks of organized offenders contain many rapists who beat up women, they reported, because the women did not stimulate them to orgasm.

Organized offenders are angry at their girlfriends, at themselves, at their families, and at society in general. They feel that they've been mistreated during their entire lives and that everything is stacked against them. If they're so smart and clever, why haven't they made a million dollars or—as Charlie Manson wanted—had a career as a rock star? They all believe that society has conspired to keep them down. Manson felt that had he not been in jail during his early life, his songs would have been very popular. Manson's rhetoric led his followers to believe they were stimulating class warfare by their murders. Ed Kemper believed he was taking victims from the rich and the middle class, and in so doing striking a blow for the working stiffs. John Gacy thought he was ridding the world of no-account punks and "little queers." In their murders, these men strike back not only at the individual victims but at society as a whole.

Two men included in our study of the backgrounds and offenses of serial murderers provide classic instances of the patterns of organized and disorganized offenders. In our road shows, when I used to display the slides and give the lecture about the organized offender Gerard John Schaefer, someone in my audience would accuse me of having taken the characteristics of that sort of offender right from the details of Schaefer's case. That's not so, but it is true that the patterns associated with the organized killer are starkly apparent in his instance.

In 1973, the police in rural Brevard County in Florida were in the process of putting together a task force to investigate a handful of cases in which women were reported missing. Then they got a break. Two distraught and alarmed young women stumbled out of the swampy woods, found a passing motorist who took them into town, and made their way to a police station, where they told a harrowing tale of abduction.

They had been hitchhiking and were picked up by a normal-looking, neatly clothed man in a car that resembled a police vehicle. He told them he'd drive them to their destination. Instead, he took them into the woods, tied them up at gunpoint, and told them they would be sexually assaulted and murdered. He told them he had done this to many women before them. After roping these two, however, the man looked at his watch and said, "Uh-oh, I gotta go; I'll be back," and he jumped in his car and drove away. The women managed to wriggle their way out of their bonds and get to the road. They took the police back to the spot where they had been tied up, and showed them how they had been immobilized. One strange sidelight to this part of the story: The police asked them to re-create what had happened, to demonstrate the immobilization in detail, and the women, who still must have been terrified by their recent and narrow escape, donned the ropes willingly, and the police photographed them in position. They had their hands tied high, with the rope thrown over a tree from which, they said, the man had intended to hang them.

Searching and excavating the area nearby, the police found partially decomposed body parts and some pieces of women's clothing. On one pair or jeans, there was quite a distinctive hand-stitched pattern; that pattern matched the description of a pair of jeans that a girl had been reported as wearing when she was reported missing. Discovering this evidence, the police began to take the stories of the escaped women even more seriously. The two women were able to describe in excellent detail the car in which they had been abducted and the physical attributes of their abductor. For instance, they said that the car had a bumper hitch, which they remembered because their abductor had tied one end of the rope to it and thrown the other over the tree; he had said he was going to use the car to haul them up to a height from which he could hang them. The car also had a fraternity sticker in the window, they said.

Before going further with the story, let me point out the attributes of the organized offender that are present so far in the narrative. The abductor personalized the victims by talking with them, used his own vehicle, and conned the women into his car by means of his verbal skills. He brought his own threatening weapon to the scene and took it away with him, had a rape kit, and was plainly planning to complete sexual acts with the women prior to torture and murder. After the murder, he was going to hide and dispose of the bodies. He displayed mobility and adaptive behavior during the crime when he left the women tied up and went to pay attention to some other aspect of his life, telling them that he would return and finish them off later.

Gerard Schaefer became a suspect. He was a police officer in a neighboring jurisdiction, and a close check of his background now revealed that he had left another police organization. According to my conversations with officers connected to the case, in his earlier job, Schaefer had been cited for stopping cars driven by women committing traffic infractions, then running the women's license plate numbers through a computer check to obtain more particulars about them, and getting their phone numbers so he could later call them for dates. (As an aside, let me say that some police use their badges and authority as a way to obtain information and, shall we say, introductions to women—but very few use their authority to take women into the woods for rape, torture, and murder.) The authorities deduced that when Schaefer had left the women tied up in the wooded area, he had gone to answer a police roll call, and had planned to return to the site, in uniform and driving his official vehicle, to finish them off. Schaefer's own car matched the description given by the two abducted women, and a search of his home turned up all the evidence needed to indict him for the murder of the missing girl who had once worn those distinctive jeans, as well as for the abduction of the two hitchhikers who had managed to escape before being murdered.

Schaefer denied the crimes entirely, but his denials were contradicted by the living witnesses as well as by the evidence, and he was eventually convicted and is still in prison in Florida. How many women he may have killed is still in question; the estimate went as high as thirty-five. Since he denied the crimes and would not help the police in their searches, we don't know whether some missing bodies that were found could be attributed to him, nor do we know whether any of the women whom he might have killed are still lying somewhere, their bodies unidentified.

From my point of view as a researcher into the minds of murderers, Schaefer's home was a gold mine, not only because it contained evidence of his crimes but also because it gave us testimony to the sort of offender he was. Women's garments were found in the home, and jewelry, as well—in my terminology, these were clearly trophies that he had used to relive his crimes. Questioned about these items, Schaefer said that as a patrolman he had picked up the clothing along the highway, and from time to time would give it to Goodwill; he had simply not had a moment in which to donate this batch. He had even given one of the necklaces to a girlfriend. In his home were stacks and stacks of soft-core pornography and detective magazines. Leafing through them, the authorities discovered that he seemed most interested in stories about women being hung, strangled, and otherwise choked.

That the hanging and associated torture were major elements of his fantasy was shown by stories that he'd written himself, and by drawings that he made over the surfaces of pinups. All of them had the same theme. For instance, there was a relatively normal pinup photograph of a young woman leaning against a tree, with her hands behind her back. Schaefer had drawn lines over this to show bullet holes in her, ropes around her arms, and that she had defecated in her panties—the latter, an action commensurate with the loosening of muscles that usually accompanies death by hanging. On another photograph of three posed and nude woman who face a single man, he had written a balloon commentary: "These women will please me. If not, they will be taken to the plaza square and entertain the villagers as they dance on the end of my rope." In other collages, he made cutouts to enhance the photo of a young woman who had been depicted as lying down, so that she looked as if she, too, had been hung. Still other photographs in his home were originals, probably taken by him, and depicted women who were actually being hung—his victims.

Schaefer's home and life, then, displayed many articles that reflected the attributes of the organized offender. He had a relationship with a woman, had steady employment, kept trophies of his crimes, used pornographic materials, and in his crimes clearly sought to realize his fantasies. His choice of victims seems to have been of young hitchhiking women who might not be missed for some time after they disappeared, since they were likely to be transients in the area.

During his trial, Schaefer flirted with the press, and was gregarious and outgoing; his standard line to reporters was that this was all a mistake, and that he would be exonerated. In one newspaper photograph taken at the time of the judicial proceedings, four law-enforcement officers are guarding the prisoner as they are moving him from one location to another; Schaefer is the only one among the five men who is smiling, well groomed, at ease in his surroundings—

the organized offender, attempting to control the situation even when apprehended and on trial for his life.

Herbert Mullin had been all right, most people who knew him during his childhood in Santa Cruz agreed, until he graduated from high school in the late 1960s. Though relatively short and small, five seven and 120 pounds, he had been a first-string guard on the varsity football team. In addition, he was a good student, popular with both sexes, always polite to everyone, and voted "most likely to succeed." By his senior year, however, the appearance of having it all together was masking quite another reality: Herb Mullin was on the skids. The reason was a paranoid schizophrenic disorder, beginning to take hold in him, and accelerated (not caused!) by experimentation with marijuana and LSD.

Once out of high school, he went through a series of personality transformations of the sort that are characteristic of paranoid schizophrenics. Let me say at once that schizophrenia is completely misunderstood by the lay public. Schizophrenia is the most prevalent of all the psychoses, and paranoid schizophrenics are the most common of the schizophrenics. Most paranoid schizophrenics are not violent, however; in fact, the vast majority are harmless. The percentage of harmless people among schizophrenics may well be lower than it is among the normal population. No matter, though, for the crimes that are committed by paranoid schizophrenics are so gross that when brought to light, they bring censure down on all of the mentally ill. Herbert William Mullin was one of those who give mental illness a bad name.

During the late 1960s in northern California, a great many young high school graduates were "trying to find themselves," and some of Mullin's transformations didn't seem all that far from the norm for young men Herb's age. He went to college but couldn't hack it. For a while, he wore beads and long hair, and when that did not gain him the sexual experiences he sought, he cut his hair, put on a suit and tie, and appeared as a businessman. From time to time, as each experiment failed, he would enter a mental hospital for a spell, only to be released because he seemed relatively harmless to himself and others. Deciding he should be married, he would ask girls on the street or at a party whether they would marry him. When he was turned down by women, he decided this must mean that he was a homosexual, and so he went into the gay districts of San Francisco and asked men on the street whether they would like to live with him. The gays didn't want him, either. He stood up in a Catholic church and shouted that this was not proper Christianity; then he studied to be a priest but gave that up. Similarly, he showed up one day at a gymnasium and studied to be a boxer; he fought with such ferocity in his first bout that his handlers told him he had a good career ahead of him, but he soon walked away from the ring as well.

A year after registering as a conscientious objector, Herb applied to join the armed services; his father was in the military, but all the services rejected him except the Marines, who allowed him to go through basic training and then realized his mental instability, refused to put him on active duty, and cashiered him out. He lived with a mentally ill older woman for a time, during which he took up Eastern religions and mysticism. He went to Hawaii to pursue these but didn't get very far; he returned to the mainland and told a friend that he had also been in a mental institution in Hawaii.

By this time, in his mid-twenties, Mullin was completely socially unfit. He had tried everything and everyone but fit in nowhere and with no one. Though he worked sporadically, he couldn't hold a job for more than a few weeks at a time, and his parents continued to support him. By this time, too, he had a full-blown case of paranoid schizophrenia.

Schizophrenics characteristically take information from various sources and synthesize it in their minds, weaving it together in such a way that it makes a delusion and distorts the actual meaning of the information. Mullin had seen or read information about the possibility of future earthquakes in California, and he had a delusion about preventing these. He came to believe that California had been kept from having a calamitous earthquake in the previous half-dozen years because the war in Vietnam had produced a sufficient number of American casualties; that is, nature demanded blood sacrifices in order to keep from destroying the natural world. In October of 1972, however, the Vietnam War was rapidly winding down, insofar as American involvement was concerned, and Mullin's mind discerned a potential catastrophe looming. California would suffer a cataclysmic earthquake that would drop it into the ocean, he concluded, unless the amount of human sacrifices to nature was raised. It was for this reason, Mullin later said, that his father began to order him, by telepathy, to take some lives.

Very often, we find that the disorganized offender has led a life decidedly free of antisocial behavior prior to his crimes. Such offenders are not criminally oriented, not hostile or particularly violent prior to the time that they erupt into murder. Mullin followed that pattern. He had been unable to fit properly into the social fabric, had not been accepted either professionally or sexually by anyone. He had been stopped several times for possession of pot, but he had not raped, robbed, stolen, gotten into fights, or exceeded speed limits prior to the moment he was able legally to buy a gun and began killing people.

Although the tale of murders I am about to recount has a certain amount of coherence, I want to point out that at the time of Mullin's murders, the police suffered from what is known as linkage blindness—they were unable to relate one of these killings to another because of two factors. First, the murders did not seem to be connected by use of a similar weapon or a similar MO. The victims differed from one another in age, sex, and other characteristics, and so did the circumstances of their deaths. The second reason was that Ed Kemper was also operating in the same approximate area at the same time.

Herbert Mullin's first victim was a male hitchhiker of fifty-five, apparently a vagrant. Mullin must have noticed the man walking down the highway, and driven past him. Then he parked his car on the shoulder and began to look under the hood as the man approached. The man asked whether he could help in return for a ride, and Mullin let him get under the hood to peer at the engine. Then Mullin reached inside the car for a baseball bat and smashed the man's head in. Mullin dragged him into the woods not far from the highway and left him. The body was found the next day.

Two weeks after the first murder, Mullin's father directed him to kill his second victim as a sacrifice, and also to test the hypothesis that the environment was rapidly being polluted and that an earthquake might be nigh. Accordingly, he picked up a female hitchhiker on a highway and then plunged a knife into her chest as he was driving. In the woods, he undressed her, spread-eagled her legs, and cut her abdominally, in order to investigate his hypothesis of pollution. He took her organs out and examined them, hanging them on nearby branches so he could see them better. She was not found until several months had gone by, and by then, only her skeleton remained. Therefore, the first and second murders were not considered linked by the police.

Mullin was a disorganized offender, and I have said that disorganized offenders don't drive cars, but Mullin did. That just goes to prove that every single attribute on our list does not apply to every single killer. In a sense, that's why profiling remains an art and not a science, and why we resist our students' wishes that we profilers

provide them with a checklist that would make easy their own assess-
ments of crime scenes. Although Mullin differs slightly from the classic
disorganized killer in being able to drive a car, he shares many of the
other characteristics of the disorganized offender: the chance victim,
the chance weapon, the mutilation of the body, and no real attempt to
hide the body or prevent identification. The reason that the second
victim was not found until months later was pure luck, not something
that happened as a result of planning or guile by the murderer.

On a Thursday afternoon, four days after cutting up the young
hitchhiker in the woods, Mullin appeared to have doubts about the
appropriateness of what he believed to be his father's instructions, so
he went to see a Catholic priest in a confessional booth at a church
fifteen miles from Santa Cruz. As Mullin later related the incident, he
told the priest about the sacrifice program and that his father had told
him to start on it and to take certain victims. The priest asked him,
"Herbert, do you read the Bible?"

"Yes."

"The commandments, where it says to honor thy father and
mother?"

"Yes," Mullin responded.

"Then you know how important it is to do as your father says."

"Yes."

"I think it's so important," the priest said (in Mullin's recollec-
tion of the encounter), "that I want to volunteer to be your next
sacrifice."

Mullin kicked and hit and stabbed the priest a half-dozen times,
then left him bleeding to death in the confessional booth and rushed
away.

A parishioner saw the struggle and the assailant and ran for
help. Mullin escaped and the priest died, but the parishioner gave a
description of the killer to the police; unfortunately, it described the
killer as tall as well as thin, and so was not much help in the investigation.

Brooding, Mullin tried to figure out what had gone wrong in
his life, and his thoughts came to center on the time in high school
when a teammate first gave him marijuana to smoke. As he became
more and more mentally ill, Mullin had actually stopped using drugs,
and now had taken to blaming them for his problems. In early January
1973, he went to a remote area of cabins without telephones on the
outskirts of Santa Cruz, where he thought the teammate might still
reside. He went to the door of a house occupied by a woman who lived

there with her common-law husband and children. The husband was involved in selling illegal drugs but was not home. The woman answered the door and told Mullin that the man he wanted to see lived down the road. In his memory, she also insisted to him that she and the children would like to volunteer as human sacrifices, as the priest had. He killed them all with a pistol. Then he knocked on the door of the football teammate's home.

The former teammate invited Mullin in, and a confrontation began. This man, too, was now a drug dealer, and drug paraphernalia lay about the house. The teammate was unable to answer questions about why he had ruined Mullin's life with an early toke of pot, so Mullin shot him. Dying, the man crawled upstairs and into the bathroom, where his wife was in the shower; he shouted for her to lock the door, but Mullin broke it down and fatally shot her, too. When police found five people dead in two neighboring homes and learned that the men had been involved in the drug trade, they thought the murders were drug-related—a deal gone wrong, revenge being wrought. They did not suspect these killings to be connected in any way to the death of the priest or of the two hitchhikers.

A month later, Mullin was in a redwood forest area and walked in on four male teenagers in a tent. He asked them their business and they said they were camping. He claimed to be a forest ranger and said that they were polluting the forest and ought to leave; moreover, the campsite was not in an area that was legal for camping. The four young men shooed Mullin away; the presence of their .22 rifle in the tent may have helped them do so. He said he'd come back the next day to see whether they had gone. The teenagers remained in the tent. Next day, Mullin came back and killed them all with the .22. They were not found until the following week.

By that time, Mullin had killed again, and had been apprehended. His father's supposed instructions to kill came to Herb while he was driving his station wagon with a load of firewood in it. He noticed an Hispanic man weeding his garden across the street. He made a U-turn, came back down the street, stopped, took out the rifle, put it across the hood of the car, and shot the man. He committed this murder in full sight of the dead man's neighbor, who managed to write down the license plate number of the station wagon as Mullin calmly drove away from the scene of the crime. Within minutes of the description being put out on the police radio, a patrolman spotted Mullin driving down a road, ordered him to pull over, and arrested him; when apprehended, he was docile and did not attempt to grab or use the recently fired rifle on the seat next to him. Also in the station wagon was the .22 pistol that had been used several weeks earlier to kill the people in the cabins.

Mullin's disorganized characteristics were apparent by his demeanor in court—he had to be restrained by chains, and he submitted rambling written discourses to the judge that had nothing to do with the matters at hand—and in the way he had behaved during those four months in which he executed thirteen people. The logic that connected these murders existed only in his tormented brain. However, the jury judged him to have been legally sane at the time of the murders, and convicted him on all counts.

When I attempted to interview Mullin in prison, I found him docile, polite, and handsome, but uncommunicative. Every few minutes, as I tried to question him, he would ask, "Sir, can I go back to my room now?" He stated that he had committed his crimes only in an attempt to save the environment. Mullin displayed all the signs of serious mental illness. That he was in a penitentiary with career criminals was ridiculous at best, and unwise; he should have been in a mental institution.

Organized and disorganized: two types of killers. Which are the more prevalent and dangerous? That's hard to answer, but perhaps we can approach an answer by means of our research and some educated guesses about modern society. Our research into murderers is acknowledged to be the most broad-based yet completed. In it, we judged two-thirds of the murderers to be in the organized category, as opposed to one-third in the disorganized; perhaps those ratios carry through in the overall population of killers, only some of whom are behind bars, as our interviewees were.

My guess is that there has always been a certain unchanging fraction of disorganized killers in society, from the earliest days until the present—men who are quite deranged and who now and again go on killing sprees that stop only when they are caught or killed. We can't do much about the disorganized murderers; there'll probably always be one or two among us. It is my sincere belief, however, that the number and percentage of organized killers are growing. As our society grows more mobile, and as the availability of weapons of mass destruction increases, the ability of the antisocial personality to realize his rapacious and murderous fantasies grows apace.

7

WHAT PLUS WHY
EQUALS WHO

When I arrived at the Behavioral Sciences Unit in 1974, I became an apprentice in profiling to the Mutt and Jeff team of Howard Teten and Pat Mullany. Mullany, a former Christian brother, had been at the task since 1972, and Teten, a former San Leandro, California, evidence-unit specialist, had been working on profiling since 1969. Teten, in turn, had received guidance from a psychiatrist in New York, Dr. James A. Brussel, who had astounded the country in 1956 with a prediction about the personality of a "mad bomber" who had left thirty-two explosive packages in New York City over a period of eight years. Brussel studied crime scenes, messages from the bomber, and other information, and had told the police they would find an Eastern European immigrant in his forties who lived with his mother in a Connecticut city. The psychiatrist said the man was very neat; he deduced from the way the bomber rounded off the points of his *W*'s that he adored his mother—the rounded *W*'s looked like bosoms—and hated his father. Brussel even predicted that the bomber, when arrested, would be wearing a double-breasted suit, neatly buttoned. When taken into custody, George Metesky was indeed wearing a buttoned double-breasted suit, and fit the profile in many other regards, except for the fact that he resided with two unmarried sisters rather than with his mother.

Profiling had somewhat fallen into disrepute during the 1960s, when a committee of psychiatrists and psychologists guessed very incorrectly about the identity of the Boston Strangler, but the need for profiling kept growing because violent crimes against strangers—the most difficult of all crimes to solve—kept increasing in number. In the 1960s, in the majority of murder cases, the killer had some relationship with his or her victim. By the 1980s, some 25 percent of murders were "stranger murders," in which the killer did not really know the victim. The reasons for the steady rise in the statistics, sociologists believed, could be found in the sort of society we had become: mobile, in many ways impersonal, flooded with images of violence and of heightened sexuality.

Profiling was even less of a science then; it was an art that had to be painstakingly learned over a period of years by means of an apprenticeship. Even in the FBI, it was not a regular bureaucratically designated activity but, rather, one that was pursued by a handful of people when local police would see fit to refer a case to us that seemed beyond their own capabilities, or when an officer was smart enough to know when he or she needed help. I was fortunate to begin in profiling as Teten and Mullany tackled a difficult case.

Pete Dunbar, an agent in the Bozeman, Montana, office, brought to our attention an unsolved kidnapping in that state. The previous June, while the Jaeger family of Farmington, Michigan, had been on a camping trip, someone had put a knife through the fabric of a tent and snatched away their seven-year-old daughter, Susan. Teten and Mullany had put together a preliminary profile of the likely suspect in the kidnapping. They thought it was a young white male who lived in the area, a loner who had come across the family during a night walk. The profilers concluded that Susan was probably dead, though when no body was found, the family continued to hold out hope.

Dunbar had a logical suspect, a twenty-three-year-old Vietnam veteran named David Meierhofer. An informant had provided the name, and it happened that Dunbar was acquainted with Meierhofer, whom he characterized as "well-groomed, courteous, exceptionally intelligent . . . polite." Meierhofer was a good match with the Teten-Mullany profile, but there was no evidence to tie him to the abduction, and he was not charged with the crime. The Jaegers went back to Michigan to resume their lives and Dunbar went on to other work.

In January of 1974, however, an eighteen-year-old woman who had rejected Meierhofer as a suitor was also missing from the Bozeman area, and Meierhofer was again a logical suspect. He volunteered to take a lie-detector test and to be given truth serum. He passed both those tests in regard to both crimes, and his attorney pressed for Meierhofer to be unconditionally released and for the authorities to keep away from him.

However, more information was obtained from the second crime, and this enabled the profilers—myself included, now, as a neophyte—to refine the profile. It pointed to the sort of person Meierhofer was, and the fact that this suspect had been able to get past the truth serum and polygraph tests did not sway us. The public thinks these tests are a good way to discern the truth, and that is so for most normal people. Psychopaths, however, are known for their ability to separate the personality who commits the crimes from their more in-control selves. Thus, when a psychopath takes these tests, the in-control self manages to avoid all knowledge of the crimes, and very often the result is that the suspect passes the tests. Meierhofer was in control at some times, and at others, horrendously out of control. We convinced Dunbar that Meierhofer had to be the killer, and that even though he had passed the tests, Dunbar should not let the matter go. Teten and Mullany thought that the killer might well be the sort of man who telephones the relatives of his victims in order to relive the crime and its excitement. Accordingly, Dunbar asked the Jaegers to keep a tape recorder next to their telephone.

On the first anniversary of the seven-year-old's abduction, Mrs. Jaeger answered a call at her Michigan home from a man who claimed he was keeping Susan alive. "He was very smug and taunting," Mrs. Jaeger later told a reporter. The unknown man said that he had spirited Susan away to a country in Europe and was giving her a better life than the Jaegers could have afforded to give her. "My reaction was not what he was expecting," Mrs. Jaeger recalled. "I felt truly able to forgive him. I had a great deal of compassion and concern, and that really took him aback. He let his guard down and finally just broke down and wept."

The caller did not admit that Susan was dead, and hung up before the call could be traced. An FBI voice analyst went over the tape and concluded that the taunting voice had been David Meierhofer's. However, the analyst's evidence was not then considered sufficient in a Montana court to obtain a search warrant of a suspect's premises, so the authorities had no way of getting at Meierhofer. Dunbar spent some time tracing the call; it seemed to have come from an open area, possibly from someone tapping into phone line on poles above a neighboring ranch. Dunbar traced Meierhofer's service record and learned that Meierhofer had learned to tap into field telephone wires in Vietnam. However, this, too, was not hard evidence.

Mullany listened to the tape of the Jaeger-Meierhofer conversation and initiated a bold move. "I felt that Meierhofer could be woman-dominated," he later recalled; "I suggested that Mrs. Jaeger go to Montana and confront him." She did so at his lawyer's office in Montana, but Meierhofer was calm and collected, very much in control of his emotions. Shortly after Mrs. Jaeger returned to Michigan, though, she received a collect telephone call from a "Mr. Travis" in Salt Lake City. Travis wanted to explain that he, not someone else, had taken Susan. Before the caller could go on, Mrs. Jaeger interrupted him and said, "Well, hello, David."

Now Dunbar had enough evidence, in the form of an affidavit from Mrs. Jaeger, to obtain a search warrant of Meierhofer's premises, and in them found remains of both female victims Meierhofer was confronted with these remains and other evidence, and confessed not only to those two murders but also to the previously unsolved killing of at least one local Montana boy. After the confession, Meierhofer was put into a cell alone, and, the next day, he hung himself.

There was no doubt in our minds that the profile put together at Quantico had helped solve the case. If there had been no profile, Dunbar would have had no reason to be quite so interested in a suspect named by an informant. Later, after the second murder and after Meierhofer had passed the polygraph and truth-serum tests, the Quantico profile assisted Dunbar in sticking with the case and firming up his inner conviction that Meierhofer was the culprit. Finally, Mullany's guess that Meierhofer could be swayed by Mrs. Jaeger because of his confused psychological responses to women was the blow that finally cracked open the killer's defenses.

This early case demonstrated to me both the power and the possibilities in profiling. Profiling had helped identify the most likely suspect and had given the agent in the field reason to keep after him, even when many factors argued against continuing to do so. Moreover, the Meierhofer case showed that the more experience we had, and the more information about violent criminals we amassed and comprehended, the better we would become at profiling.

No two crimes or criminals are exactly alike. The profiler looks for patterns in the crimes and tries to come up with the characteristics of the likely offender. It's fact-based and uses analytical and logical thinking processes. We learn all we can from what has happened, use our experience to fathom the probable reasons why it happened, and from these factors draw a portrait of the perpetrator of the crime; in a nutshell: What plus why equals who.

The real task is to whittle down the universe of potential suspects, to eliminate the least likely ones and allow the on-site investigators to focus on realistic targets. Thus, if we are able to say with a high degree of probable accuracy that the suspect in a crime is a male, we've eliminated about 50 percent of the population who are not males. The category "adult males" is a smaller fraction of the population; "single white males," an even smaller number. By making such choices, we very quickly narrow the search. Every added category makes the band of possible suspects slimmer—for instance, we might suggest that the likely criminal is unemployed, or one who has previously received treatment for mental disease, or that it is a person who lives within walking distance of the crime scene.

I taught class after class at Quantico and did road shows about profiling, and I found that no matter how intensively we tried to instill the principles in our students, they wanted more direction. Didn't we have a workbook from which they could learn what questions to ask, to figure out what characteristics of a crime scene were the most important? Police officers, and even our in-service agents, wanted a checklist, so they could profile, as it were, by the numbers—put in this and that detail of evidence from the crime scene, push a button or apply a formula, and have a perfect profile pop out. In the future, we hope to have a computer program that can perform in that way, but we've been working on it for a half-dozen years and haven't perfected it yet. Profiling is still best done by people with a lot of experience, particularly by those who have studied psychology. And there's a lot of work involved, work in the sense of applying one's brain to what is usually a complex puzzle.

At the heart of the puzzle is the crime scene, which generally contains the best evidence that is available to us. We try to analyze it exhaustively, in an attempt both to understand the crime and, by reflection, the nature of the person who committed it. A good example is that rooftop in the Bronx where a special-education teacher was murdered. Virtually everything at the site came from the victim—the handbag used to strangle her, the comb placed in her pubic hair, even the felt pen with which the killer wrote obscenities on her body. That proved to be important in assessing what sort of a killer this might be; we thought it was a person who hadn't planned the crime, that it might have been somewhat spontaneous. In other instances, an abductor might bring with him what we have come to call a rape kit, with tape, ropes, and possibly a gun, all of which could be used to control a victim.

As I reported briefly in an earlier chapter, the absence of such a rape kit was a factor in another classic murder case in which I became involved as a profiler. The thoughtful reader would surmise that a city the size and sophistication of New York would catch on quite early to the idea of psychological profiling as an investigative aid, but that sort of acceptance had to wait awhile, until we had helped to unravel this particularly perplexing murder of the young special-education teacher.

On an October afternoon, the nude body of this young woman was found on the roof of the Bronx public-housing project in which she lived. Francine Elverson had been a small woman, under five feet tall and weighing less than a hundred pounds. She lived with her mother and father in an apartment in that building, and had not been seen since early morning, when she had left for her job teaching handicapped children at a nearby day-care center.

Her body was arranged in an odd, almost unnatural position that made no sense until investigators described it to her parents, who told them it resembled the letter *chai* of the Hebrew alphabet, the letter that had been on a chain she had worn around her neck; the chain was missing from the scene. This, however, was not an anti-Semitic crime but a brutal sexual murder. On either side of the victim's head, the killer had placed the earrings she had worn; her nylons were tied loosely around her wrists and her underpants had been removed and pulled over her head to cover her face. The rest of Francine's clothing lay nearby, and under it was the place where the killer had defecated. The young teacher had been beaten about the face, strangled with the strap of her purse, and severely mutilated after death. Her nipples had been cut off and placed on her chest, there was a lot of blood smeared about, bite marks on her inner thighs, an umbrella and a pen had been jammed into her vagina, and a comb was entwined in her pubic hair. The killer had written on her thigh and abdomen in ink: "Fuck you. You can't stop me."

Semen and a single black pubic hair, not the victim's, had also been found on her body; that hair served to lead the police astray for some time. When New York Housing Authority homicide detective Thomas Foley got around to sending us the crime-scene photos and other investigative information, the police had twenty-two suspects, some of them quite promising. That wasn't surprising, because New York is a very large city in population as well as in area, and there are a lot of strange, potentially violent people within that number. For instance, one obvious suspect was a man who lived in the building and who had previously been incarcerated for sex offenses. Another was a black man who had formerly been a janitor in the building and had never turned in his keys. A third was a fifteen-year-old boy who found Francine's wallet on the stairs in the morning as he was on his way to school but did not give it to his father to return until later in the day.

I looked at the crime-scene photos and the other evidence and concluded that the black pubic hair was irrelevant. Another profiler disagreed with me but I argued that this was a crime of a mentally ill person; the level of violence to the body showed that. The absence of a rape kit showed a lack of complete premeditation and stalking; real stalkers bring with them the things they need to restrain the victim. This was clearly a spontaneous, blitz-style assault, committed during a chance encounter between killer and victim. Though the scene had been made to appear a bit as if a gang had done this, I thought not. Our profile told Foley that he ought to be looking for a white male aged twenty-five to thirty-five who knew the victim and lived and worked either in that very building or in one that was nearby. I thought it likely that the killer was mentally ill, and, as with Richard Chase, the disease had been bubbling within him for ten years before it had erupted into a mutilation murder. Most people who have full-blown mental illness do not range far from their homes to commit this sort of crime, and that was why I thought it probable that be lived nearby, either alone or with an indulgent single parent. The notes and arranging of the body suggested that this was not a well-schooled man, probably a school dropout who had gotten his ideas on what to say in his note and how to mutilate the body from an extensive collection of pornographic materials. Because I felt certain that he had a history of mental disease, I thought it likely that he had been released by some mental-care institution within the past year. I also suggested that there would be severe precrime stresses that might have provoked the murder. Given the level of police work that had already been put in, we all concluded that the cops had probably already interrogated the killer.

This profile enabled Foley and his men to refocus their investigation. They could put the former janitor on the shelf for a while, since we said the crime had been committed by a white man, and they could also more or less eliminate the man who had had prior sex-crime offenses, who was now happily married, employed, and considered as having put his past behind him. Another suspect who had been previously dismissed could now be brought to the fore, however. Earlier, the police had spoken to a man who lived on the fourth floor of the building (the same floor as the victim) and shared the apartment with his son, who had been in a mental institution. The mother had died when Carmine Calabro was nineteen years old, and that was eleven years earlier. When interviewed in October, the father said that Carmine had been in the institution at the time of the murder—and the police had not triple-checked this alibi. Now, it was scrutinized more closely.

Calabro was a high school dropout who had spent more than a year in a nearby mental hospital, then had gotten a job as a stagehand, from which he had recently been fired. He had first told police that he was an unemployed actor, but he later admitted to being an unemployed stagehand. The Calabros' apartment was full of pornography. When the police looked into security at the mental hospital, they discovered that it was so lax, it would easily have been possible for Carmine to have slipped out of the institution, committed the murder, and returned without anyone having noticed he had been gone or being able to say that he had been absent. At the time of the murder, he had been wearing a cast on his arm, and it was surmised that he had used this cast to render the victim unconscious. By the time the police caught up to him, the cast had long since been thrown away; fortunately, it was not needed to prove that the former mental patient was the killer. One of the key clues came from the victim's body: she had been bitten. Three forensic odontologists, including Dr. Lowell Levine, were able to match the bite marks to the prime suspect's teeth—and the case was solved. Calabro was convicted and sentenced to twenty-five years to life.

Further investigation revealed that this former stagehand had a long history of violence toward himself, including repeated suicide attempts, and was described by many people as being insecure with women. His inability to connect with a woman seems to have been the starting point of the crime.

It turned out that Elverson's body had been transported to the medical examiner in a body bag that had previously been used for a black male and had not been properly cleaned before transport. The unexplained pubic hair had come from that earlier murder—not from Elverson's body at all.

When the Elverson-Calabro case was all over, Lt. Joseph D'Amico, Foley's boss and a former student of mine at Quantico, told a reporter, "They [the profilers] had him [the suspect] so right that I asked the FBI why they hadn't given us his phone number, too." While we liked that compliment, we liked even better the fact that this case helped open the eyes of New York's police community to the idea of profiling as a way of narrowing the field of suspects in a difficult case.

In court, Calabro never admitted his crime. However, after an article including information about the BSU's profile of the case had appeared in the magazine *Psychology Today*—an article that did not mention the name of the killer or of the victim—Calabro wrote us a letter. That he would write to us directly and make reference to the case summarized in the article was as much an admission of guilt as he ever made. The letter said that some points in our psychological profile "I personally believe [are] correct."

I was on the interstate, traveling in a Bureau car to Richmond, Virginia, to give a lecture, when a call came over the FBI radio asking me to turn around and return to Quantico. When I protested that I was expected to show up and talk to a prestigious group, I was informed that I was needed because President Reagan had been assassinated. I turned around. On the way back, I tuned in to commercial radio stations, from which I learned the good news that the President had been shot but was alive and expected to recover, as were the other victims. Driving back, I alternated between listening intently to the reports and churning over in my mind some details of my earlier interviews with such assassins as Sirhan Sirhan, Arthur Bremer, and Sara Jane Moore. My visit with Arthur Bremer had been almost a carbon copy of the one I'd had with Sirhan; the two assassins were two peas in a behavioral pod, paranoid schizophrenics to the core. Bremer had been bizarre in appearance, something like Howard Hughes in his reclusive state— wild hair, flowing beard; his eyes darting about. He carried with him two shopping bags that contained all of his earthly belongings. Yet Bremer had seemed somewhat in control of his actions at the time of his attempts on the life of Governor George Wallace. I thought also on this ride back to Quantico of David Berkowitz, who was not an assassin but who had many of the personality characteristics that I associate with assassins: He had stalked a particular type of victim much as Bremer had stalked Wallace.

At Quantico, I went to Assistant Director McKenzie's office, where it was obvious that I had been expected, and I was put on the hot line to headquarters, where I spoke with Frank W. Waikart, the agent who had been put in charge of the case. Waikart told me that the authorities already had John Hinckley in custody and needed some assistance on what to look for when they searched his motel room. I asked for whatever details he could provide me about Hinckley.

The FBI had worked quickly. My colleagues already knew that Hinckley was a white male in his midtwenties. They learned he was single, a college student from Denver, and that his family appeared to be fairly wealthy. After his shooting spree, he had submitted rather easily to the Secret Service and other agents who immobilized him, and now appeared to be calm. The FBI had the key to his motel room, but the motel and room had also been discovered by the press, and the authorities were nearly having to beat off the press to prevent unauthorized people from entering and trashing the assassin's quarters.

Although Hinckley was in custody, many, many things could go wrong in this stage of the investigation, when the shock and panic had not worn off. First of all, Washington, D.C., is a multijurisdictional area, and lots of different police authorities might want to push their way in and seize evidence. There was the extreme danger that if the evidence was not properly seized, it could be thrown out in court, and that might put the entire prosecution of Hinckley in jeopardy. What was essential was to get a search warrant that listed items for which the prosecution would specifically look. It must not seem as if the search was a random one.

What was required, then, was more than a profile; it was a journey into the mind of this assassin to see who he might be, and what evidence of that personality he might have left around him. I told Waikart that all the facts he had given me pointed toward the notion that Hinckley was a mentally disordered type of assassin, though not so disordered as to be actually beyond understanding what he had done or what was happening to him. I did not see him as a paid assassin or as part of a conspiracy but, rather, as a loner, an introvert. He would be the type, often recognized on college campuses, who had no successful relationships with women, didn't fit into the dating scene, wasn't a member of sports teams or even of clubs, the sort of person who wasn't very good academically and who found his rewards in fantasy. And so I told Waikart to look in Hinckley's motel room—and in his car and his Denver home—for evidence of such loneliness and fantasy.

The searchers should seize materials that were reflections of the fantasy: diaries, scrapbooks, reading material. I cautioned Waikart to seize all reading material, no matter how innocuous it might appear, because it would be a window into Hinckley's personality. There might be, for instance, magazine articles or books where specific passages were underlined, and the underlining would tell us what Hinckley thought was significant. High up on my list of what to look for was a tape recorder and audiotapes, because this sort of lonely person often makes audiotapes and uses them as sort of diary. Another important item would be credit cards and receipts, because we'd need to trace his steps back at least six months and possibly as long as a year. Assassins such as Bremer had stalked their targets, and I thought it likely that Hinckley had also done so. Hotel bills might contain records of phone calls; he might even have a telephone credit card that we could use to find additional records of his movements and interests.

My list of a dozen items was turned into a search warrant listing those items, and was used by the authorities to seize items from Hinckley's motel room and other rooms used by him. Nearly every item I had suggested as important was found. For example, there were tapes of his conversations with Jodie Foster. There was a postcard with a picture of the Reagans that Hinckley had addressed to Foster, with this text:

> Dear Jodie: Don't they make a darling couple? Nancy is downright sexy. One day you and I will occupy the White House and the peasants will drool with envy. Until then, please do your best to remain a virgin. You are a virgin, aren't you?
> [signed] John Hinckley

He hadn't sent the postcard, but he had written it. Another item seized was a letter to Foster that said he was going out to shoot Reagan and knew he might not return, but that he wanted her to know he had done this deed for her. (This letter, among other items, was evidence of a premeditated attack against Reagan and of the fact that he knew what he was doing was legally wrong.) There were diaries and comments in the margins of papers; one read, "Everything whirls / and still the young girls / laugh and mock my name." There was an annotated copy of the script of *Taxi Driver*, the film about an assassin in which Jodie Foster had starred. All of this material fit quite well with my snap evaluation of John Hinckley as a loner who was unsuccessful with women and who lived in a fantasy world.

One thing we in law enforcement are never able to forget is that murder is a horrific crime that scars the family, friends, and associates of the victim. This bedrock belief was all the more reason for me to feel the necessity of doing what I could to help when a call came from Dr. James Cavanaugh in Chicago. Years earlier, I had enlisted Dr. Cavanaugh as an adviser to my Criminal Personality Research Project. He was medical director of the Isaac Ray Center of Rush-Presbyterian St. Luke's Medical Center in Chicago, which deals in forensic psychiatric issues.

One of Cavanaugh's medical students, a young woman named Lori Roscetti, had been found murdered at the side of some railroad tracks not far from the medical center. Roscetti had been a bright, gentle, straight-A student who had just finished a campaign to reinstate a campus escort service for women, which had been dropped as a result of a budget crunch. Her efforts had failed. Lori was liked by everyone at the center, and the staff and Cavanaugh were quite upset by her death.

The formal request for my presence was initiated by Tom Cronin, a Chicago police officer who had been a police fellow at the FBI Academy and a student of mine. Tom sent me a batch of materials. He facetiously noted that a reward for information leading to the arrest of the murderer had already reached $45,000, of which half would be mine if we did a good profile. (In the middle of serious business, law-enforcement people often try to maintain a level head by making jokes; we are, of course, precluded from seeking or accepting monetary rewards.)

From the materials, I learned that the young student had been studying in a room with several others until about 1:30 A.M. on a Saturday in October. She and a male student had gone down to the garage to get her car, carrying books and bags, and she had then driven the male student up to another level of the garage, where he got out of the car and slammed the door. She must have assumed the door was locked, since that male student and others had told the police that Lori was always quite conscientious about such matters; the medical center was in a bad neighborhood at the edge of the University of Illinois Circle campus, and she was always cautious about traveling to and from the area.

At five-thirty that same morning, her body and her car were found next to a railroad trestle adjoining an impoverished black community and not more than half a mile from the hospital. The medical examiner's report showed that she had been badly beaten about the face, that there were considerable trauma injuries to her midsection, and that she had been repeatedly sexually assaulted. It seemed that her car had actually been driven over her body. The doors and trunk of the car were open, and her empty wallet was found on the scene.

The police had no suspects but were interested in a young man who had been a platonic friend of the victim's. He had sought a closer relationship with her and had been spurned, but he had been unexpectedly in town on Friday night and on the morning of the murder. They were also looking into her relationships at the medical

Suspected serial killer Gerard Schaefer led from the courtroom by Florida sheriff's deputies. Note that the only man in the picture who seems at ease is the suspect.

Surviving victim of "cop gone bad" Gerard Schaefer, reenacting her treatment at his hands.

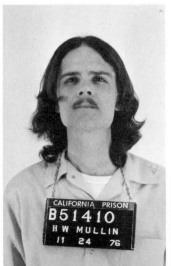

Herbert M. Mullin, serial killer of fourteen people near Santa Cruz, California.

Victims of the psychotic Mullin.

Tent showing the hole that David Meirhofer used to remove a child victim, whom he later killed.

Wrapping on a piece of meat, showing the initials ''SMDS,'' which indicated the name of a previous Meirhofer victim, Sandra Marie Dykeman Smallegan. The pack contained the hand and two fingers of that victim.

John W. Hinckley poses in front of Ford's Theater in Washington, D.C., where President Abraham Lincoln was assassinated. This photograph was taken shortly before Hinckley shot and wounded President Reagan.

Duane Samples at the time of his arrest for the evisceration murder-mutilation of two female victims in Silverton, Oregon.

The deadly fish-filleting knife used by Samples to kill and eviscerate his victims.

Samples's automobile, during a police search.

Robert Ressler (seated) with Pierce Brooks, founder of VICAP.

Pierce Brooks (top center) and members of the FBI's VICAP team: Anna Boudee, Ken Handfland (front left), Dr. David Icove (front center), and Jim Howlett (front right).

Brooks leads the search for bodies of the victims of 1960s serial killer Harvey Murray Glattman in the desert outside of Los Angeles.

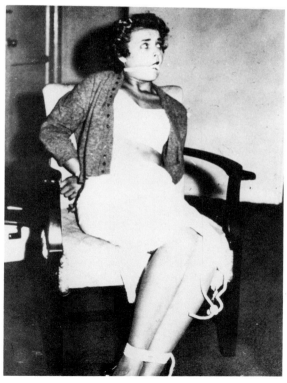

Glattman took this photograph of his frightened victim before killing her to add to his collection of victim souvenirs and later relive his murderous fantasies.

Arrest photograph of John Wayne Gacy taken in Northbrook, Illinois, three years before he murdered the first of thirty-three Chicago-area boys.

Dr. Robert Stein, medical examiner overseeing crime-scene search in the crawl space of Gacy's home in 1979.

Infamous "crawl space" under Gacy's house, with markers indicating the twenty-seven bodies buried there. Two more were found at the rear of the property and four more were thrown into local rivers.

Collection of pornography owned by Gacy, which police found during a search of his residence.

Left: *Painting of clown made by John Wayne Gacy in prison and presented to the author.* Above: *Back of clown painting showing inscription.*

Author Ressler, then an FBI Special Agent, and serial killer Edmund Kemper.

Edmund E. Kemper leading local police to grave sites near Santa Cruz, California.

A grave marker locating the site of a buried skull of one of Kemper's victims.

Monte Rissell at the time of his arrest for the murder of several Washington, D.C., women.

Body of Rissell victim found near his home in, Alexandria, Viginia.

The face of a monster: confessed serial killer Jeffrey Dahmer.

Both experts, good friends, on opposite sides of the Dahmer trial—psychiatrist Dr. Park E. Dietz for the prosecution, Ressler for the insanity defense.

center—focusing, for instance, on a janitor who had access to the garage—as well as canvassing in the area where she lived. They were attempting to trace people who drove trucks near the railroad tracks and a nearby viaduct—in short, going out in all directions.

In terms of profiling, the case was easy, and after viewing aerial photos of the crime-scene area, the medical examiner's report, and all the other documents, I gave an oral profile to Tom Cronin at his home.

My guess was based on what I thought was likely to have happened after Roscetti had left the garage. She had probably stopped at a light in this run-down district, and some people had come up to her, blocked the car, and one had pulled a door, which happened to be open, even though she had thought it was locked. These people then forced her to drive to the somewhat isolated location, where they had raped, killed, and robbed her.

To my mind, this had been an opportunistic crime; the attempt to rob had been the primary motivator, and the sexual assault was secondary. The murder had probably been committed to prevent the victim from identifying her attackers, and it reflected the psychopathic nature of the group of attackers. The presence of a good deal of seminal fluid made it likely that there had been more than one killer. It had all the hallmarks of a gang event. I told the police to look for a group of black youths, somewhere between three and six males, ranging in age from fifteen to twenty, who would previously have been in jail, and who lived close by the scene of the abduction and the railroad trestle where Roscetti had been killed. In white middle-class neighborhoods, kids tend to hang out in single-age groups—all fifteen-year-olds, for example, or all eighteen-year-olds—but in black neighborhoods, there is often a mixture of ages, with young ones accompanying older ones. This murder took place well before the rape of the jogger in Central Park by a bunch of kids who had gone "wilding"; if I had known the term *wilding* then, I would have used it to describe what I thought had happened in the murder of Lori Roscetti. The anal assault convinced me that at least some of the gang members had already been incarcerated, because such assaults are common in prisons.

Was this an obvious profile? Yes and no. As I indicated earlier, the police were intensely investigating people linked personally to Roscetti, and continuing on that path would have taken them further and further astray. The profile allowed the police to refocus the investigation, and thereby sped up the case. Armed with the profile—and the lure of reward money for information—police put the word out on the streets of the black neighborhoods adjoining the crime sites that they were looking for young black men who had bragged of taking money from a woman medical student, or of doing anything else associated with Roscetti's murder. The community rather readily came up with a number of nicknames—Shim-Sham was one—that were tracked down, and youngsters were hauled in for questioning. The youngest of the four suspects was fourteen; interrogated, he admitted to the crime, as did two other perpetrators, aged seventeen and sixteen. Between them, these latter two already had more than two dozen arrests and convictions for previous offenses, and both had served time in youth reformatories. A fourth youth was still being sought when the whole story emerged. After a night out, the foursome had run out of money and were looking for a car to rob. They waited about fifteen minutes until they saw a car with a lone white female stopped at a light. Two had stood in front of the car, betting that the driver wouldn't run them over, while another tried the doors. Finding a door open, he climbed into it and opened the other doors for his companions. After that, the foursome had driven Roscetti to the trestle site, where they stabbed her with a sharpened stick she had kept in the car for protection, and had put her over the hood of the car and raped her before beating her into unconsciousness. When she stirred again, they smashed in her head with a piece of concrete wrapped in a plastic bag, and ran her car over her body. Then the attackers had walked to the Abla projects where three of them lived and where the fourth used to reside.

The fourth suspect, eighteen, eventually surrendered in the custody of a local television newsman who was known for such assistance. Later, several of the suspects tried to recant their early confessions and claimed these had been coerced by the police. The jury evidently didn't believe the recantations, and all four were convicted. Three were sent to prison, and the youngest to a youth facility. The escort system Lori had fought for was reinstated. Neither the convictions nor the beefed-up security brought Lori Roscetti back, of course, but the law's vengeance and the future protection of other potential victims were the only solace available to the community, to Lori's family and friends, and to Dr. Cavanaugh and the staff of the medical center.

Many of the cases that the FBI profiles have to do with offenders who have already been caught but whose crimes are so unusual that the local authorities seek guidance on how to proceed. One morning during Thanksgiving week of November 1985, a teenaged girl, nude, handcuffs on hands and feet, and quite weak from loss of blood, crawled along a road near Malabar, Florida, seeking help. Several trucks passed her by, but then a motorist stopped.

"You're not going to take me back to that house, are you?" the terrified girl asked.

The motorist responded that he would help her, and got her into the car. She asked him to "remember that house," which she pointed out to him, a few doors away, a place with a well-kept lawn, many trees, a swimming pool and patio. The motorist took her home and called the police and an ambulance. At the hospital, it was determined that she had lost between 40 and 45 percent of her blood and that there were ligature marks on her neck as well as on her hands and ankles.

As she recovered, the nineteen-year-old told the police that one day earlier she had been hitchhiking in Brevard County on her way to a friend's home and had been picked up by a man wearing a sport coat and a tie. He offered to take her most of the way but said he had to stop at his home and pick something up. At the house, he asked the hitchhiker to come inside. When she said no, he went around to the back of the car, got in behind her, and threw a nylon rope around her and choked her into unconsciousness.

The hitchhiker awoke to find that she was tied to a kitchen countertop, arms and legs immobilized. A video camera had been set up, along with lights. The man raped her and videotaped the action. Then he inserted needles into her arm and wrist and carefully extracted blood and began to drink it, telling her that he was a vampire. After that, he handcuffed her and put her in the bathtub, returning later for another round of sexual assault and blood extraction. The next morning, after a third round, the man handcuffed the hitchhiker and left her in the bathroom, saying that he would be back later for further assaults, and that if she tried to escape in the interim, his brother would come and kill her. It was after the attacker had left the house that she was able to push out the bathroom window and crawl to the road. Had she not escaped then, doctors believed, she might well have died from a further round of blood extraction.

The house that she described to the police belonged to John Brennan Crutchley, thirty-nine, a computer engineer for the Harris Corporation, a NASA contractor. He was married and had one child; both his wife and child were in Maryland, visiting her family for the holidays. A search warrant was obtained and served on Crutchley's home at two-thirty the next morning. During this serving, Crutchley was arrested, some obvious items of interest were seized, and photographs were taken of the residence. The hitchhiker initially did not want to file charges against Crutchley, but she was convinced to do so by a rape counselor, on the grounds that convicting Crutchley would prevent him from assaulting other women. The victim took and passed a lie-detector test about the rapes, and Crutchley was charged with sexual battery, kidnapping, and aggravated battery of the hitchhiker, as well as possession of marijuana and of drug paraphernalia.

The well-meaning police search had seized some of the obvious items, such as the video camera, the hook in the ceiling where the hitchhiker had been tied, the marijuana, and some of the other paraphernalia of the assaults, but they had not been in time to prevent the erasure of the sections of videotape. According to the victim, this video would have contained the record of the assault on the hitchhiker. After the search, it was not entirely clear what the police had and what they had missed, nor even what they ought to be looking for in further searches. The police authorities contacted me for assistance, and, during a trip to Florida for other purposes, I went to Titusville to render it.

I was very glad they asked me to get involved in the case, because while the police knew they had caught a dangerous rapist, after I found out a few things about Crutchley, I thought it probable that they had a serial killer in custody.

One of the greatest problems in law enforcement today is that the police don't know how to deal with unusual cases; specifically, they don't know what to look for at a crime scene, and in a search that doesn't grab everything that could be of interest, time is allowed for the suspect and his associates to hide or destroy what could be of vital importance to the case. It was my task initially to tell the police what to look for in a second search. For instance, the police photographs of Crutchley's house showed a stack of credit cards, several inches thick; by the time of the second search, these had been removed and had presumably been destroyed.

Those credit cards and such things as the presence of a dozen or more women's necklaces that hung on a hook in Crutchley's closet (and which I thought were trophies), as well as the presence in the house of identification cards from two other women, pointed me in the direction of believing that the abduction of the hitchhiker was not Crutchley's first offense. When asked about these identification cards, Crutchley said he had given rides to the women and they had left the cards in his car and he had had no opportunity to return them. He avowed that the necklaces belonged to his wife, and said that the hitchhiker had been a "Manson girl" who had solicited kinky sex from him.

There had been a four female bodies found in remote sites in Brevard County during the previous year, and police investigated whether Crutchley might have killed these women, but authorities could find no evidentiary connection between Crutchley and those bodies. The second searches that I recommended included excavations on his property and searches of his offices at the Harris Corporation. These turned up the fact that the stack of credit cards had disappeared and that Crutchley appeared to have illegal possession of a great deal of highly classified information on naval weaponry and communications. Some of this was on diskettes that he had protected by a code, which authorities were able to break. Other federal agencies considered opening an espionage case against him. We found a stack of seventy-two three-by-five-inch cards containing women's first names, their telephone numbers, and Crutchley's evaluation of their sexual performances. Some of these women were telephoned by the authorities, and they gave some indications that they had been restrained or assaulted by Crutchley, but the majority said only that they had participated in kinky behavior with him. There were indications that his wife had done so, as well.

I insisted that Crutchley's actions be traced back in time. We learned that in 1978, Crutchley had been the last person to see alive Debbora Fitzjohn, a secretary in Fairfax County, Virginia. She had been in his mobile home before her disappearance, and police in Fairfax were investigating whether Crutchley had any connection to her death. (No charges were brought.) We learned that wherever Crutchley had been in residence, in Pennsylvania, for instance, there were reports of missing women or bodies found in remote locations—though none of these missing-person cases have to date been connected to Crutchley.

In April of 1986, as the case was ready for trial, Crutchley decided to plead guilty to the kidnap and rape charges in exchange for the dropping of the charges stemming from the blood drinking (grievous bodily harm) and the possession of drugs. After his plea, he held a press conference to downplay what he had done. Echoing his line, his wife later suggested that the crime had been "a gentle rape, devoid of any overt brutality."

State's attorney Norman Wolfinger asked me to enter the case again at this stage, because the state wished to press for a more severe sentence than would normally be given to someone convicted of a first-time charge of kidnap and rape. The usual penalty was twelve to seventeen years; with time deducted for good behavior in prison and so on, Crutchley could be out in four to five years, and the state did not believe that was in society's best interests. I agreed, and began to look into the case, prior to going to Florida to give testimony at a presentencing hearing.

I learned that Crutchley's family was well educated. But Crutchley's mother had dressed him as a girl until he was five or six years of age, and there were other instances of childhood abnormalities. Crutchley told a psychiatrist at the time of sentencing that he remembered seeing a psychiatric counselor in his youth. Friends and a former wife said that he liked to control people and would often make them do his bidding, and that he was a sexual sadist. Others said they knew of group sex in which he had been involved. There were indications of his bisexuality, and it was clear from interviews with some of the women named on the three-by-five-inch cards that Crutchley was into unlimited sexual experimentation. Such unlimited experimentation was one of the categories of behavior I had documented as being frequently associated with serial killers.

In June, the presentencing hearing was held, and the courtroom was packed. The blond, slight, erudite-appearing Crutchley decided to take the stand in his own defense. In a tearful two-hour presentation, he said that he was just a sexual experimenter and that the behavior for which he had been convicted was private and not within the court's jurisdiction. Although the charge stemming from the blood drinking had been dropped from the indictment, it was an issue in the sentencing hearing, because it showed how much harm Crutchley had done to his victim. He tried to explain it away by saying that he had learned blood drinking from a nurse, fifteen years earlier, as part of a sexual ritual, and that if the drinking of blood was really important to the sentencing, it should be thrown out, because he hadn't really drunk the blood in this case. Why not? Because it had coagulated, and he couldn't get it down. Such answers, of course, did him very little good. Crutchley admitted that "I need treatment," which ought not to include extended jail time. His wife sat in the courtroom but would not take the stand in his defense, though she later told reporters that he wasn't really guilty and was just "a kinky sort of guy."

When I took the stand, as sometimes happens, my credentials were brought into question. The defense attorney was contending that this case was so unusual that no one could claim to be an expert on things of this nature. He asked me how many blood-drinking cases I had seen. I gazed toward the ceiling for a moment and counted them in my mind before saying, "Oh, a half-dozen."

People in the courtroom gasped. Which ones? The defense attorney challenged. I rattled them off, beginning with Richard Trenton Chase. After that demonstration of my experience, I had smooth sailing. I made a strong plea for sentencing that exceeded the guidelines. To go beyond those guidelines, the state had to provide good reasons; in this case, the reasons were that there had been extensive physical and mental injury to the victim, excessive brutality and premeditation of the crime; and taking advantage of a vulnerable victim. The presence of the video camera and other evidence, such as his family's absence, showed that the crime had certainly been premeditated, and Crutchley's repeated savaging of the hitchhiker even after she had lost a lot of blood demonstrated brutality and taking advantage of someone who was vulnerable. Crutchley had told the hitchhiker that he would continue to assault her again and again, and this was certainly mentally as well as physically injurious.

I further testified that John Crutchley had all the hallmarks of a serial killer, and gave my reasons for saying so—the stack of credit cards and other "trophies" I believed to have come from missing women, the unlimited sexual experimentation, the fact that the hitchhiker would have died if she had been subjected to the blood draining for another day, the Fitzjohn case in Virginia, and so on. I drew similarities between Crutchley and Ted Bundy, who was then awaiting execution and whose maneuvers to delay that execution shared headlines with the Crutchley case in Florida.

The judge did exceed the guidelines and gave Crutchley twenty-five years to life in prison, and fifty years of parole, a sentence that would keep Crutchley more or less under the state's control for the rest of his life.

Norm Wolfinger sent a letter of thanks to Director Webster for allowing me to testify, and told me personally that had I not testified, Crutchley's sentence might not have exceeded the guidelines. That was nice to hear, because I believe that Crutchley ought to be behind bars for a long stretch, but there are times when I wonder whether pursuing these dangerous people so assiduously is accomplishing the protection of society. With good time, law-enforcement people figure, Crutchley will be out in 1998, and maybe even sooner. In the criminal-justice system, nothing means anything anymore: Life imprisonment doesn't mean life, death doesn't mean death, and twenty-five years means twelve and a half, or maybe even six. But don't get me started on that!

*　　*　　*

In October of 1989, I was preparing to retire from the Bureau, and had long since turned over the day-to-day work of profiling to others at Quantico. However, men who had worked with me in the Bureau, or whom I had taught at the academy, were all over the country, and when they called to ask for assistance, it was me personally they wanted, and I always said yes. That's how I got involved in a case that took me back in time, both in the type of crime and in its location.

In broad daylight, on a weekday afternoon just prior to Halloween, twelve-year-old Amy Mijalevic disappeared at a small shopping center directly opposite the police station in Bay Village, Ohio. This happened right down the road from the site of the osteopathic hospital of Dr. Sam Shephard, near Cleveland; Shephard's was the most notorious murder case of the 1950s and 1960s in the Cleveland area.

Amy's photograph, peering out from a "missing girl" poster, could have been that of any of ten thousand twelve-year-old girls in America's heartland, a blue-eyed, brown-haired, freckle-faced girl with outsized earrings and a turquoise jumpsuit. You looked at that photo and hoped that it was all a mistake, that she'd turn the corner and come home soon; and yet you knew there was slim chance of that.

I had been an agent in the Cleveland office of the FBI before transferring to Quantico, and so I was a former colleague of John Dunn, who became involved in the case of Amy's disappearance. Another agent concerned with the case, Dick Wrenn, had also worked with me on a case in Genoa, Ohio, in 1980. Both men asked me to come and have a look at the evidence. I was attending a conference of the American Academy of Forensic Sciences, held in Cincinnati, and over a weekend I drove to Bay Village.

The FBI had gotten into this case quickly, and our involvement followed the model established in the Joubert murders. I had frequently lectured about the interagency coordination that had been the key to success in that case, and the Joubert task-force model had been followed in several subsequent cases. When I arrived in Bay Village, Dunn had already established his task-force headquarters in the suburban police station, and he had two dozen agents assisting the local authorities.

Amy had been abducted, but nothing more was really certain. There had been no ransom demands, no body found, no signs of a struggle. The main witness was Amy's younger brother, who told us that in the days prior to the abduction, Amy had received a series of telephone calls at the house from a man who the brother said had given

Amy the following pitch: "I work with your mom, and she's just been promoted and we want to get her a present; meet me in the shopping center after school and help me pick out a gift. Keep this a secret, and don't tell anyone, because we don't want your mom to know about the gift."

Amy had asked whether she could tell her brother, and the man said she shouldn't. Amy agreed, saying that her brother was a real blabbermouth. After she hung up, however, she did tell her brother, who later recounted the conversation to the authorities. Several people had seen Amy talking to a man in a car at the shopping center, and they gave partial descriptions that were made into a sketch that filled the lower part of Amy's "missing person" poster and flier. The sketch was of a white man, fairly youthful but otherwise undistinguished in the witnesses' minds, who might or might not have worn glasses.

Dunn, who had been a priest and a police officer before joining the FBI, sat down with me and we made a profile. If John Joubert had been on the streets, I would have suspected him, or someone quite similar to him, although Joubert killed boys and not girls. Many of the characteristics that I felt were important were similar to those of Joubert. I wanted the police to look for a man in his late twenties or early thirties who was introverted and a loner, relatively unsuccessful in life, unmarried, not overly educated but not stupid. This would be a man with no military service but with a propensity for spending a lot of time around kids. His smoothness in conning Amy into the car argued for his knowing something about children and the way their minds work, and I thought it likely that a person who preferred children's company would not have put himself in a situation such as the military, where male bonding is part of the experience. It might just be children of both sexes he was after, but it was more likely he sought out only girls; in either case, he would be uncomfortable with male and female adults. I felt strongly that Amy's abduction was his first offense, because there was no record of any similar abductions in the area and because the abductor had exposed himself to so much danger by his phone call and by making the abduction in such a public place as the parking lot, where many people could see him. I thought that the abductor might have conned Amy into his car, taken her to his home on the pretext of getting money or a greeting card or some such, even offered her cookies and milk, and played with her until she became frightened and started to resist, at which point he might have been convinced that he had to kill her. I told the authorities to keep an eye out for a person who might try to interject himself into the investigation.

It wasn't much, but there was very little to go on.

In January, I returned to Bay Village, where the authorities had leads on four or five suspects who more or less fit the profile. One was a stablehand who worked at a place where Amy had taken riding lessons; I thought he was more mentally disordered than the man who had smoothly talked Amy into a car. Nonetheless, the police hauled him in and gave him truth serum; he easily passed that test. Another suspect was a police officer, and a third was a fireman. I didn't think they fit the bill, either, because education, discipline, successful adaptation, and male bonding are essential to obtaining and keeping such jobs as they held.

A fourth suspect was a youngish man who had come to the police department and volunteered to distribute the handbills with Amy's picture. Now many other people in the community had also volunteered, but Dunn and Wrenn had felt that this particular man, named Strunack, was a very likely suspect. He was single, in his early thirties, lived alone, and worked as a stockboy at a discount-price club; he had graduated from high school but had no further education, and no military service. He did, however, have a very severe skin problem that caused his face to break out so badly that he was taking medication for the condition. It was thought that his skin condition prevented him from having relationships with women. In addition to volunteering, Strunack had sent a sympathy card to Amy's mother, from "a concerned friend," and signed his name. In it were two cheap decorative pins, with a note saying that the mother could wear one and that when Amy returned home, Mrs. Mijalevic could give her daughter the other one.

I agreed with Dunn and Wrenn that this was a likely suspect, and I wanted to know where the pins had come from. We determined that they were sold in the place where Strunack worked.

Under the guise of trying to thank him for his volunteer work, Dunn and I went to see Strunack. He lived in a studio apartment in an inexpensive town-house complex. The place had a fold-up bed and a tiny kitchen and bathroom. After bringing up the volunteer work, we asked Strunack some questions about himself. Yes, he said, he had a girlfriend. We later learned that she was a woman with a small child from an early marriage. I doubted there had been any sexual activity between them.

After a while, we deliberately turned up the heat. Why was he so involved in this investigation? Was it possible that he was the one who had picked Amy up? I tried to minimize what he might have done, saying that it was possible that the child had had some difficulties, maybe fell down and hurt her head, and that he'd been afraid to tell anyone about it. Maybe there'd been an accident. Strunack protested vehemently, saying that he had had nothing to do with Amy's disappearance.

We had no authority to search the place, but when Strunack went to the bathroom, I looked it over as best I could. My focus was to see whether there was anything in the apartment that could have been a trophy of Amy or of any other child. I felt it likely that he might have killed her in this apartment and taken her elsewhere, and I had the task force prepared to move in and open the drains, take the hair out of brushes, and so on, if we got the slightest hint of involvement. There was no such hint, however, and we left Strunack in his apartment.

Coming out of the interview, I told Dunn that my gut said this was the guy, and he thought so, too—but there was no proof.

Three weeks later, Amy's body was found about fifty miles away. She still wore her turquoise jumpsuit, but it had been taken off her body and put on again after death. The dump site was a field just off an exit to I-71, the main highway that connects Cleveland with Cincinnati. Amy's body was well preserved and had not been there very long, perhaps a week at the most. The coroner thought it likely that she had died in October and that her body had been preserved by cold until the moment of dumping.

The day that the finding of Amy's body was reported in the newspapers, Strunack mixed dry gas in a glass of Coke and drank it, committing suicide.

As soon as the police learned of his death, Dunn and I recommended a quick search of Strunack's apartment. They obtained a warrant and went to the town-house complex, only to learn they were too late. Even before the wake, his family had already cleaned the place down to the walls and given his clothes to Goodwill.

Amy Mijalevic's abduction and murder is still being carried on the Bay Village police books as an unsolved crime, and we will probably never know the truth of the matter. However, there have been no similar crimes in the community in the past two years, and maybe that's all that can be hoped for.

8

STAGING: PATTERN OF DECEIT

In this chapter I'll take you through a handful of cases that initially baffled the police because the criminals had been so clever at "staging" the crime scenes. One of the helpful consequences of our experience in profiling, and our research into the minds and criminal methods of incarcerated murderers, is extra knowledge about how some organized criminals work hard at throwing the police off their track. (A disorganized violent criminal never bothers himself about deliberately misleading the police.)

You already know about stagings from detective novels or from reports about such common occurrences as husbands who have killed their mates in a fit of anger, then tried to make the scene appear as if a burglar had come in and murdered the poor wife. The police almost always see through such stagings quickly. The cases in this chapter follow a similar pattern but are far more ingenious; indeed, in all instances, they had the regular authorities pretty much fooled—for a while.

In Columbus, Georgia, one February evening in 1978, a group of middle-aged and elderly women were at a party together, and the main topic of discussion was the mysterious series of killings of seven other elderly women in Columbus. At one point during the evening, in a demonstration of how completely the fear of the killer had gripped the city, seven of the women guests emptied their purses, revealing seven handguns that fell out onto the carpet. In fact, the killings were terrible—elderly women, some of whom had been raped and all of whom had been strangled to death with nylon stockings in their own homes. Everyone was terrified of the "stocking strangler." Some forensic evidence obtained at the crime scenes suggested that the killer was a black male, but the police had been unable to narrow the search beyond that.

There was tremendous community pressure on the Columbus police and their chief. Fortunately that chief was not the stereotypical backwoods lawman but one who had an advanced degree in police sciences. Nonetheless, he was reluctant to do as the media asked— call the Georgia Bureau of Investigation and the FBI for help—because he didn't want to lose control of the case.

Then the chief received an unusual handwritten letter on U.S. Army stationery, addressed to him. It is reprinted (in part) just below. In the original, the capital and lowercase letters are all about the same size.

DEAR SiR:

WE ARE AN ORGiNiZATION COMPOSED OF 7 MEM-BERS. I'M WRITING ThiS LETTER TO INFORM YOU THAT WE hAVE ONE OF *YOUR COLuMBUS WOMEN* CApTiVE. HER NAME iS GAiL JACKSON. SiNCE THAT COrONER SAid THAT THE S-STRANgLER iS BLACK, *WE dECidED TO COME hERE* AND Try TO CATCH hiM OR PuT MORE PrESSuRE ON YOU. I SEE NOW, MORE PrESSurE iS NEEDED. AT THiS POiNT GAiL JACKSON iS STiLL LiViNg. IF THAT STrANgLER iS NOT CAUgHT BY 1 JUNE 1978. YOU WiLL FiND GAiL JACKSON'S bODY ON WYNONTON RD. IF hE'S STILL NOT CAUGHT BY 1 SEPT 1978. THE ViTIMS WiLL doublE. . . . YOu hAVE uNTiL SuNDAY FOR REplY. DON'T THiNK WE ARE bluFFiNg. . . . WE ARE *CALL* THE: ForCES OF EViL.

The letter cautioned the authorities not to make too much of the fact that the letter was written on military stationery; anyone could get hold of that, the writer suggested. The message of the letter seemed to be clear: An organization of white men was going on a vigilante offensive, and black women were going to die until the black killer of the elderly white women was caught. Succeeding letters announced that the Forces of Evil had come from Chicago, and that the police chief was to communicate with the organization through radio or television messages. A demand for ten thousand dollars in order to keep Gail Jackson alive was also made. The chief at first disregarded the letters, but then he sent them to the newspapers, hoping perhaps to flush out the sender. And he also rechanneled some of his resources from going after the stocking strangler into chasing the Forces of Evil organization. He and his policemen looked hard for seven white men, even telephoning to Chicago to see what the police there knew about such a white supremacist group.

Then came a phone call to the MP desk at Fort Benning, Georgia, the large military reservation that abuts Columbus; a caller, claiming to be a representative of the Forces of Evil, said that Gail Jackson was going to be killed and asked why didn't the police do something about it.

Two days after that phone call, at the end of March 1978, I was in Atlanta, Georgia, having dinner with an old Army CID buddy, Tom McGreevy, who had become deputy director of the Georgia Bureau of Investigation, for whom I was conducting a course at the Georgia Police Academy. Tom told me something about the Columbus case. He had become involved after the Columbus chief had finally realized that it was no longer in his interest to keep the state authorities at arm's length. He showed me the Forces of Evil letters and asked whether I could help. In addition to the letters, we had available some recorded telephone calls to the MP desk.

Analyzing the communications, I immediately discounted the idea that Gail Jackson was about to be killed by a group of seven white men in reaction to the death of the seven elderly white women. The evidence pointed precisely in the opposite direction. I thought the probable culprit was a single black male. The style of writing in the letters, as well as the accent of the voice on the telephone-call tape, made that a reasonable assumption. Once I had figured that out, the rest was easy: The letters seemed quite clearly to be an attempt to lead the authorities away from the most likely suspect, a person who was a known associate of Gail Jackson's. But what other reason would the killer have to write such a letter? Possibly to prevent the police from getting close to him, because he had already killed Jackson. It seemed likely that he had penned the letters in order to disguise the death. My analysis of the letters and the voice on the calls was seconded, independently, by the FBI's psycholinguistic consultant, Dr. Murray Miron.

The MP desk at Fort Benning received another call on the third of April that said Gail Jackson's body could be found "one hundred meters" from Fort Benning. A quick search did locate her body, and the information went from the base authorities to McGreevy to me.

Jackson had been a prostitute, well known in some of the bars in the vicinity of the military reservation. The medical examiner estimated that she had been dead about five weeks; that is, she had been killed prior to the time the letters had been written, as I had suspected.

Now, with some more details in hand, I was able to come up with a more detailed profile. Often, the best way to approach a profile is through victimology, through looking at the victim's background. Was this a low-risk or a high-risk victim? What areas did she frequent? What was her daily routine? What was her lifestyle? Who would she be likely to consort with in such a lifestyle? Jackson, also known by several other names, had been a black prostitute who plied her trade among the black servicemen of the large military installation at Fort Benning, and she had frequented the streets and bars near the base. I concluded that the killer was someone so close to Gail Jackson that his name or identity would inevitably be turned up in any investigation of her life, and that had been the reason for his attempt to lead the authorities 180 degrees in the opposite direction; that is, away from his own characteristics. He had chosen to portray Jackson's abductors as seven white men from Chicago.

I pegged him as a single black male, twenty-five to thirty years of age, an enlisted man on the Fort Benning complex, possibly a military policeman or artilleryman. I was certain the killer was in the military because of the references in the letters and phone calls to "meters" and the way he kept calling automobiles "vehicles." His inadequate English made it certain that he was not a college graduate, therefore not a commissioned officer, and I thought it likely that his rank would be no more than an E-6. As for his age, the reader already knows that most serial killers are in their twenties or thirties; I guessed he was in his late twenties because that would be commensurate with a person of modest education in a middle-ranking military position.

The latest Forces of Evil letters had mentioned the name of another black woman, Irene—whose last name the writer did not know—and said she, too, would be killed if no action was taken. I guessed that she was also already dead, and I recommended that all the phone booths on the base be kept under surveillance. They were, and the recording system was in operation, but when a call came in, the MP at the desk was so upset that he forgot to turn on the recorder. Following the instructions of the caller, authorities found a second black female, Irene Thirkield, dead on a rifle range at the fort. She, too, had been a prostitute.

Armed with my profile and the knowledge that both women had been prostitutes, GBI narcotics agents interviewed the patrons of a nightclub on the outskirts of Fort Benning frequented by black soldiers. Several people knew both prostitutes and readily named a man who had acted as their pimp. Two days after the profile was circulated, the military and civilian authorities arrested William H. Hance, a specialist fourth grade attached to an artillery unit at the fort. Confronted with the handwriting, voice evidence, and shoe prints taken at the crime scenes, Hance admitted that the letters had been a complete hoax, and confessed to the killing of the two women, who he said had been involved with him in prostitution and low-level drug trade, as well as to the killing of a third female at Fort Benning in September of the previous year. Later, he was identified as the murderer of another young black woman at another post where he had been stationed earlier, Fort Benjamin Harrison in Indiana.

As McGreevy said in a letter of appreciation to the Director of the FBI, "The profile data turned out to be right on the nose in every respect," and on behalf of his agency and that of the Columbus police, he expressed his gratitude to me and to the Bureau for the "whole-hearted, professional and immediate efforts" that supported the investigation "when we needed all the help we could get."

I had initially thought it likely that Hance had also committed the strangulation murders of the elderly white women, but this possibility was dismissed when the forensic evidence did not match. Released from chasing the figment of Hance's imagination, the Columbus police and the GBI continued their investigation. Good police work finally paid off. In one of the early murders, a pistol had been stolen from the victim's house, and later the police got a tip concerning this pistol. The weapon was traced to Kalamazoo, Michigan, then to some other cities, and ultimately to a small town in Alabama, where the man who admitted having it said it had been given to him by his nephew, Carlton Gary, who lived in Columbus. Gary, it turned out, was a black man who had killed in New York and gone to prison for his murders; then he had escaped, hidden out in South Carolina, and robbed many restaurants before returning to his place of birth. His mother had been a maid in many of the homes of the women that Gary had strangled. Gary was apprehended, convicted, and sentenced to death. He is still in prison, as is William Hance.

Just after the Forces of Evil case, the army requested that the FBI conduct training sessions for the Army in hostage negotiations, and I donned my military hat and went over to Germany to teach at the school.

Thereby hangs a long story, but, to shorten it, I'll just say that during my twenty years in the Bureau, I maintained my reserve status in the Army. Since this was technically speaking against Bureau policy, I now and then had to do a bit of tap dancing to be permitted to keep my commission. Every other government agency not only allows but encourages its employees to be in the reserves—the CIA even has its own reserve unit that meets at Langley—but the FBI doesn't like divided loyalties. Nonetheless, from time to time, the Army would request that the Bureau provide experienced teachers for hostage nego-tiations or other similar subjects, and the task would fall to me. On this particular trip, I asked my associate John Douglas to come along as my backup; John had participated in a tense hostage negotiation in Milwaukee that was successfully resolved, and had also followed me in teaching our hostage-negotiation course at Quantico.

On the way home from the school, we stopped by prior arrange-ment at Bramshill, the British police college about a hundred miles from London that is the leading training facility for law enforcement in the British Isles, the counterpart of Quantico. I hoped to establish some contacts there and stir up some interest in an exchange program. We met the commandant of the college and some other high-level officials, conducted a few guest lectures, and sat in on some classes.

The British expressed quite a bit of skepticism about what we American blokes said we could tell about a case just from looking at crime-scene photographs, and this became the meat of an after-hours session at the local lounge to which the lawmen regularly repaired at the end of the day. Douglas and I sat in that lounge drinking beer with John Domaille, a police officer attending the college just then, and a man who was investigating the most notorious multiple slaying case that had surfaced since Jack the Ripper. The unknown killer was called the Yorkshire Ripper, and he had murdered eight women in Yorkshire, most of them prostitutes, over the course of the previous four years. There were three survivors of his attacks, but all they had been able to agree upon was that the attacker had been a white man of adult age and average size. The police had no good suspects. For instance, they were suggesting to police stations that the killer would be a man born between the years of 1924 and 1959; that is, anywhere between twenty and fifty-five years of age.

Domaille described the crimes to us. Much in the manner that we would later come to associate with Ted Bundy, the killer bludgeoned women and then sexually assaulted them as they lay dying; after death, he mutilated their bodies with a knife.

In the past year, Domaille told us, Chief Inspector George Oldfield had received two letters in the mail from "Jack the Ripper," and then a tape-recording, also sent through the mail. A third letter had been received by a major newspaper. These had become the focus of a renewed manhunt. Oldfield, near retirement age, was under considerable public pressure to find the killer before he struck again. This was the largest case ever in Oldfield's jurisdiction; he had many people trying to second-guess him and criticizing the police for not being able to apprehend the killer. Oldfield had the tape electronically analyzed, the background noises amplified so they might be identified, and was going all out to share his information with the public. A lot of time and money was being spent on tracking the killer through use of this tape. You could telephone a number and listen as the tape was played for you, then offer your comments if you thought you recognized the voice or even the precise origin of the fairly thick backcountry "Geordie" accent. Hundreds of police officers were roaming the area of the murders with tape recorders, playing the tape for the citizenry and soliciting their comments, and the tape was also being broadcast on radio and television.

We said we wanted to see the crime-scene photographs, and offered to do a profile of the likely offender after we'd seen them, but such photographs weren't available at Bramshill just then. However, someone had a copy of the tape-recording and proceeded to play it for us. The speaker was an adult male and spoke with a slow, measured voice. There was considerable background noise, and the tape lasted about two minutes.

> I'm Jack. I see you are still having no luck catching me. I have the greatest respect for you, George, but you are no nearer catching me now than four years ago when I started. I reckon your boys are letting you down, George; ya can't be much good, can ya? The only time they came near touching me was a few months back, in Chapeltown when I was disturbed. Even then it was a uniformed copper, not a detective. I warned you in March that I'd strike again . . . but I couldn't get there. I'm not quite sure when I'll strike again but it will definitely be some [time] this year, maybe September, October, even sooner if I get the chance . . . there's plenty of them knocking about. They never learn, do they,

George. . . . I'll keep on going for quite a while yet. I can't
see myself being nicked just yet. Even if you do get near,
I'll probably top myself first. Well, it's been nice chatting to
you, George. . . .

"Jack" also encouraged Oldfield to listen to the "catchy tune"
on the tape, which turned out to be an extract from a record entitled
Thank You for Being a Friend.

By the time we finished listening to the tape, more than a few
people had gathered at our table. Under the needling stimulus of the
Brits, I said to Domaille, "You realize, of course, that the man on the
tape is not the killer, don't you?"

He was thunderstruck. John Douglas concurred in my evaluation of the tape. It was a hoax designed deliberately to flummox the
police, and perpetrated by someone other than the murderer. The two
of us then lit into the subject. We told the assembled crew why it was
quite clear that the tape was the product of a hoaxer: Because what the
person on the tape said seemed totally inconsistent with the crimes as
Domaille had described those killings to us. We thought that the killer
was not the type of extroverted man who would be communicating
with the police, that he was the quiet, introverted, woman-hating type.
Didn't they understand that his style of quickly rendering the victims
unconscious and his postmortem mutilations showed that hatred of
women?

The voices around the table took on tones of distinct challenge.
If the tape's sender was not the killer, then what sort of man did we
think the killer was? We were being asked to do an instant profile, just
the sort of thing we are most reluctant to do. We protested that we
didn't have crime-scene photos, but the officers gave us more details
and would not be denied. Put up or shut up. Fortified by another round
of beer, we winged it. The killer, we said, was undoubtedly in his late
twenties or early thirties, probably a school dropout or a man who had
not been through higher education. We postulated that he was able to
enter the areas of the murders in a way that rendered him near invisi-
ble—he got there without people paying attention to him, because his
business regularly took him to various areas; he would be a cabdriver
or a truck driver or a mail carrier or possibly even a policeman. We
thought that he was not a total loner, and would have a relationship
with a woman, even though the absence of sexual penetration of the
victims suggested that he had some serious mental problems that had
taken years to develop.

By the time we were finished elucidating this rump profile and defending our conclusions, Domaille invited us to go to Yorkshire to look at the crime-scene photos. We were unable to do so because we had to get back to Quantico, so I invited him to bring the crime-scene materials to us in the United States as soon as he could.

He didn't come and the materials didn't arrive. I later learned that Chief Inspector Oldfield was adamantly opposed to showing us those materials, and totally disagreed with our rump profile. He could not stomach our explanation of the crimes and the fact that the audio-tape demonstrated so easily that he had been misled, and that thousands of police man-hours had been wasted in a fruitless search for the wrong man.

Sometime—and more victims—later, Oldfield was replaced as chief of the investigation. The hunt for the killer had cost nearly $10 million; the police had questioned 200,000 people, made 30,000 searches of homes and 180,000 vehicle searches. It was not until 1981 that the case of the Yorkshire Ripper was solved: During a routine police check in a prostitution area, a man was stopped, and evidence later connected him to thirteen killings and seven other assaults. As we had predicted, Peter Sutcliffe was a thirty-five-year-old, married truck driver for an engineering firm and he regularly traveled around the country for the purposes of his job. After Sutcliffe's apprehension and conviction, some further spadework finally revealed the identity of the man who had perpetrated the audiotape hoax: He was a retired police officer who hated Chief Inspector George Oldfield and had sent the tape to vex him.

In the small town of Genoa, Ohio, in late February of 1980, teenager Debra Sue Vine left her friend's house at eight in the evening and headed for her own home, two blocks away. She never arrived. The next morning, her father, vice president of a local bank, reported her missing. A search of the area between her home and the friend's home turned up one of Debra's mittens. Later that morning, an aunt who was staying at the Vine home received a telephone call from someone she described as a white male in his late teens or early twenties with a Southern or New England accent. He said, "We have your daughter. We want eighty thousand dollars or you will never see her again." The aunt asked to speak to Debra, and the caller hung up.

The aunt told police that because of the unique characteristics of the Genoa telephone system, she believed the call had been a local rather than a long-distance call. The following day, Debra's father received another call at his residence, from a man he thought was speaking with a Mexican accent. The man claimed to have Debra and wanted fifty thousand dollars. Mr. Vine, too, asked to speak with his daughter, and the caller said that Vine would just have to trust him, and that instructions for delivery of the money would be given later. The phone call was recorded.

Because ransom demands had been made, the FBI was able to enter the case. Genoa is twenty miles from Toledo, and the Cleveland office of the FBI became involved. What seemed like a big break came the next day—three days after the abduction. Some of Debra's clothing was recovered about two miles west of Genoa, at the side of a county road, and the remainder was found the following day on another county road in the same general area. Near her sweater was a crumpled-up handwritten map, on yellow legal paper. The map depicted the general area where the clothing was found, and markings on it seemed to indicate that a search ought to be made near a bridge over a river. The authorities went to the bridge and found tire tracks and two sets of footprints that indicated someone had dragged something to the bridge. A police dog, brought along to sniff, was quite excited by these findings, but a search of the river found nothing.

The police thought it certain they had found the dump site of the body, and they continued to search along the river. A tape recorder had been set up to monitor the Vine family's phone, but no further messages from the abductor were received just then.

In my early days at the Bureau, I had been assigned to the Cleveland office, and still knew many of the agents there. As so often happened, I was in the area of the crime, conducting a road school, and the Cleveland office learned about this and contacted me.

From FBI agents Dick Wrenn and George Steinbach, I learned the details of the abduction (such as were then known), heard about the sequence of finding the clothing, looked at the map, listened to the tape-recording of the ransom-demand phone call, and came to an immediate conclusion. The clues had been deliberately staged and were misleading. The police had been directed to the supposed dump site by a detailed map, and they were meant to believe that the body had been thrown into the river.

When I encounter a deliberate staging, the immediate need is to look in precisely the opposite direction from the one the perpetrator wants me to face. Since the caller avowed that Debra was alive and that there would be more ransom demands, I told my colleagues from the Cleveland office, and the local Genoa authorities, that the staging indicated that Debra was almost certainly dead. Given the usual patterns of these sorts of crimes, it was likely she had been picked up by someone and then raped or sexually assaulted, and most likely had been killed during the assault. It was probably not a well-planned abduction, more of a spur-of-the-moment thing, and the death had been unexpected. After the killing, the killer had had some moments of panic, then had settled down to make a plan for keeping the authorities at bay. The abductor must have felt that any real investigation of the victim would lead to him as a likely suspect, and he had staged the dropping of the clothing and the map and the tire and drag marks by the river as attempts to steer the investigation in precisely the wrong direction. "He's trying to lead you to a place where you'll never find the girl," I concluded.

The phone call also seemed deliberately phony, especially the Hispanic accent—"'Ey mon, I need de mawney ri' now.'" It seemed like the comic José Jimenez accent, not the real thing. The tape was sent on to Dr. Murray Miron of Syracuse University, the Bureau's psycholinguistic consultant, for more precise analysis, but in light of all the other evidence, I was certain that it was just another aspect of the staging. I thought to myself: This is a community of two thousand people; the likelihood is that the abductor is so visible to the police that he knows the investigation will stumble across him unless he keeps it away from him by every means possible.

I sat down and worked up a profile of the likely offender. He would be an athletically built white male in his late twenties to early thirties. I thought he was athletically built because he had been large enough to abduct Debra from the street without interference, and also because I guessed that he was the sort of antisocial personality who compensated for his personality by muscle building, driving souped-up cars, and wearing cowboy boots. Reasoning along the same lines, I described him as a macho, aggressive sort of individual, one who would be very neat in his appearance and might well have the reputation of a ladies' man. Believing that this was a spur-of-the-moment crime, I thought that the precrime stresses most likely had to do with the man's trouble with a woman; this had been an affront to him, and in reaction, he had grabbed the first attractive, vulnerable young woman he came across. The ransom notes, drawings, and staging of the scene made it a virtual certainty that the perpetrator had been someone extremely familiar with police procedure. I postulated that the abductor had been a police officer, a private detective, or a security officer but that he was now unemployed and had been so for six to nine months.

I thought it likely that he'd been in a number of scrapes in his life, one of which might have led to the termination of his most recent employment, and possibly to the end of his relationship with a woman, since I was equally certain that he would have been divorced at least once, and in trouble with a woman, either a former wife or a girlfriend. During this unemployed period, I guessed, he would also have had a scrape with the law that would have resulted in an arrest. For most people whose personalities tend to get them fired, troubles do not come singly, and they pyramid after such a basic prop as a job is removed. This man's rage was great enough so that he would most likely have been unable to stay out of trouble once he had lost his job and his wife or girlfriend. I guessed that as an ex–law-enforcement man he would be driving something that resembled a police car, a late-model automobile, a sedan painted in dark colors, with a CB radio or a device to monitor police frequencies, and the antenna on the car positioned on the rear fender or in the center of the hood.

As the reader will have discerned from many of the other cases reported in this book, many killers like to take on the color of authority in order to control situations and victims. In some instances—and not as rarely as I would like, since I've spent my professional life in law enforcement and have great respect for the vast majority of officers who uphold the law—the same urge to use the color of authority for nefarious purposes is present in people who manage to get themselves on police forces. Sometimes it happens that an officer is kicked off one force for infractions that don't quite add up to an indictable crime but are serious nonetheless. He tells the next force to which he applies that he was severed, say, because of a personality conflict with a superior—certainly a common-enough occurrence—and manages to get hired again. In Chapter 6, I discussed Gerard Schaefer, whose employment history as a police officer fit that pattern.

In the Genoa case, my profile produced two prime suspects, one of whom was a thirty-one-year-old officer recently fired by the Genoa police department for cohabiting with an eighteen-year-old girl; and a second who had at one time been with a neighboring police department, had most recently been a railroad detective, and who had been fired from that last job nine months earlier. The first man had been hanging around the fringes of the investigation and making himself overly cooperative. That sort of behavior often masks guilt, because the offender tries to learn what the police know, so he can stay one step ahead of the authorities. Though I advised the Cleveland office against a polygraph on either of the likely suspects, because true psychopaths are frequently able to "beat the box," the Cleveland office decided to give the first suspect a lie-detector test. Then they called me to tell me the suspect had passed. I asked whether his alibi had been verified, and the answer was, "What for? He passed the polygraph test." I requested that they verify his alibi nonetheless, and that was done. This first former police officer was eliminated as a suspect.

The second man's name was Jack Gall, and he seemed to fit the profile extraordinarily well. He was having difficulty with his former wife, with whom he jointly owned a several-cabin resort on a Michigan lake that they were trying to sell. While in Michigan, after his separation from the railroad detective force, Gall had been arrested for a burglary. He owned a late-model Monte Carlo, complete with CB radio, and so on. In fact, he fit the profile so precisely that it was decided to keep only a loose surveillance on him in hopes that he would tip his hand.

Several weeks went by before the victim's father received another phone call at his residence from the man with the Mexican accent, telling him there would shortly be instructions on where to drop the ransom money. One of the Genoa officers on the case, listening later to the tape, said that he was now sure the caller was Jack Gall, because Gall had sometimes regaled fellow officers with his Mexican-accented stories. A fourth call came the next day, April 10, and was successfully traced to a pay phone on the outside wall of a Woolco store a few miles from Genoa. Surveillance was put on that pay phone in hopes that the kidnapper would use it again. That simple, obvious step led directly to the conclusion of the case.

Watching the phone paid off almost immediately. The next afternoon, agents in a van parked near the wall phone saw Gall approach and make a call. At the same time, Mr. Vine received a call at his home. The caller said, "Tonight's the night," and told Vine that precise instructions would follow in the evening. Agents in the van snapped photos of Gall making the call at the same time that the message was being recorded from Vine's phone. After hanging up, Gall reached into his shirt and drew out a folded-up note, which he attached right under the phone-booth table, being careful to do so with white-gloved hands that would not leave fingerprints for the police to collect and identify.

Gall then sped away. After pursuing him for a few blocks, the agents decided not to track him farther, because he seemed to be "tail-conscious." Anyhow, his residence was known and was also being watched. In the evening, Vine received a call telling him to go to the

Woolco phone booth, where he would find further instructions. They were in the note taped under the table, and that note was the first in a series of nine that Gall had block-lettered and cached in similar places. Vine and some agents hidden in his car were taken on a several-hour chase all around the county, kept running from pay phone to pay phone, told to switch vehicles, and so on, until they were at last directed to a location where Vine was supposed to leave a suitcaseful of money and be told where to retrieve his daughter. The whole chase was watched by a Bureau aircraft and sophisticated surveillance machinery, and Vine finally left the suitcase at a remote spot near a river. It was not picked up, nor was his daughter returned; five hours after making the journey to the river, Vine retrieved the suitcase and took it home.

The cruel charade had been tolerated on the slim hope that the kidnapper still held Debra alive, but it produced nothing. This part of the hoax was mounted, it seemed, in an attempt to give Gall an alibi, since during the several-hour chase from phone booth to phone booth, Gall's car was observed in his own driveway. That actually did not provide him with an alibi, since all the latter moves were directed by the series of nine notes, and Gall could have called the pay phones from his home number.

Though the body of Debra Sue Vine had not been found, the authorities now had ample evidence on which to indict Gall for extortion, and they did so. He was quickly convicted and sentenced. Genoa Chief of Police Garry Truman recently told me that he believes this case would have gone unsolved if the authorities had not had my profile and the assistance of the FBI. The police pursued Gall for murder, especially after the victim's body was eventually found. Debra's body was discovered in a deserted location near to Genoa but opposite from where the "X marks the spot" site had been indicated on the phony map. The body was wrapped in an electric blanket, and there was hope that this blanket could be identified as one stolen in the Michigan burglary for which Gall had once been charged. As of this writing, the murder charge has not been brought, but Gall is still incarcerated for extortion.

The veneer of incomprehensibility in a crime scene not only covers the evidence in the cases of violent murder and rape that make up the bulk of this chapter but also in cases that are far less bloody, far more common, and seldom make the headlines. One such interesting crime scene became a recent assignment for me in 1991, months after I'd retired from the FBI.

A psychologist in a major city on the West Coast had been retained by an insurance company to evaluate a claim of $270,000 for damages to a home, damages apparently caused by vandals. Faced with a crime scene that was difficult to assess, the psychologist wanted me to evaluate it and to do a profile of the likely offender or offenders.

I was a good choice, because in thirty years of law-enforcement work, I'd seen hundreds of vandalism scenes on military bases and installations, government buildings, private property—virtually every sort of place that could be hit by vandals. The psychologist planned to send me color photos of the scene, the police reports on the incident, and his comments on the matter. I told him to go ahead and send the photos and police reports but to hold back his own comments until I'd made my evaluation. That was the procedure we'd followed for years in the FBI. In an attempt to give an independent opinion, we'd try not to look at anyone else's conclusions before making our own evaluation. We'd routinely ask police departments seeking our help to send us only firsthand reports and photos. If they insisted on shipping their conclusions anyway, we'd ask to have them sent in a separate and sealed envelope, and once we received that envelope, we'd put it aside until after we'd made our own judgments. Any other way of working would have prejudiced independent examination of the evidence.

A few days after my conversation with the psychologist, a packet of photos and police reports arrived in the mail, and I spread them out on a desk and began to peruse them. There were dozens of photos of a single home that was in a complete mess. At one time, it had been a lovely suburban house, but it had been trashed, apparently by vandals. The owners were seeking more than a quarter of a million dollars from the insurer. That was a sum large enough to prod the insurer to obtain some outside opinions on the damage.

Peering at the photos and reading the police reports, most observers would see at first glance that the home had been overturned and was in total chaos, with spray-painted graffiti, upended and broken valuables, smashed doorjambs. Damage was spread through the living room, halls, kitchen, main bedroom, and bath. Walls, furniture, paintings, clothing, vases, jade carvings, and other items had been broken and defaced. Curtains were down. Glass over art prints had been cracked. Spray-paint graffiti could be made out in various locations, on walls, furniture, and the like, in single-word clusters, such as "Asshole," "Ass," "Suck," "Cunt." There was also a two-word inscription: "Fuck Me."

You may have seen such a scene yourself, though probably not in real life; more likely, you saw it in a film or on a television show, with the damage attributed to teenage males, misunderstood rebels who were "acting out" their aggression against society. It's a familiar fictional theme.

These photos didn't show me that, however. First glances can be deceiving. The vandalism wasn't exactly what it appeared to be, and certainly didn't reflect what I knew about teenage male offenders. Vandals usually travel in groups—packs, if you like—composed of a strong leader and several inadequate and subordinate followers who take their cues from the leader. Sometimes a vandal is a single individual, a lone, antisocial adolescent male whose act is a deliberate lashing out at society at large, or against an authority figure known to him. Damage from such vandals is usually random, indiscriminate, and accompanied by obscene writings and sometimes by obscene acts performed at the location of the vandalism. The graffiti in particular will reflect the interests and lifestyle of the vandal or vandals; in most cases of adolescent male vandals, these graffiti will have to do with musical groups, or will incorporate symbols of satanic or occult origin, such as pentagrams or inverted crosses—iconography and music that we often find to have attracted the focus of emotionally unfulfilled youth. Occasionally, in conjunction with such graffiti, we'll find that sexual acts have been carried out at the scene, acts that reflect the vandal's state of mind in that place. He feels he has total freedom of action in the arena he is trashing, that he is entitled to take women's undergarments and masturbate in them, or defecate on the rug or urinate in a closet. Theft of items is common, and food and alcohol belonging to the owner of the site are usually consumed right there and then— actions that also reflect the vandal's feelings of entitlement. As a matter of course in the usual teenage male vandalism act, damage is total and few items of value or endearment survive.

These photos, however, showed me a different pattern of vandalism. The destruction was not total, but selective. Some of the paintings were damaged, yes, but in some instances only the canvases were damaged and the ornate frames were left intact. The real damage was to paintings that did not seem particularly valuable. Some Indian art prints—objects whose value I happened to know about—were damaged in an interesting way: The glass over the prints was broken,, but the prints underneath were left unharmed. The most intriguing lack of damage was to a large oil painting of a little girl; it was left untouched. Certain vases, statues, and jade carvings seemed to have been tipped over onto the floor with some care, and none appeared to have been broken. The usual teenage vandal would not have left such art objects intact. Moreover, an entire shelf of plants had not been touched.

Although the kitchen and the bathroom were extensively trashed, there had been no real damage to countertops, mirrors, appliances, or fixtures. Doorknobs had been damaged, but not the doors themselves. Other than some minor ceiling damage, no wallboards had been kicked or knocked out; such kicking is a favorite act of adolescent male vandals. A curtain rod seemed to have been placed gently down on the floor without harming or wrinkling the curtains on it. Some clothing had been damaged, but the torn items did not appear to be particularly stylish or valuable. Was it possible that the vandals had missed virtually all of the expensive or sentimentally important items?

The spray painting was also incomplete and inconsistent with the acts of true vandals. It seemed to have been directed at locations that could be easily cleaned, painted over, or—in the case of furniture— reupholstered. The pattern of the spraying went around art objects and the more delicate valuables. No fetish sex acts had taken place in this particular vandalized suburban home.

Finally, there was the graffiti. Single-word obscenities are not common to the usual teenage vandal; today's young trashers are more apt to leave slogans and names of musical groups, such as Slayer, Motley Crue, Public Enemy, or Terminator X. Among the specific terms used by the spray-painter was *Cunt*, and in teenage usage, this term has been replaced by *Pussy*. Last of all, and especially meaningful, I thought, was the inscription "Fuck Me." "Fuck You" would have been more typical of a hostile and arrogant young male. But "Fuck Me"?

Taking all these factors into consideration, I wrote up a profile of the probable offender.

I specifically rejected the idea that the vandals had been a group of adolescent males. The vandalism was too benign, too carefully done. All the clues pointed away from a group of males and toward a different possible perpetrator. The author of this damage and destruction, I said, was a lone white female, over forty and less than fifty years of age; specifically, someone who had no current familiarity with teenagers. She would be an extremely narcissistic woman and intimately involved with the items and the collectibles that were passed over in the vandalizing of the house. I postulated that she would be a woman who had difficulty with interpersonal relationships, someone who had been through several divorces during her lifetime. I theorized that she would be a close family member of the owner or renter, and that she had a vested interest in making the acts of violence selective, so that she would not wipe out items that she deemed to be irreplaceable.

This woman, I guessed, had staged the vandalism to make it look like her conception of a typical act of male adolescents. Her attempts at reproducing youthful graffiti dated her and revealed her sex and age. No young male vandal would write "Fuck Me." This was a middle-aged and rather confused woman at work. She was probably not comfortable with the use of foul language, and the inscribed words reflected her notion of what she fantasized male hostility and antisocial behavior were all about. In contemporary terms, however, her choice of obscenities seemed childlike.

If she had any children, I wrote, these would probably not include a teenager, and not a boy. I thought it likely she was the mother of only one child, a daughter, and that the daughter did not currently reside with her. My reason for this (aside from her lack of familiarity with teenagers and male children in general) was the presence of the oil painting of the young girl in the home, and the fact that it was undamaged; such an icon usually suggests an absent but favored relative.

I thought that there had been a specific triggering event for this behavior on her part, that the perpetrator was probably responding to stressful events that had occurred days or at most weeks before the act of vandalism. There could have been, I said, a matter of money, or of men, the loss of a job, or something that caused her immediate future to appear uncertain.

Summing up, I said that the motivation for the vandalism was one or a combination of three factors. An angry woman committed the act of vandalism to retaliate against a family member. Looking for attention, this woman transformed her act into the sort of false allegation that we often see in trumped-up rape cases. The woman sought insurance money because she had undertaken improvements or renovations to the place and could no longer afford the renovations that she had ordered previously.

I put these conclusions and the reasoning behind them down on paper for the West Coast psychologist and sent my findings to him. After he read my document, he called to tell me that the profile described almost perfectly the owner of the home, the woman who had reported the damages to the police and had made the claim for insurance money. White and in her forties, she had broken up with her boyfriend, had money problems, had a daughter who lived with her former husband, and matched in many other details the personality I had postulated. The psychologist was rather amazed at my perspicacity. I wasn't. Compared to the profiles of unknown, vicious, antisocial criminals that I had struggled to compile and make accurate over the past seventeen years in the FBI, this attempt at puzzle solving was kid stuff.

9

TO KILL AGAIN?

Police officer Kilburn McCoy looked like a cowboy, with Clint East-wood–type good looks, and both he and his police officer wife, Janet, were attending a class I was teaching at an academy near Salem, Oregon, in 1980. At the end of the week, McCoy asked me to go down to his police station and look at the files on a murder committed in 1975 by a Vietnam veteran named Duane Samples, who was now in prison. McCoy thought Samples would be an excellent addition to the murderers we were interviewing for the Criminal Personality Research Project, because even though Samples was not a serial murderer—he had been convicted of killing just one person—he was articulate, a college graduate with a degree in psychology, and seemed to have the sort of overwhelming violent fantasies characteristic of serial killers.

Samples's crime had taken place during one terrible night in the small town of Silverton, Oregon, on December 9, 1975. Fran Steffens, her eighteen-month-old daughter, and her friend Diane Ross were in Fran's apartment, and a casual acquaintance, Duane Samples, came over for some beer, marijuana, and conversation. Samples was a counselor in a local drug clinic, a Vietnam vet in his early thirties who had knocked around quite a bit and had had fleeting relationships with several women in the area. He was interested in Fran, but his interest was not really reciprocated, though Fran did not send him away. As the evening wore on, the women became tired. Fran went to bed alongside her daughter, and Diane sat on the couch, listening to Samples. He was boring her stiff with his stories of Vietnam, and she finally told him that she was tired and that he ought to leave.

Samples left. Diane drifted off to sleep on the couch, then woke up to a strange, warm, sticky feeling—and discovered she had been cut severely: on the throat, across her body under her breasts, and from the navel upward. Two feet of her intestines were hanging out. It wasn't even the cuts that had awakened her; it was Fran's screams as she was being dragged into the bedroom by a knife-wielding Samples. Diane somehow held her arms around her torso and ran out the door. With two hands wrapping her gut, she couldn't hold up her pants, which had also been cut. She stepped out of them and stumbled down the block and into a neighbor's house, through the kitchen and into the bedroom, where she told them, "I've been cut. Call a doctor; I'm dying." She worked hard at not giving in and falling asleep, thinking that she would die if she did. When the ambulance came, she heard someone say, "No need to hurry. She won't make it."

However, they did hurry and Diane Ross did make it. She remained alive, and was able to tell the police that Duane Samples was killing Fran Steffens.

The police rushed over to Fran's residence but found Fran already dead, cut in a similar manner to Diane, around the neck and on the torso, blood and intestines spilled out over the bed she shared with her daughter, who managed to sleep through and escape Samples's slaughter. Blood was smeared on Fran's thighs, evidence of post-mortem attack on the body. There were also defensive wounds on the hands, showing that Fran had attempted to fight off her attacker.

Samples was actually well known to the police in the area, principally through his counseling work, but also because he even played softball with some of the cops. An all-points bulletin alerted a pair of officers, who drove to the apartment Samples shared with two other men in a nearby town: he wasn't there, but they found him shortly, and he surrendered peaceably. In his pocket, the police found a handwritten note to Fran dated "Mon. Dec 8" in which he asked her to show the letter to the police so that she could be exonerated from killing him. It said that he "set forth to threaten Fran w/her life" unless she did as he instructed her, "eviscerates & emasculates me." She was instructed either to do this, or he would "gut & mutilate her & her kid." The note went on to say that being killed by a beautiful woman was a "life long fantasy come true," and that a part of him could "hardly wait to see" the blade cutting "murderously" into him.

Samples claimed he had taken this note to Fran, who had refused to kill him, and this refusal had triggered his killing of her. It was a remarkable note, and we'll come back to it later in the case.

Police and psychologists who interviewed Samples that night and in the following days said that he was oriented, knew who he was and where he was, knew right from wrong, and knew enough to ask for a lawyer. There seemed to be no evidence of psychosis as the basis for the crime. There was clear premeditation and thought involved in the crime: Samples had left the house, gone to his car, taken a fish filleting knife, and come back with the intent to kill both women. Diane even believed she had heard him coming down the block after her as she struggled to reach the neighbor's home. He was arraigned and charged with one count of murder and another of attempted murder.

During the pretrial period, Samples and his attorney reviewed their options and Samples weighed the issues very methodically, even putting them down in rows and columns on a piece of paper later obtained by the prosecution. His very deliberate actions in this regard show that his mind was working rationally at that time. Samples faced three choices. He could plead not guilty, stand trial, and risk having Diane Ross take the stand and testify to very damaging things about him. If he pleaded not guilty by reason of insanity, Diane could still be called to testify, and her story might outweigh his contention (supported by the note of "Mon. Dec. 8th") that he had not been in his right mind when he committed the murder. Samples and his attorney seriously considered the insanity defense for a time, and unearthed his diary and other evidence of his long-standing preoccupation with disembowelment for use in such a defense. The "Mon. Dec. 8th" note was also going to play a large role in that defense: It could be construed to show, more than premeditation, clear mental instability. (In my view, the note was actually too well composed and thought out to reflect real instability—it was the creation of a semitrained psychologist, working hard at creating an alibi.) The third option, which Samples eventually embraced, was essentially a plea bargain. He pleaded guilty to murdering Fran, in exchange for the charge of attempted murder of Diane Ross being dropped; this meant she would never be able to testify against him. In return, Samples received the maximum sentence available in the state of Oregon, fifteen years to life; with good time and a little luck, he figured, he might be out of jail in seven or eight years.

After Samples pleaded guilty, was sentenced, and began serving his time, the media lost interest in his case. Diane Ross recovered and moved to California, and Fran's daughter was raised by other members of her family. The prosecutor's office later admitted that because of the guilty plea, the prosecution had not looked extensively into Samples's background. Some evidence had been gathered, however. The note of December 8 referred to a lifelong fantasy of disembowelment by a beautiful naked woman, and this had indeed been a recurring theme in Samples's life for some time. At age five, he slept in a bed between his mother and his pregnant aunt. The aunt had a hemorrhage and lost of a lot of blood in the bed before miscarrying; the idea of spilling out internal organs seems to date back to this time. Later in childhood, he was stimulated by seeing an ant on his belly and felt that he wanted the ant to bore a hole through him. At the age of thirteen, playing Russian roulette, he accidentally shot himself in the abdomen. In a journal entry made after his experiences in Vietnam, he wrote that this was the fulfillment of a fantasy dating back to childhood, a "gushing compulsion to feel steel in his guts." Initially, the fantasy had been of his own murder, committed by an "Amazon" woman "spearing" him during the sex act. Fran Steffens had been a relatively large and tall woman. He told a psychiatrist that his activities in his youth included (in the words of the psychiatrist's later report) "pricking himself with pins or knives while enjoying these fantasies, which he found added to his erotic stimulation." Later, the fantasy included killing the woman. He had actually written out his intended MO in a threatening letter to a former lover, well before the murder of Fran Steffens. This letter had many linguistic similarities to his "Dec. 8" note. It warned her that when she was in bed with a new partner he would "erupt from the bowls [sic] of darkness to open with razor knife his taught [sic] throat." The letter goes on to explain in excruciating detail how Samples was going to disembowel both his former girlfriend and her new lover, sadistically torture them, and partake in their sexual act so that semen, blood, and other bodily fluids would all intermingle in orgasm and death. It would be the greatest sexual experience any of them had ever had, and it would be their last, himself included. After he had fatally wounded them, he also planned to turn the knife on his own gut, so that they would be "mutually dead together."

From an initial look into Samples's background, a picture emerged of a smart man, in the top 5 percent on the intelligence scales, a Stanford University scholarship student who had received his degree in psychology in 1964, then gone into the Army. He claimed to have served in Vietnam as a "forward observer," calling in artillery strikes against Viet Cong positions. He came back to find life in America had drastically changed, enough so, he later said, to dash his idealism. After his Vietnam service in 1966 to 1967, he had become a drifter, with his own drug and alcohol problems. He was a bartender here, a social worker there, unemployed for a long stretch of time, moving from town to town, steadily north and west. He was evidently unable to hold a steady job until he translated his own problems into an ability to talk to people about these addictions, and won a counseling position for college students and teenagers in the area near Salem. Friends and colleagues considered him a good counselor, and he had many allies in the social-work community. In light of his background, many people would have concluded that the murder Samples committed was an isolated, bizarre event, perhaps induced by drugs—an aberration. Most people who knew him casually, however, saw only the surface and had no access to his depths or insight into understanding the complexities of his character.

On another visit to Oregon, during which I was also going to interview several other murderers in the state's prison system, I decided to try to see Samples. He came readily to the interview, a balding, thin man nearing forty, with wire-rimmed glasses and an intelligent gaze, a thoughtful and soft-spoken man. He worked in the psychology section of the prison as a clerk, and was a willing worker, participating in such experimental programs as biofeedback to teach inmates how to deal with aggressive feelings. I made my pitch and asked him for an interview that would help fill out the fifty-seven-page questionnaire that we were then using as the basis for our statistical analysis of the lives of murderers. He said no. Samples explained that he did not see himself as being the same sort of person as the serial killers and mass murderers whom I had been interviewing, and therefore did not want to be included in the program. He did talk to me unofficially for about an hour, during which he said that he was studying as well as working in the psychological section of the prison and planned after he was paroled to get his Ph.D. in psychology. He wondered whether, having completed his doctorate, he could get a job with the FBI's Behavioral Sciences Unit. Incredulous, I told him that the FBI would probably not agree to hire anyone with a prison record. I felt that in talking to me at all, Samples was merely stroking his own ego and fighting boredom. Since he hadn't agreed to participate in the interview program, there was no pledge of confidentiality given; I took no notes and did not run a tape recorder.

I thought that was the finale of my involvement with Samples. From the pictures of the crime scene and other materials I'd seen, the experts I'd talked to, and my brief brush with Samples, it was clear to me that he was a classic sadistic sexual psychopath. He had refused to consider himself as such or to be lumped into a category with the others, but he displayed all the signs of such killers, from the quiet demeanor to the long history of fantasy that drove the murder he committed. In our terms, it was a "mixed" case, which showed dynamics of both the organized and disorganized killer. The crime scene was disorganized because of the gross disembowelment, the mutilation of the body, the blood smearing, and the lack of sexual assault. Samples had been organized in his planning of the murder, however; with a calculating mind, he had gone back to the car to get the filleting knife, and then had tried to kill both women. After the murder, he had had the presence of mind to remove his jacket and clean up the crime scene. At the time of the murder, he was a person locked into a sexual fantasy involving violent behavior. Through the presence of drugs and alcohol, he was in the mood to realize his fantasy and had the opportunity, because both women were vulnerable. I thought it even more likely that Samples had written the "Mon. Dec. 8" note *after*, not before, the murder, in an attempt to provide himself with ammunition for a plea of not guilty by reason of insanity. It was the act of a man who thought ahead, possibly not at the moment of his destructive act but certainly in the hours after it, when the realization hit him that Diane had gotten away and that she would certainly be able to identify him.

The next I heard about Duane Samples, in early 1981, was that Governor Vic Atiyeh of Oregon had commuted his sentence and that he was expected to be released shortly from the Oregon prison system. Samples had actually begun the application for commutation in 1979, and I had been unaware of that at the time I tried to interview him. His concealment in this matter had also caused turmoil in the Marion County District Attorney's office. When the request for commutation was first made, there had been some notification to then District Attorney Gary Gortmaker, who had not responded; that first request had been turned down by the governor, but a second request had been made and granted. In the interim, Chris Van Dyke, son of actor Dick Van Dyke, had taken over as Marion County District Attorney, and he and his assistant Sarah McMillen had gotten into the act; McCoy had given them my name as a person who could possibly help reverse the commutation. Local Silverton authorities had been alarmed when the commutation had gone through, and they had made their strong protest known to the county attorney's office. Van Dyke had become outraged that the governor would have made such a commutation without allowing the prosecutor's office an occasion to present a recommendation against Samples's release. McMillen wanted to know whether I could come out and testify with the prosecution against letting Samples out of prison. I agreed that he should not be released, and told her that

I might be able to testify but that a request for me to do so would have to go through proper channels. Had Samples previously agreed to take part in the Criminal Personality Research Project, I would have disqualified myself, but since he hadn't, I was available if the Bureau chose to allow me to go. Shortly, Chris Van Dyke sent a letter of request to Director Webster, and eventually an arrangement was made that would permit me to travel to Oregon to testify.

Samples had asked for a commutation based on two factors, his own rehabilitation and the notion that he had been mentally ill at the time of his crime but that psychiatry only just recently had begun to understand and recognize the disease he had had in 1975, so a proper defense had not been available to him at that time. As for his rehabilitation, many people who spoke with him concluded that he had put his crime behind him and had been a model prisoner. He displayed all the correct behavior of a properly rehabilitated man: He wept when discussing the murder, said that it was a terrible thing, and argued that he could now control his aggression and would never commit such an act again. In the United States, Samples's defenders argued, we do not judge people before crimes are committed. Therefore, Samples should not be prejudged as to any future crimes, and he should be given a chance to redeem his life.

Samples's rehabilitation claims were of the usual sort. What was unusual was his innovative assertion that the murder of Fran Steffens had been a direct result of his suffering from Post-Traumatic Stress Disorder (PTSD), and that therefore he had not been responsible for that murder. This particular mental disorder had not been recognized by psychiatry in 1975, when the second edition of the *Diagnostic and Statistical Manual of Mental Disorders* had been the standard reference, and so hadn't then been available for his defense. Part of what Samples said was true. All he could have found in the 1975 edition was something called "transient situational disturbance," sometimes observed in veterans, a disturbance that had to do with sleeplessness, inability to hold a job, irritability, and sexual problems as a result of stress from a variety of sources, one of which was the stress associated with being in combat. In 1980, the third edition, known as *DSM-III*, had been published, and in it, "transient situational disturbance" had been upgraded from a rainstorm to a typhoon; that is, there were a few paragraphs about PTSD. Most of the description made reference to stress that was other than war-related; nonetheless, the definition was there. This was the straw at which Samples grasped. His experiences in Vietnam, Samples claimed, had left him shattered, and, after years of torment, had tragically surfaced in his murder of Fran Steffens. With counseling in prison, Samples now felt he had conquered this disorder that had once pushed him to snuff out a life. He hadn't been responsible for the murder in 1975, he contended, because of his PTSD, but now he had triumphed over the post-traumatic stress, and, moreover, he was rehabilitated, and so should be set free.

Two psychologists supported Samples's claim. One was in private practice and was receiving Veterans Administration funds to see Samples in prison on a regular basis; the second was an academic who had extensively studied veterans suffering from what was just becoming recognized as post-Vietnam stress syndrome. Lawyers who spend their time working for business corporations know enough to stay out of a complex criminal case, though they have a degree that says they are capable of handling one; frankly, I thought these mental-health professionals in the Samples case were similarly out of their depth. For example, the vast majority of the cases of PTSD that dealt with post-Vietnam stress had to do with veterans who couldn't hold a job, had sexual problems in their marriages, couldn't sleep at night, and had other similar complaints. To my knowledge, there were no other cases at that time in which PTSD was extended beyond these rather ordinary complaints to cover the disemboweling of two women. I did not doubt that Samples might well be suffering from some sort of stress as a result of his having been in combat in Vietnam; but the fantasies that had directed him to kill one woman and nearly kill the second had begun well before his Vietnam experiences, and were the controlling aspect of his motivation to murder. PTSD aftershocks usually occur within weeks or months after a precipitating traumatic event. Samples's murders had been committed ten years after he returned from Vietnam.

High in the pantheon of Samples's arguments for commutation was his contention that while in Vietnam, he had watched two fellow officers die rather horribly, of disemboweling wounds; Samples even remembered their names, Hugh Hanna and Randy Ingrahm. Their deaths had scarred him mentally, he said. According to the academician's report, Samples watched Ingrahm, a "close friend literally being shredded by a claymore land mine"; he recalled "placing the bleeding parts of his body into a basket for Medevac and seeing the blood run out of the basket as it was lifted up into the helicopter." Samples also avowed that he was a war hero, decorated for bravery in Vietnam, but that in his dreams he now saw his medals as being "the color of dried blood."

While in prison, Samples had married a woman who worked for a prominent advertising and public relations firm that was well connected in political circles in Oregon, and she had helped push for commutation. I thought it a bit out of character for Governor Atiyeh to have turned down the request the first time but to have agreed the second time to commute the sentence. Atiyeh was a former business-man and state legislator known to be very much on the side of law enforcement, and publicly so. An antique gun collector, Atiyeh would later pose for an advertisement for the National Rifle Association, which included a statement that said, in part, "As a governor, I'm concerned with crime protection and Oregon's penal system. And like other NRA members, I want guns to be used safely and legally. We believe strict punishment is the best solution to crime with a gun." In his several years as governor, a hundred commutation requests had crossed his desk; he denied all but four, and the other three were virtually without controversy; one of these, for example, was of a wife who had killed the husband who had abused her for a decade. Well, perhaps the governor had been given bad advice about Samples, or had decided that releasing Samples would be a gesture of goodwill toward the community of Vietnam veterans, who had not been well treated by the public at the time of their return from the service but who were being hailed in retrospect as heroes by incoming President Ronald Reagan.

I had some time before I was expected to go to Oregon, and in the interim I did some digging. As a reserve officer in the Army's CID, as well as being an FBI agent, I not only had access to Army records but also the experience to know how to evaluate those records. I asked the Army to check and see whether officers by the name of Hanna and Ingrahm had been killed in 1966 or 1967, and obtained a copy of Samples's discharge form, a DD 214; everyone who is discharged from the services gets a copy of their own 214, and it shows their service record, including all medals and citations. Samples's 214 showed no medals for bravery. Another document in those records were special orders addressed to Hanna that covered many topics, among them ones that mentioned Samples's name and in another paragraph also mentioned a Randy Ingrahm. The Army further informed me that while men with the names of Hanna and Ingrahm had been wounded in that time period, neither had died; nor were there dead officers with names that were somewhat similar but spelled differently.

Interestingly, the two mental-health professionals who were willing to testify on Samples's behalf appear not to have researched his claims about his war service to the point where they could have better determined whether or not the patient was telling the truth. I thought it likely, though, that Samples had requested and received his army documents. He conducted an extensive correspondence from prison, for instance, managing to win a monthly disability check based on his stressful experiences in Vietnam—that was why the VA sent a private practice psychologist to see him on a regular basis. To obtain that stipend, he would have had to cite his records.

Samples was quite concerned with records and documentation. John Cochran, a forensic psychologist who worked regularly in the Oregon prison system, believed that Samples, as a clerk in the prison's psychological section, had altered and retyped his own prison records so that they would show he had been rehabilitated. This allegation of tampering with the records was never proved, however, as some of the records disappeared entirely. Cochran was used to working with inmates, and thought Samples was a classic sexual sadist. Cochran repeatedly told the authorities and the press that such a condition was not really curable; in other words, that despite the outward signs, Samples was not rehabilitated, because he could not be. There was reason to believe, Cochran said, that if Samples was released, he would kill again; he recommended against the commutation, but his expertise was disregarded.

When it came time for me to go to Oregon to see the governor, my wife was in the hospital after a serious automobile accident; though she was injured, she still urged me to fly out and fulfill my obligation. The controversy over Duane Samples had already reached the press in a big way. The commutation battle had also become a political one, with the Oregon legislature beginning consideration of bills that would undercut the governor's power to issue such commutations.

Statements in the pages of the Oregon newspapers and on television news programs articulated the arguments of both sides. One side said that Samples had been rehabilitated and that if our society believed at all in the rehabilitation of prisoners and in the possibility that mental disease can be treated and reversed, Samples should be given his chance at a new life outside prison walls. Many psychologists and psychiatrists—though not those who worked regularly in prisons— held this view, as did Vietnam vets and their political supporters and many liberals. It was an attractive view to hold, one that saw human beings as capable of change and growth, one that believed in the ability of psychiatry to treat mental disease, and in an optimistic prognosis for a man who seemed to have been rehabilitated.

The other side contended that Samples was a sexual sadist whose outbursts had been constrained only because he had been behind bars, that there was a distinct chance that if released he would repeat the murderous behavior that had already landed him in prison, and that therefore he should not be released. It was in a sense a pessimistic view, one implying that psychiatry can understand mental disease but that some conditions are beyond treatment, and that had reference to the fact that many, many inmates in prisons are recidivists who repeat their crimes after their release and have to be caught and incarcerated again.

To my mind, both arguments were a little windy. I prefer to reason from facts, and the facts I had found all indicated that Samples fit the pattern I had already observed in so many cases of serial murder, in which a man whose violent fantasies had been developing since childhood eventually realized those fantasies and murdered someone. Samples's own writings, his drifting, drugs, and bad relationships with women in the years prior to the murder, the details of the murder itself, and his lying about his military record and the source of his problems all were indications of recognizably psychopathic behavior. The Oregon prison system already held several men who had similarly fit the pattern and become serial killers, including two who had been prematurely released after committing early murders and who had killed again within a relatively short time after their release. Jerome Brudos and Richard Marquette had been captured and convicted again in Oregon. In nearby California, Ed Kemper had killed many more people after his own premature release from an institution where he had been placed for having murdered his grandparents when he was a teenager. None of their murderous fantasies had subsided, even after incarceration. They were stable while in custody, but that was not an indication that they would be capable of living on the outside without again resorting to murder.

Near the end of June 1981, and the night before we were to see the governor, the prosecution's team sat down together. In addition to Van Dyke, McMillen, and myself, there was Dr. John Cochran of the Forensic Psychology Service of the Oregon State Hospital, Steven H. Jensen, unit director of the correctional treatment program at the hospital, and Dr. Peter DeCoursey, a Portland psychologist who had evaluated Samples in 1975, just after the murder. We discussed what we would do the next morning, and in the course of it I suggested to Van Dyke that since Samples was basing his commutation on post-Vietnam stress syndrome, that his claims could be verified or refuted through examination of his military records. Van Dyke had had these in his hands but hadn't looked at such things as the DD 214, which showed no awards for valor in combat, and certainly no Bronze Star. Nor had the prosecutors thought to ask the Army, as I had, whether Hugh Hanna or Randy Ingrahm had really been killed in combat. Sarah McMillen asked me if I could find out whether Randy Ingrahm was alive, and I said she ought to do it officially, but said I'd make a try, as well, when I returned to Quantico.

Next morning, we went to the state capitol building to make our presentation. I was up first, and I found Governor Atiyeh visibly nervous. He asked me whether I was from the local FBI office, and when I said I had come from Quantico, he wanted to know what this issue had to do with the FBI, since it was not a federal case. I explained that I was an expert on violent criminal behavior, and had come at the request of the Marion County authorities, a request that had gone through proper channels at the FBI.

We had expected this sort of challenge. I had even discussed it with the legal counsel people at Quantico and at FBI headquarters before traveling to Oregon. We had all agreed that it would be wrong for me to comment specifically on Samples, and so I confined my remarks to Atiyeh and his aides to six similar cases that I knew very well, including those of Brudos, Marquette, and Kemper. I hit hard on such matters as Brudos and Marquette, stressing that these men had been prematurely released from prison after early murders, and that because of their lifelong violent fantasies that they could not control, they had killed again shortly after release. My presentation was scheduled for twenty minutes. After the first ten, Atiyeh left the room and did not return. We were told he had an important matter to address. I got the distinct impression that the governor had realized the information and advice he had previously received was insufficient for him to have agreed to the commutation. He seemed to prefer to be seen as somewhat distanced from this matter, not personally involved, that it was really a matter to be dealt with by his aides. Those aides listened politely but appeared to make no notes as I continued my presentation. Then the mental-health specialists made theirs, which described Duane Samples specifically as a danger to society and a man who would most likely remain so in the future.

I flew back home, believing the controversy was now behind

me. We had given the governor the information he had previously not had, and now the matter was in his hands. But the shouting wouldn't stop. Before Governor Atiyeh even rendered his decision, Marquette filed an appeal for commutation similar to that of Samples. Marquette's was summarily turned down. Atiyeh's decision on Samples was eagerly awaited but was not forthcoming. In the next month or so, under the prodding of Sarah McMillen, I managed to locate Randy Ingrahm, who was an insurance salesman in Illinois; he had been an enlisted man, not an officer in Vietnam, and had been wounded, but he said he didn't remember Samples, though he had been with Samples's artillery unit. I conveyed this information to McMillen, who publicized it widely. Then Samples struck back: The man who had died, he said, was named Ingraham, not Ingrahm (as he had previously insisted); the Army confirmed that a man with that name had died in Vietnam during 1966 or 1967 but had had nothing to do with Samples's unit.

Samples's other blow was to insist publicly that the prosecution team's presentation was faulty, since it spoke of a sexual crime, and, he said, there had been no sexual attack during the murder. How could there be a sex crime without sexual contact? he argued. As the reader knows from the earlier cases and examples in this book, the lack of penetration of the victim's body is characteristic of certain types of disorganized murderers who are nonetheless fulfilling sexual fantasies in their killings—but this explanation requires a lengthy narrative to be effective, and in the arena of the public mind is not able to over-whelm the sort of phrase that Samples used, the sort that fits neatly into a television sound bite.

The controversy interested the CBS program "60 Minutes," which did an "investigative" segment that was fairly shallow. Post-Vietnam stress syndrome was an idea whose time had come, and Duane Samples was an articulate man: Together, those elements proved irresistible to the news program. CBS presented a sympathetic view of Samples's plight. By this time, Samples knew all the right things to say and what to display in his behavior. How could such a polite, contrite man be disbelieved? The United States was putting the Vietnam War behind it, and we had to be understanding about its last victims, our soldiers who had fought and come home to dis-dain. CBS seemed to feel that the clinching argument in the case was that the attempt to impugn Samples by reference to Randy Ingrahm's nondeath had failed.

Those attempts were still not complete, however. While in Europe on an Army assignment, I managed to locate Hugh "Bud"

Hanna. He had become a major, assigned to SHAPE headquarters in Belgium, and I talked with him there. He remembered Samples vividly, because Samples was supposed to have been his replacement in that forward observer position, and there had been a problem with Samples. The Stanford graduate had been counseling enlisted men against the war, and was considered less than stable. Rather than send Samples into combat right away, the brass had decided to return Hanna to that post and see whether Samples straightened out. While in that forward post, Hanna was shot, hit in the mouth, tongue, and palate. When it came time for him possibly to testify against Samples for his antiwar activities, Hanna could hardly speak, and the issue was mooted. I conveyed what I knew about Hanna's physical health and other comments to Van Dyke's office, which passed them on to the governor's aides. The summer wore on, and the governor still wasn't making public his decision.

Then Samples's former commanding officer got into the act. Toward the end of August 1981, Col. Courtney Prisk told reporter Bob Smith that he had known Samples in Vietnam "as well as any commanding officer knows a lieutenant in his unit. Probably better, because we talked often." In Smith's article, printed in the *Silverton Appeal-Tribune*. Prisk went on to say, "Duane showed concern for the 'enlightenment' of the times. . . . He was a guy I thought needed frequent counseling to keep his spirits up. He was strange—not peculiar—but strange. He was disturbed by things that did not disturb others." Prisk pointed out the fact that Ingrahm and Hanna were alive, not dead, and recounted that there had been one casualty in his unit from a claymore mine, but it had been three hundred yards from Samples, and he doubted that Duane had even seen the event, though it had been talked about in the unit. Prisk summed it up for the reporter: "I believe Samples has taken two or three things he saw or heard about and fabricated them into something. . . . [Duane Samples] was a good soldier and did a good job in Vietnam. There's no question about that. That's why that whole stress thing is just so much bull—."

Maybe it was the commanding officer's statement that finally swayed Atiyeh or his aides, maybe it was the convincing presentation that I and the other members of the district attorney's team had made, or maybe it was the public outcry that expressed itself in pressure from the state legislature in the form of pending legislation to limit the commutation powers, and in alarm from many ordinary citizens expressed in the letters-to-the-editor columns of the newspapers—but in late 1981, Atiyeh reversed his commutation decision. Samples would serve out the remainder of his sentence, until the parole board—if ever—saw fit to release him from prison.

After the commutation decision, Samples came to believe that I was the culprit, the man who had unfairly confined him to jail, and he mounted a campaign against me that took several reams of paperwork and several years to resolve. The bogeyman could not be someone like John Cochran, who had known him well, or any of the other mental-health professionals who had treated him and who had been in the forefront of recommending that he be kept in prison for a good long time; no, the culprit had to be the hired mudslinger from Washington, the man who had wanted to interview him officially but whom Samples had turned down. Samples enlisted state legislators and even a United States senator in the process, writing letters to ask them to prod the bureaucracy for an investigation of my role in the whole affair. I had slandered him in front of the governor, Samples alleged; I had no business saying anything about his crimes or those of serial murderers; I wasn't a Ph.D. in criminal psychology and therefore was not academically certified enough to know anything about anything. As is usual when the bureaucracy is prodded, an investigation is undertaken and everyone has to spend a lot of time and paper answering the inquiry. That's what happened as a result of Duane Samples's typing away in prison and trying to get me. Fortunately, both Van Dyke and I had proceeded precisely by the book and had a lengthy paper trail to cite and to show to anyone who was interested. Eventually I had to give a sworn deposition to the FBI's Office of Professional Responsibility. Their decision that I had done nothing wrong ended the official inquiry into the matter.

Duane Samples was released from prison in 1991. I certainly hope that he has been truly rehabilitated and will not repeat the sort of crime for which he had previously been convicted. Only his continued proper behavior will demonstrate that of course.

10

TIGHTENING THE NET

Back in the 1950s, a serial rapist and killer was slashing his way through the Los Angeles area, but only one investigator suspected that several seemingly unconnected murders of young women were attributable to that lone killer. The search for that killer led, a quarter century later, to the formation of governmental structures for tightening the net around all future serial criminals.

Harvey Murray Glattman was a killer ahead of his time. In the 1950s, he put advertisements in newspapers that promised women auditions for modeling jobs. His ads said that professional models were not wanted, but that good pay could be obtained by young women with no experience in modeling. Women answered his ads, and when they did, he offered more money than they were making in their current jobs for a few hours of discreet posing. He'd convince them to go to a secluded apartment, then ask them to take off more and more clothing as he photographed them. Glattman understood that it was most likely the women had not told friends or relatives where they were going, in case they might disapprove; therefore, the women who posed for him would not be missed for some time. Glattman seems to have told himself that because these women were willing to take off their clothes in front of a stranger, they were inviting rape, and so he raped them; then he killed them so they wouldn't talk about the rapes. It's a pattern that was later replicated by other killers—Jerome Brudos in Oregon, for instance.

I say that Glattman was a man ahead of his time because the idea of putting personal ads in the newspapers was new in the 1950s; today, it's commonplace, with fringe newspapers and sometimes even mainstream magazines printing personal ads enabling two strangers to meet. You've seen or heard of such ads: young bachelor, handsome, seeks woman interested in sharing experiences, skiing, dancing. Most of the ads are legitimate; a few disguise a rapist or killer looking for victims. In Glattman's case, the ads were a reflection of fifteen years of fantasy development, during which he had steadily escalated from infantile sexual experimentation to making passes at girls, to minor sexual assault, and then to rape and murder.

Los Angeles homicide detective Pierce Brooks was the man put in charge of the investigation of two seemingly unrelated murders of young women in the area. Brooks was already an unusual man, a naval officer and blimp pilot who had become a top investigator in Los Angeles. He was frustrated during his investigation because although he felt that one man might be responsible for both murders, and possibly some others in the area, he had no systematic way of checking his hypothesis. So he personally combed the newspaper files in several counties surrounding his own, and local police files, to see whether other murders had been committed that matched the MO of the killer he believed he was chasing. To make a long story short, this spadework eventually led to the capture of Glattman, who when confronted with the evidence confessed to the murders.

Glattman's extensive confession, obtained by Brooks, is one of the earliest documents of a serial killer's mind that we have, and it reflects many of the factors that I have outlined in other chapters of this book. Among the most interesting aspects of the confession were Glattman's rationalizations and reports of his conversations with the women after they had been raped. As with many killers, Glattman became annoyed when a woman would try to control him—for instance, by saying that she would not tell her roommate about the rape if Glattman let her go—and that made him angry enough to kill her. Actually, the chances of his having let her get away after the rape were near zero, for he was in the clutches of a fantasy that had been forming in his mind for many years, a fantasy that included murder. Glattman was tried and convicted, and then executed in 1957; Brooks attended the execution.

If any of this sounds familiar to you, that is because both the killer and the detective in the case have become the subjects of fictional treatments. In a seminar for mystery writers a few years ago, I presented the case of Glattman, and Mary Higgins Clark asked me for more details, which I furnished her: She used the Glattman story as the basis for her recent best-selling novel *Loves Music, Loves to Dance*. Years earlier, the detective in Joseph Wambaugh's celebrated book *The Onion*

Field was Pierce Brooks, though that book deals with a case other than the Glattman matter.

Brooks's experiences in trying to pry information from other police jurisdictions in the vicinity of Los Angeles led him to propose a system for linking all the departments in California, so that future criminals could be tracked and trapped more easily. He envisioned doing this by computer, because teletypes, another option, were clumsy and not conducive to sharing information. In the late 1950s and early 1960s, computers were quite new, very large, and very expensive, and California said it couldn't afford to buy computers and use them for such police purposes. So Brooks put the idea on a back burner and went on with his career, becoming chief of homicide detectives in Los Angeles and, later, chief of police in Springfield and Eugene, Oregon, and in Lakewood, Colorado.

In the mid-1970s, when I first began seriously looking into the personal histories of serial killers, the Glattman case caught my attention, and I studied it from the public records. As the reader knows, I spent the late 1970s putting together the Criminal Personality Research Project, getting it approved by FBI headquarters, and obtaining a Justice Department grant to interview convicted murderers. In that project, and in the growth of the Behavioral Sciences Unit, we were beginning to institutionalize some of the personal initiatives that I had made. By this time Teten and Mullany had retired, and I was the FBI's senior criminologist and criminal profiler; from what had been almost an ad hoc handful of men looking into murders, rapes, and abductions, we had become a formal group of people who profiled cases for local police and were reaching out to do research in the prisons. In addition, and despite some foot dragging inside the FBI, I had managed to start a program to train experienced field agents as profiling coordinators, bringing them to Quantico in 1979 for an intensive course in what was becoming a bit more of a science and accordingly less of an art, then sending them back to their field offices. There, fifty-five newly trained agents became the resident experts in profiling, aided in our research, and acted as coordinators when there was a case where our help was sought; they funneled information to us and took our analysis back to the local police departments.

In 1981, Quantico director Jim McKenzie and I were sitting at a bar, drinking beers after work, and I was waxing philosophic.

We had already established the greatest training facility for law enforcement in the country, perhaps in the world, and our fingerprint files and our evidence-analysis laboratory had long been considered the best available anywhere. I reminded Jim that the laws had recently changed, and that the FBI had new latitude to work in the areas of violent crime that had heretofore been solely the province of local police departments. And I suggested that we now ought to develop at Quantico, with our growing resources in behavioral sciences and our field coordinators, a National Center for Violent Crime Analysis. Under that umbrella, I'd put the CPRP, special training for police interns, programs to take the results of the research projects and apply them to such areas as assisting police in making out behaviorally oriented search warrants and conducting interviews, and other aspects of our in-service training for local police and for our own agents. Deadpan, McKenzie said that it ought to be the National Center for the Analysis of Violent Crime—and that by switching two words, the concept had become his idea. We both laughed, understanding the joke about the way in which bureaucracies worked and management superiors took credit for everything. McKenzie recognized that the National Center was my idea, and that it was a good one. In the years following, McKenzie fought hard to make the NCAVC a reality, and it certainly would not have become more than an idea without his tireless endeavors; organizational change does not take place in the federal government without a well-placed and indefatigable champion of the cause.

The NCAVC eventually absorbed all of the behavioral sciences programs at Quantico with which I had been associated. The reader will recall that Quantico began in 1972 as a training facility for in-service agents and visiting police, as well as for new agents. Much of that training of experienced personnel was later subsumed under the NCAVC; in addition, the umbrella idea incorporated a lot of research and information-gathering programs that had never been done at Quantico before I started going out on my own to interview convicted murderers in prisons. From the original Criminal Personality Research Project, for instance, similar projects were developed that looked more closely at child abuse, at arson, at rape, at the minds of assassins, at spies and counterpies, and at other important subjects in criminal justice. The NCAVC became, in effect, the behavioral sciences research and training arm at Quantico. The Behavioral Sciences Unit had enlarged its universe considerably.

While we were looking into the possibility of establishing the NCAVC, I learned that a man named Pierce Brooks had obtained a small grant from the Justice Department to study the feasibility of establishing a Violent Criminal Apprehension Program. After more than twenty years, he had revived his dream of the late 1950s, and had done so in a day when working with computers had become much more acceptable and a lot less expensive.

In the interim between the era when Harvey Glattman was an active killer and the early 1980s, there had been a large and significant change in the landscape of violent crime in the United States. In the 1950s and 1960s, virtually all of the homicides in the United States were solved within a year of the time they had been committed. That was because most of the approximately ten thousand murders committed during any one year fell into the category of murders perpetrated by someone known to the victim—by a spouse, another relative, a neighbor, or a coworker. Statistically speaking, very few had been done by a stranger or were for other reasons "unsolvable." By the 1970s, however, the earlier situation had changed drastically. Now, of the approximately twenty thousand murders committed annually in the United States, about five thousand a year were going unsolved—about 25 to 30 percent. It was this fraction of the murders that Pierce Brooks hoped to address with his VICAP system. In the intervening twenty years since he had initially formulated the idea, Pierce had broadened it considerably; he wanted the system to be countrywide, not just in California, and he wanted all police departments to be able to feed in data and to use the data that was stored in the system to evaluate their own unsolved crimes.

Learning of the National Institute of Justice grant to Brooks, I got in touch with him and invited him to be on the board of advisers of our Criminal Personality Research Project, and to visit us at Quantico. When he saw what we were doing, he invited me and my immediate superior to join his own task force, which was operating from the good offices of Professor Doug Moore and the Sam Houston State University in Huntsville, Texas, one of the nation's academic centers for the study of law enforcement.

I never saw anyone milk a federal grant the way Pierce Brooks did. Any person knowledgeable about the ways of government would have asked Justice for a couple of million dollars to study the feasibility of a nationwide computer system; Brooks had asked for and received around $35,000, and he shepherded every penny of the public's money. He had assembled a stellar board of experts in homicide and other relevant fields. To attend a conference in Texas, we were asked to book our air tickets months in advance and to take supersavers to keep the costs down. At Sam Houston State, we stayed in dormitories, and, when it came time for a meal, Brooks had buses to ferry us to fast-food restaurants. No lavish expenditures here. While I admired his husbanding of the public's money, I felt that Brooks's initial plan for VICAP would shortly become unworkable, however.

His idea was to have the national headquarters for VICAP in a room or two at the Lakewood police department. There would be ten or fifteen terminals around the country, only in the largest localities, which meant that each terminal would have to service two or three states. To actually run the system, he'd have to apply for federal grants each year; that was when he planned to add several goose eggs to the amount he'd requested for the initial study.

After he and I had gotten to know one another, I leveled with Pierce and advised him on my view of the realities of government and grants and the like. The federal government being what it was, I said, even though he might obtain a large grant in 1982, there was the likelihood that if the administration changed in 1984, a new administration would not renew the grant and that the project would die due to lack of funds. However, if the program was part of an already-existing government agency, the refunding of it could become a part of the permanent appropriation for that agency, which would mean it was much less likely to be dropped at the time of an administrative change. Moreover, I argued, if we put the VICAP program under a federal agency, there would be offices and personnel already in place, telecommunications on site, possibly even a computer system with excess capacity already installed, and the new money could be better used. One could put such a program under the auspices of the Post Office or the Department of Health, Education, and Welfare—but the most logical home for it was the FBI. Even though a lot of local police departments resented the FBI—remember the one-way street?—it was clear that the FBI was the correct setting for the VICAP program, especially in conjunction with the NCAVC, whose establishment we were concurrently exploring.

Brooks had to agree with the logic of my argument, and we began to set the wheels in motion to bring the VICAP program under the aegis of the FBI, as part of the NCAVC; when the new and larger grant was obtained, Brooks would come to Quantico to manage the program during its first year. With those concepts in mind, Brooks and the FBI applied for a grant of millions of dollars to begin the VICAP and NCAVC programs.

My reasons for being so interested in VICAP were rooted in the work I had been doing for the FBI during the previous decade. In too many cases, police who were confronted with "stranger" murders did not act on them in the most optimal way in the early stages. David Berkowitz had killed several people before the New York City police began to acknowledge that there was any connection among the victims or the crimes. If VICAP had been in full operation, the connection would have been made sooner, and the arrest might have taken place in time to prevent the later murders. Similarly, during Wayne Williams's series of killings in Atlanta, for over a year the police denied that they had a serial killer's work on their hands.

VICAP was needed to help the police in those cases, and VICAP was needed to tie into the NCAVC and other existing government programs such as those dealing with missing persons for another very good reason—to release people such as the parents of Johnny Gosch from their agony. One can get over a death, even the death of a child, but the uncertainty of not knowing anything keeps wounds open and hurting. Ten years after the abduction of their son, the Gosches would like to know whether he's dead or alive, whether his remains have ever been found, whether his killer has ever been caught and incarcerated, perhaps for a different crime. They need to put the matter to rest, and to do so, they need information. VICAP and the NCAVC could help to provide the information that would make them rest easier.

The establishment of VICAP and the NCAVC was no exception to the rule that making institutional change takes a while. Discussions on VICAP continued for a year. During one of our sessions in Texas, a member of the VICAP task force, a former reporter, burst into the room bearing the news that a man named Henry Lee Lucas had confessed to over one hundred killings in nearly every state in the union. Here, said the former reporter, was a perfect case on which to hang the need for VICAP.

Those of us with more direct experience in homicide investigations looked more askance at the Lucas case, even though we did agree that its very existence might be helpful in convincing the public of the need for VICAP.

Henry Lee Lucas was a one-eyed drifter in his late forties when he was convicted of killing an elderly woman in a small town in Texas in 1983. At the time of his sentencing, Lucas told the judge that although the authorities had nailed him on this charge, it was no big deal, because since getting out jail in 1975—he had been sent there for the murder of his mother—he'd killed hundreds of other people across the nation, some by himself and some in conjunction with another drifter, Ottis Toole, whom he met first in 1979. That admission, and his later detailed confessions, kept Lucas off death row and sent law-enforcement people throughout the country into a remarkable frenzy that lasted several years.

The first people that Lucas roped in were the Texas Rangers. There were lots of inquiries coming to Texas from police and sheriff's departments in many states, seeking to find out whether Lucas had had anything to do with some of the unsolved murder cases they still had on their books. The Rangers quietly let it be known that if you had such an unsolved case in your jurisdiction and would send the particulars to them, they'd begin an inquiry and advise you whether you ought to come to Texas and put your questions directly to Lucas.

Let's say your police department in southern Illinois had an unsolved homicide, a young woman raped and knifed to death behind a convenience store, and the signs seemed to point to the murderer having been a transient. You sent the case jacket to the Rangers and they took up the matter with the prisoner. Instead of asking indirect questions to learn whether Lucas had been in Illinois on the dates in question, or whether he'd ever killed anyone near a convenience store, the Rangers asked especially leading questions of Lucas, questions that gave him the race, sex, and age of the victim, and sometimes even showed him the crime-scene photographs—to jog his memory—and then asked him whether he had committed the murder. Lucas was shrewd enough to say no to more than half the cases, but he also said yes to a large percentage. And when he said yes, a representative from that police department would go to Texas to interview Lucas personally, and then, often as not, would arrange for Lucas to take a trip to the state in which the murder had occurred, to visit the crime scene, testify in a trial, and so on. Almost always, there was no other evidence and no witnesses on which to base a conviction for that crime. Incredibly, police from thirty-five states used this process to close the books on 210 unsolved murders.

In the process, of course, Henry Lee Lucas got to leave his non-air-conditioned cell in Texas for large periods of time; on his excursions, he was conveyed to distant locations by airplane or car, stayed in motels, ate well in restaurants, and was generally treated as a celebrity. At one point early in the game, a sort of convention was held in which police officers from all over the country went to a central location to "discuss" the Lucas cases. I didn't attend, but I was told that this was the pinnacle of chaos; observers likened the atmosphere to the pit of a commodities market, with everyone yelling and screaming and making hand gestures to try to claim certain cases as their own. My impression is that this fiasco was fueled not only by the need of police departments to close their difficult unsolved murder cases but also by the boredom of local policemen, many of whom convinced their superiors that it was important for them to go to Texas on a sort of paid holiday in order to join the queue waiting to get in to interview Lucas.

One of my superiors wanted to get in on the action and go to Texas to interview Lucas—not really to obtain information but just to be able to say he'd been there and interviewed such a heinous criminal. Since I controlled the purse strings of the CPRP grant on which he wanted to travel, I was able to veto that idea. One agent from our Houston office did interview Lucas, and asked him whether he had committed the murders in Guyana. "Yep," Lucas said. The agent asked him how he had gotten to Guyana. "Drove my car," Lucas responded. Questioned further, Lucas said he wasn't certain of the exact location of Guyana, but thought it was Louisiana or Texas. In short, he freely admitted that he had been responsible for the many hundreds of people who had died at the hands of Jim Jones in the Jonestown murder-suicides, several thousand miles away from the continental United States, when he obviously had had nothing to do with them. This was a clear indication that his confessions about the hundreds of other murders were just as false.

Eventually, records of Lucas's employment in the mushroom fields of Pennsylvania, sales of scrap metal in Florida, credit-card receipts, and other evidence were compared and tallied, and the discrepancies in his stories were made manifest. Some of the most important work in this regard was conducted by Hugh Aynesworth and Jim Henderson of the *Dallas Times Herald*. Such diligent spadework established that, for instance, Lucas had physically been in Florida when a murder to which he later admitted was being committed in Texas.

By the time I interviewed Lucas, years after the controversy had died down, the dust had settled and Lucas said that he had actually committed none of the murders to which he had previously confessed. Under closer questioning, he did admit that since 1975 he had "killed a few," fewer than ten, perhaps five. He just wasn't sure. He had told all those lies in order to have fun, and to show up what he termed the stupidity of the police.

It took several years for the Lucas fiasco to be resolved. The task-force member had been right, though: If we had had VICAP up and running at the time Lucas made his first startling admission, it would have been easy to see what was truth and what was falsehood in his confession. First, we would have asked the police departments to fill out VICAP forms on their unsolved murders and enter them into the computer system. Then we would have analyzed them by date, location, and MO, and would quickly have been able to show that several of them had been committed on the same date in widely separated locations, thus eliminating the possibility that they were committed by the same man. By such processes of elimination, we would have narrowed the field very quickly and allowed investigators to concentrate on the real possibilities.

While we were still developing the prototype VICAP form, the police in Los Angeles were in the midst of a major case that they called the Night Stalker. They weren't completely sure but thought that a single person was responsible for a series of killings in the Hispanic areas of that city. We sent out some people from the emerging VICAP unit to give them technical assistance, primarily to help determine which victims could be attributed to the single killer and which could not. Most of that was fairly obvious to experienced investigators such as Frank Salerno of the LAPD, who had earlier been the point man on the Hillside Strangler case and who was in charge of the Night Stalker operation, but we were testing our form and also trying to be helpful without inserting ourselves into the limelight of the investigation. The goal was to show the police that they could use the FBI as a resource without running the risk of being upstaged. Richard Ramirez, the Night Stalker, was caught with very little assistance from the FBI, but the case did help us to revise our form, which was initially too lengthy and tried to accomplish too much—as often happens when a project is put together by a committee. Later, we made the form shorter, though it is still quite detailed and takes about an hour for a policeman to fill out.

The mid-1980s, when we were gearing up to ask for funding for VICAP and the NCAVC, coincided with a period that Philip Jenkins of Pennsylvania State University has called ''the serial killer panic of 1983 to 1985.'' An article by Jenkins in the *Criminal Justice Research Bulletin* (1988) cited numerous stories in newspapers and magazines during that period, all making the point that there were lots more unsolved murders in the United States than there had ever been before, that a large number of these were serial murders, and that new criminal-justice-system elements were needed to attack the growing problem. Jenkins cited the Lucas case as evidence that such matters were blown out of proportion. As I've reported earlier in this chapter, the trend certainly did show more and more unsolved "stranger" murders in the 1970s and 1980s than in early decades, but Jenkins was basically correct in his thesis: There was somewhat of a media feeding frenzy, if not a panic, over this issue in the mid-1980s, and we at the FBI and other people involved in urging the formation of VICAP did add to the general impression that there was a big problem and that something needed to be done about it. We didn't exactly go out seeking publicity, but when a reporter called, and we had a choice whether or not to cooperate on a story about violent crime, we gave the reporter good copy. In feeding the frenzy, we were using an old tactic in Washington, playing up the problem as a way of getting Congress and the higher-ups in the executive branch to pay attention to it.

The difficulty was that some people in the bureaucracy went too far in their quest for attention. Pierce Brooks and I had urged the formation of NCAVC and VICAP on good grounds, but in our minds, these were long-term projects that might not pay off right away, at least not insofar as capturing criminals at the first touch of a computer-terminal button. I recall saying to Pierce that if VICAP began officially in 1985, it would not be fully operational until 1995. My reasons for this prediction were simple to understand. Filling out VICAP forms and sending them in to Quantico would be a voluntary procedure on the part of local police departments; it would take time to make those departments recognize the advantage to be gained by filling out and sending in the forms, and it would also take time to build a sufficient data base and to perfect a system able to retrieve the information in a way that would be helpful in solving crimes.

President Ronald Reagan announced the formation of the NCAVC at the annual convention of the National Sheriffs Association in Hartford, Connecticut, on June 21, 1984. He said that its primary mission was the identification and tracking of repeat killers. Pilot funds were provided by the National Institutes of Justice. Pierce Brooks came on board, spent nine months with us, and, at the end of May 1985, sat down at a terminal at Quantico and watched as we entered data from the first real, incoming VICAP form into the computer. It had taken twenty-seven years, but his dream of a way to match data from one violent crime to another had finally taken operational form. Three days later, Pierce was on his way back to Oregon, and the program was turned over to me to manage.

I didn't want it. VICAP is a number-cruncher's dream, and I'm more interested in behavioral sciences and in active, ongoing investigations. The best man for the job was a Department of Justice supervisor, Robert O. Heck, who had shepherded the large grant through the bureaucratic mills, had done a tremendous amount of work on the project, and had expected to run the program after it was fully established. Higher-ups in the FBI had even promised that job to him. Once the FBI obtained the grant money, however, the management told Heck that they were going to administer it, not him. Heck was bitter, and so was I. Nonetheless, things kept rolling onward. In October of 1985, the entire cost of funding the NCAVC was absorbed into the regular annual budget of the FBI; its four basic programs were Research and Development (mostly consisting of my Criminal Personality Research Project), Training (of field agents and local police), Profiling, and VICAP.

Another monkey wrench was soon thrown into the works. The original plan for VICAP called for one manager and many junior analysts to do the actual work of taking the data from the incoming forms and entering it into the computer, and others who would actively cajole local police departments into using the forms for their unsolved homicides and other violent crimes. During the first year of appropriations, the money for those subordinate jobs was channeled by my superiors into the purchase of computer equipment. So we had some shiny new electronic playthings, and no one to do the drab, time-consuming work of entering information into the system. In subsequent appropriations, my superiors decided that rather than use the money earmarked for data enterers and junior analysts, they would instead hire high-level managers and senior crime analysts who had very little to analyze because very little data was being punched into the system. It had been naively predicted that all the unsolved cases would go into the computer in the first year. Since there were about five thousand unsolved murders a year, that would have meant that by 1989, after four years of operation, there ought to have been twenty thousand cases in the computer's memory; by that time, only five thousand had been entered, and the program appeared to fail to live up to its potential. Only in the late 1980s, near to the time of my retirement from the Bureau, were we able to hire the appropriate midlevel technicians to get data put in, and simultaneously to convince enough local police departments to send us their completed forms so that VICAP would begin to have a chance to show what it could do.

There are still several major cities and states that won't fully participate in the VICAP program, and their refusal to participate means the system has a somewhat lower chance of accomplishing the goals set for it. I believe that the federal government should mandate local departments to report their unsolved violent crimes to VICAP, as they are required to do for the Uniform Crime Reporting System. If this was done, and such VICAP reporting was standard procedure in all police departments, I am certain that we could reduce the 25 percent of all unsolved homicides to between 5 and 10 percent.

Here's my reasoning. VICAP doesn't all have to do with serial murderers, who would be traced because, for example, we are able to match the pattern of knife wounds on victim A in Massachusetts to those on victim B in New Hampshire, giving police more of a lead on the killer. A lot of other crimes would feed into it. For instance, say that you had a single homicide-by-gun in New Jersey. The bullet was found but not the killer; the information was entered into the VICAP computer though. Say that two years later, in a bar in Texas, a man was arrested for an attempted rape and a gun was seized from him. Running that gun's ballistic particulars through the VICAP computer might turn up a match, and the man arrested in Texas could be tied to the unsolved single homicide in New Jersey.

We're not at that point yet, but we will be. And we need to be. As I write this in the late summer of 1991, the need for a strong VICAP is more apparent than ever. Just recently, after admitting to the killing of one ten-year-old girl, Donald Leroy Evans, in Gulfport, Louisiana, startled his captors and the nation by saying that he has killed more than sixty people in twenty states since 1977. Two of the murders have now been verified, so Evans may in fact be a serial killer of serious proportions. That is not certain, however, and the whole affair could turn into a chaotic mess of the sort that surrounded the Henry Lee Lucas confession in the early 1980s unless the crimes are examined in some detail. The best way to do that would be to enter the details of every crime to which Evans confesses into the VICAP computer, cross-check them against the FBI's Missing Persons and Unidentified Dead programs, and analyze them against his travel patterns and other particulars so the truth of his serial-killer claims can be evaluated. Using all those systems is now possible, though they are not yet interlinked. Even though certain cities and states in this country have not wanted to work with VICAP, England,

Australia, New Zealand, Korea, and other countries have shown great interest in the program. Since my retirement, I have conducted seminars in some of these countries about VICAP and criminal profiling. They are eager to join forces and submit data in the hope of more quickly apprehending violent criminals.

My original estimate that VICAP would be fully operational by 1995 seems in hindsight like a pretty good guess, after all, though I certainly took a lot of heat in the FBI for having said so in 1985.

11

TWO FOR THE SHOW

On June 20, 1988, I was the master of ceremonies for an unusual live, closed-circuit video show featuring two of the country's most notorious and dangerous serial murderers. The occasion was an attempt to get the VICAP program more widely accepted; in the service of that objective, we were holding the first ever International Homicide Symposium at Quantico. In attendance were three hundred law-enforcement officials from the United States and abroad. Our focus was to try and standardize the procedures for investigating homicides from country to country; each country—indeed, in the United States, each separate jurisdiction—seems to go about the business of examining a crime scene, questioning witnesses, and hunting killers in a different way. As program manager of VICAP, I wanted to make people aware of our national program for the apprehension of violent criminals. Bringing them to Washington, D.C., was the first part of the Bureau's plan. Giving our guests an experience they would probably never have elsewhere—something to talk about when they got home—was the second part, and that unique experience was going to be provided by live interviews of two notorious serial killers. Because of my extensive interviewing of both men, done over a period of nearly ten years each, I was able to persuade John Wayne Gacy and Edmund Kemper to "visit" with us from their prisons in Illinois and California. Both men trusted me, and, I believe, would not have consented to these unique interviews had I not been in charge of the proceedings and made the request personally. After I had made the preliminary arrangements, a Bureau paper shuffler tried to horn in on the glory and wanted to act as the master of ceremonies; I told him that if Gacy or Kemper heard his voice when he expected to hear mine, he might just refuse to go on with the show, and we'd all have egg on our faces. The paper shuffler decided that he'd have to settle for some brief introductory remarks and then sat down and behaved as a good audience member should, leaving the performance to me.

The idea of interviewing a convicted murderer by satellite had earlier been broached to me by staff members of the Geraldo Rivera television program, but I refused to get involved in asking anyone to appear on commercial television, believing that this was not a proper thing for a Bureau employee to do. The Rivera program had tried to convince the California prison system to let Charles Manson appear live but had been unable to do so; rather, the prison had allowed the program to come and do its own extensive taped interview with Manson; later, this had been broadcast in several parts, during which Dr. Jack Levin of Northeastern University and I were asked to critique what Manson had said.

Our closed-circuit program, by contrast, was "interactive." The two men faced video cameras whose images were sent to Quantico via satellite and projected on very large screens. I first presented their cases in slide lectures to our audience, then acted as a funnel for the audience's questions to them. We could see them, but they could only hear us. Each man answered questions for a period of ninety minutes, and it was quite a show, for Gacy and Kemper are both extremely intelligent and articulate, in addition to being dangerous serial murderers.

I had been driving to Chicago with my family in late 1978 for a Christmas vacation when I heard on the radio that bodies were being discovered on the grounds of a small house near Des Plaines, Illinois, a suburb of Chicago not far from O'Hare airfield and not far from where I had grown up. Several bodies had been discovered, and the radio report said that there might be many more to come.

For a man interested in multiple murder, this was too important an opportunity to pass by, vacation or not. Depositing my family at our relatives' home, I said a few words of greeting and apology and then grabbed my camera and took off for the crime scene. There were dozens of people swarming around, many of them families looking for hints of vanished relatives. I asked the local FBI agent for help, and he introduced me to the man in charge of the burgeoning investigation, Joe Kozenzack, chief of detectives of the Des Plaines department. By this time, the search and exhumation of the bodies had been taken over by the Cook County sheriff's office, and I met those investigators, as well; by chance, Howard Vanick, a lieutenant in that office, had been in my class at Quantico, and so I quickly became acquainted with the case at the time it was breaking.

Here's how it had begun. December 11, 1978 was Elizabeth Piest's birthday, and she was waiting for her fifteen-year-old son, Robert Piest, to finish up work at a drugstore in Des Plaines so she could drive him home for the family party. Robert told his mother he had to go out to the parking lot to see a contractor about a summer construction job, one that would pay him nearly twice as much as he was currently making at the drugstore. Ten minutes later, when Bob didn't come back for her, Mrs. Piest became alarmed, went home, and called the police. They told her that adolescent boys often don't come home when they're supposed to, and advised her to stay calm. By eleven-thirty that night, Mrs. Piest could wait no longer, and she insisted to the police that they start to search for her son.

About twenty thousand people a year are reported missing in the Chicago area, and probably nineteen-plus thousand of them are found within a few hours to a year. So police are often reluctant to search seriously for missing people before allowing more time to elapse than had occurred in this case. But Chief of Detectives Joe Kozenczak determined to institute a real search; he, too, had a fifteen-year-old son in the same school as Mrs. Piest, and knew the Piest boy as an all-American kid, a gymnast. This was not the sort of boy to vanish and not call home; it seemed certain that something had gone wrong. Interviewing people at the drugstore, Kozenczak learned that a local contractor, John Wayne Gacy, had been in the store on December 11, doing a remodeling estimate during which he had taken pictures of the place and written down measurements.

Kozenczak had already begun looking for previous conviction records on Gacy, but none turned up by the morning of the thirteenth, when Gacy walked in the door of the police station in response to a call to come in to discuss the matter. Gacy was thirty-six, a short, pudgy man with a double chin and a dark mustache. To outward appearances, he was an upstanding and civic-minded businessman, a contractor who also did interior design and maintenance work; he had been involved in local politics—had even led a Polish Constitution Day parade that featured Rosalynn Carter, and had had his photograph taken with the First Lady—and had dressed up as a clown in full makeup to entertain children at charitable events. He had lived in the same house since 1972 and was well known in the community.

To Kozenczak, Gacy denied knowing Robert Piest or having

any contact with him. Joe told Gacy that he had been seen in the parking lot with the boy, and Gacy changed his story slightly to cover the possibility that he might have been seen in contiguity with him at the parking lot but no further. Kozenczak told me later that he had had an intuitive feeling that Gacy was lying; the way Gacy made denials was too pat and not completely convincing. Kozenczak's men obtained a search warrant and looked into Gacy's house in a very cursory way; they found some young men's clothing and a receipt for a roll of film then being developed at the pharmacy in Des Plaines where Piest worked, a receipt not in Gacy's name. The investigation revealed that Piest had loaned his jacket to a girl who also worked in the store; she had turned in a roll of film for developing and had mistakenly left the receipt in the pocket of the jacket when she returned the jacket to Piest.

Kozenczak and his superiors felt they did not have enough information yet on which to arrest Gacy for anything—officially, Robert Piest was still ''missing''—but they did have enough to put Gacy under complete and open surveillance and to question his friends, associates, and acquaintances. This was a tight surveillance. The men were on the street with him, and when he was in his car, the watchers sometimes came close to locking bumpers with him, trying to provoke him into some action. Gacy was calm at first. He told the tailers that their stupid superiors had put them up to this and that he didn't hold them personally responsible. He'd tell them where his next destination was, in case they lost him in traffic, and at least once offered to buy them lunch at the diner toward which he was heading. In five days, under the surveillance, his behavior crumbled to the point that he stopped shaving and started drinking and using drugs and shouting at people. This did not stop him from stringing Christmas lights on the outside of his home, as had been his custom at earlier holiday seasons.

Gacy found two lawyers and asked them to institute a suit against the police for harassment, alleging that the surveillance was preventing him from doing business.

The day after the lawsuit was begun, December 20, Kozenczak finally received the paperwork that told him Gacy had been convicted of sodomy with an adolescent boy in Iowa in 1968. Gacy had spent several years in prison for that offense, and had been such a model prisoner that he even started a prison branch of the Jaycees. The sentence had been for ten years, but Gacy's sterling bahavior won him parole in 1970. After being released, Gacy had moved to Illinois, and there had been a charge against him of aggravated battery and reckless conduct in mid-1972; a young man claimed Gacy had picked him up in a homosexual district, then had taken him home and had attempted to hurt him. A few days after Gacy's arrest, Gacy told police that this young man was attempting to extort money from him in exchange for dropping the charges, and he wanted the young man arrested for that. Nothing came of either charge; when the young man did not show up in court to press the matter of the abduction, charges against Gacy were dismissed.

Armed with this new information, Kozenczak decided he had enough grounds to ask for a full search warrant, obtained one, and, together with the Cook County sheriff's office, arrived at Gacy's residence on December 21 with his men in force and began a thorough search of the house. Gacy was there, and the detectives accused him of holding Robert Piest in the house. Gacy denied it, but did say that back in 1972 he had been forced to kill one of his homosexual partners in self-defense, and that he had buried the body beneath the concrete floor of his garage. As the police watched, Gacy took a can of paint and spray-painted the place on the concrete floor where he said the body still lay. Inside the house, the police later found a trapdoor to a crawl space, crawled inside, and found three decomposing bodies and parts of others. Gacy was arrested and charged with murder. In his initial confession, witnessed by a half-dozen detectives, he confessed to the murder of Robert Piest and to that of twenty-seven other young males, most of whose bodies he said were buried beneath the house, and the last few of which—including Piest—he had tossed into the Des Plaines River. Police went to work on Gacy's home and grounds so thoroughly that when they were finished, all that was left standing were the outside walls, roof, and support beams. They were looking, the Cook County medical examiner told reporters, for "any scrap of evidence—a ring, a belt buckle, a button—that will help us to identify the victims." That was because Gacy couldn't remember more than a few of the victims' names. By the time the body count was complete, there were thirty-three victims (twenty-nine in and under the house, four in the river), more than had died at the hands of any other single individual in the history of American crime. Most of the dead were young males between the ages of fifteen and twenty. Ted Bundy might have killed more people, but not all of their bodies were ever found or attributed directly to him. John Gacy was officially the worst killer in modern times.

Gacy initially confessed to the murders in some detail, then, on the advice of counsel, said no more. The killings, Gacy had admitted, began one night in January 1972. He had trolled the Greyhound bus station near Chicago's loop for sex partners, and brought home a young man and had sex with him. According to Gacy, the next morning, he saw that young man coming at him with a knife, struggled with him, and managed to stab his attacker in the chest. He buried this young man in the crawl space. Later in 1972, Gacy married for the second time. (His first marriage, which produced two children, ended in divorce during his earlier prison term.) The second wife asked him about the wallets of young men that Gacy had in the house, but he shouted at her that this was none of her business, and she put them out of mind. Then she complained of strange odors in the home, and while she was away on vacation, Gacy later said, he poured concrete over that first body to conceal the smell. Gacy's mother-in-law and the wife's children from a previous marriage lived with the couple during the next few years, during which, according to the mother-in-law, the odor of "dead rats" continued. So did the murders.

Gacy couldn't remember precisely when he'd killed for the second time, but remembered it as between 1972 and 1975, and forensic evidence later corroborated this date. He strangled a young man, then placed him in a bedroom closet for storage before burial, and became a bit distressed that bodily fluids leaked out of the victim's mouth and stained a carpet. Subsequently, he told authorities, he learned to stuff cloths or other materials in his victims' mouths to prevent any telltale leaks.

According to that first confession, in mid-1975, John Butkovich, a twenty-year-old construction employee of Gacy's came to the house with some friends and demanded back wages owed to him; after an unresolved argument, Butkovich left. Later that night, Gacy was "cruising" in his car and picked up Butkovich. He took the young man back to the house and offered him drinks. Then he said he'd show him a "handcuff trick." Handcuffed, Butkovich was helpless, and he sputtered at Gacy that if he ever got out, he'd kill him. In response, Gacy showed Butkovich his second deadly amusement, the "rope trick," in which Gacy placed a noose around the young man's neck, stuck a stick in it, and tightened it slowly, strangling him.

Gacy's handcuff and rope tricks were later described by several young men who had been picked up by Gacy and taken to his home but had refused to participate in those "magic" demonstrations, and so had survived. Butkovich did not, and was buried in a trench at the end of a toolshed near the garage, and also covered with concrete.

The Butkovich family suspected Gacy at the time, but police did not follow up on their suspicions. "If the police had only paid attention to us, they might have saved many lives,'' Butkovich's father later told reporters. The police didn't follow up, most likely because they thought that Butkovich, like thousands of other young men around the country, had simply run away from home. Moreover, to have uncovered the crime, they would have had to have some tangible evidence even to ask a judge for a search warrant of Gacy's home, and they had none.

Later, more was learned about Gacy's techniques for luring and controlling his victims, and about his sadistic acts. He usually cruised the homosexual districts for victims, many of whom were transients who would not be missed for some time. On other occasions, he struck close to home, convincing some part-time employees to come to his residence on the promise of paying back wages. Once there, they would be plied with liquor and drugs, and then he would offer to show them movies. He'd begin with heterosexual pornography, then introduce some homosexual films. Then, if the young man did not object too strenuously, he'd bring out the handcuff and rope tricks. When a victim was immobilized, Gacy would sexually assault him. Afterward, Gacy would often put him in a bathtub, sometimes with a plastic bag over his head, and nearly drown him, then revive him in order to inflict more sexual assaults and torture.

Gacy was a smart man, with a high IQ, but more important he was a highly manipulative man with good verbal skills, able to defuse a victim's paranoia and curiosity about himself. He was a spider who had to get victims into the very center of the web before being able to kill them. Whereas Ted Bundy would hit women in the face with a crowbar, Gacy used neither guns nor knives nor blunt instruments, but immobilized his victims through trickery and deceit.

The more he got away with the abductions, assaults, and murders, the more elaborate the rituals and the torture became. With a high opinion of himself, and a low one of the police and everyone else, Gacy transformed himself into a practiced and expert killer.

In February of 1976, Gacy's second wife and her family moved out, and his killings began to escalate, at a rate of approximately one a month. As he went on, Gacy must have come to believe that he was invincible, for he was not even suspected in the murders. He became more bold and cavalier, not resorting to the anonymity of the homosexual district but taking young men right off the street—one who had been on the way home from a horseback-riding stable, others from his cadre of part-time employees. Young males between the ages of about fifteen and twenty simply disappeared, and most of the time it was

believed they had simply become runaways. While the killings continued, so did Gacy's success in the local and business communities. He
became a block captain, toured the children's wards in hospitals in his
homemade clown outfit, and threw an annual block party for four
hundred neighbors. "He was always available for any chore, washing
windows, setting up chairs for meetings—even fixing someone's leaky
faucet," a local Democratic party official told reporters, and concluded, "I don't know anyone who didn't like him."

Early stories in the newspapers stressed the idea that Gacy was
a Jekyll and Hyde character. As I have argued in other chapters of this
book, the Jekyll and Hyde story is simply not the right explanation for
this sort of murderer: The deadly side is always there, but the murderer
is frequently successful in hiding it from the outside world. When
Gacy was traced back in time, it was possible to see that the strange,
murderous side of him had been in evidence for fifteen years. Back in
the 1960s, in Iowa, when he managed three fried-chicken franchise
restaurants for his first father-in-law, he would use his position to
lure young male employees into having sex with him. In an "official
statement of facts" submitted by the State's Attorney of Cook County,
it is alleged that "young men would be rewarded with sex with Gacy's
first wife in return for oral sex with Gacy." Moreover, "when a
sodomy victim reported him to the authorities, Gacy hired another
young man to beat him up and convince him not to testify." It was
only after one well-connected victim complained that Gacy was
charged with sodomy, convicted, and sent to jail.

Class rings, car title papers, and other possessions of the dead
victims were found in Gacy's home; in one case, Gacy had sold a dead
victim's car to an employee. In fact, he had kept a trophy from almost
every victim. By early 1978, Gacy considered the crawl space and
other caches on his property to be too full of bodies to contain any
more, and he began dumping victims off bridges into the Des Plaines
River.

When Kozenczak and his investigators questioned Gacy in his
home on December 12, 1978, the body of Robert Piest was still in the
attic. Somehow, before the intense phase of the police surveillance
began, Gacy managed to sneak the body out of the house and throw
it, too, into the river; it was not even found until after Gacy's trial. By
that point, only about half of the victims had been positively identified.

At the trial, Gacy's attorneys argued that he suffered from
having multiple personalities, that "Jack Handley" had done the murders. (Gacy suggested that his "Jack" and "John" personalities were

opposites. The actual Jack Handley had been a police officer in the Chicago area whose name Gacy had appropriated.) Still later, Gacy argued that because of the nature of his business, at least a dozen men had keys to his home, and some of his associates lived there from time to time and could also have been involved in murders. He revised his own story to say that he had killed only a handful, not thirty-three, and to say that he certainly had not killed every young man with whom he had sex. Some of these theories began to surface in sixty hours of audiotapes that Gacy recorded for use by his attorneys at the trial, tapes in which Gacy also admitted to many of the murders.

The state pursued a case solely against Gacy, ignoring some evidence that there might indeed have been other people involved, two associates of Gacy's who did spend time at his home. This is something that often happens in big cases: the DA pursues the one very good suspect and doesn't develop the others because that would complicate an otherwise-straightforward prosecution. The important thing seems to be to handle the case expeditiously, and so the prosecution can be successful in obtaining a verdict against an obviously guilty man.

At the trial, Gacy and his attorneys presented a defense of him as not guilty by reason of insanity. The prosecution countered by demonstrating that the steps Gacy took to procure victims, to render them immobile, to kill them, and then consciously after death to conceal their bodies argued that Gacy's crimes were premeditated murders, and that he clearly knew the difference between right and wrong at the time of the crimes. After nearly six weeks of trial, the jury pronounced him guilty of the murder of the thirty-three victims, and Gacy was sentenced to die in the electric chair.

After his conviction, I requested an audience with John Gacy, and he consented to see me, together with some associates from the BSU. Gacy claimed to know me from his childhood. Our homes were four blocks from one other, and he remembered delivering groceries to my mother's house, even describing some unusual flowerpots that were part of the landscaping. So we talked about the neighborhood, and developed a relationship of sorts. I had learned enough about conversing with murderers so that I was able to approach Gacy on a rather objective basis, without stigmatizing him for what he had done. By this time, Gacy had become convinced that the police, the psychiatrists, and the courts were all full of fools who simply did not understand him and were beneath him intellectually—but that I was schooled in the ways of intelligent killers and could talk to him about his life in a reasonable way. Gacy states that two or three of his former employees were involved in the crimes. As part of my interchange with Gacy, I told him that I agreed that the police should have more vigorously pursued those employees who had stayed in the Gacy house from time to time. I was sincere in that belief, and still feel today that there are unexplored avenues that might be traced and might reveal others who were involved in the murders.

Gacy would not speak directly to the media and even refused monetary offers for interviews. He said he wanted to tell his story one day, and I urged him to do so. However, I cautioned that he'd have to be candid and not claim he hadn't killed all of the victims. In fact, I told him, I thought he might have killed more than thirty-three; since he had traveled widely, in fourteen states, he could have trawled homosexual transient districts for victims elsewhere. Gacy neither admitted nor denied my accusation.

Through the years, I continued to stay in touch with Gacy. In our later conversations, he devalued the young men he had killed as "worthless little queers and punks." I challenged him about that. Why was he running down his victims; if they were worthless homosexuals, what was he? Gacy's answer was that they were useless runaways, while he was a successful and busy businessmen who didn't have many hours available for dating. He told me that he found it more satisfactory to have quick sex with a young man than to wine and dine and romance a woman, which took too much time from his very full schedule. This didn't sit well with me, but I simply accepted his comment without question at the time, in order to maintain our rapport.

Gacy later made a painting and sent it to me. It depicts a clown, dressed in a similar outfit to the one that Gacy had used, posing in the midst of a grove of evergreen trees, surrounded by balloons. The inscription read, "You cannot hope to enjoy the harvest without first laboring in the fields." Some people take this as a compliment to me, with the meaning that I was able to get close to Gacy because I had spent so much time working with multiple murderers and so had been properly prepared to talk to him. On the other hand, some people interpret the inscription to mean that there are even more Gacy victims who have not yet been found. Gacy himself refuses to explicate.

People who become notorious through crime often attract outsiders to them. That's what happened to John Gacy in prison in 1986: A twice-divorced woman with eight children came to visit him, and they started an extended correspondence. Two years and forty-one letters later, the woman was persuaded to let the *Chicago Sun-Times* publish excerpts from some of the letters. They contained such passages as the following:

> I'm a gullible person, and I think you are too. But you can overcome it. And it has nothing to do with educational background. I hold three college degrees. Big deal. It doesn't mean a thing without common sense. Street-wise people you can learn from. But you've got to be on guard for the con too. I mean, what the [deleted], the state said I was manipulative or a manipulator. Hell yes. But had I not been I would not have been successful. You wouldn't be successful undercover if you didn't manipulate at times.

Forensic psychiatrist Dr. Marvin Ziporyn, who had been the chief psychiatrist at the prison where Gacy was incarcerated, evaluated the letters for the newspaper and wrote an analysis of them. Ziporyn had also interviewed Richard Speck in depth, and had written a book about Speck, *Born to Raise Hell*. Ziporyn wrote that in every letter, almost in every paragraph, Gacy displayed the two major themes of his thinking. The first was that Gacy's view of himself was as a "nice guy," which Ziporyn said meant heterosexual, "helpful, friendly, generous, loving, virile and courageous." Simultaneously, Ziporyn wrote, Gacy was at pains to deny that there was a "Bad Me, bad being weak, timorous, cowardly, and—above all else—homosexual." That "Bad Me" had committed the murders. His denial of the "Bad Me" allowed the belief in himself as fundamentally good. Here, wrote Ziporyn, was a classic sociopath, a man whose huge ego "exists solely to satisfy his own appetite for existence. His answer to the question 'What is one allowed to do?' is 'Whatever one can get away with.' His answer to the question 'What is good?' is 'Whatever is good for me.' " Even in the letters, Gacy was trying to control his new friend, telling her, says Ziporyn, "what to do, what to think, how to deal with her family, how to manage her affairs," and it was in this display that one could see Gacy's need to control and dominate, the dynamic that led to his involvement in bondage and murder.

In later years, Gacy has come to believe that his troubles are traceable to his early childhood. Born of immigrant parents (Polish and Danish), he grew up in a household where discipline was strict, and his father drank and often bullied family members. He claimed to have been molested at the age of five by a teenaged girl, and at the age of eight by a male contractor. By the age of ten, he was having epileptic seizures, and his medical conditions kept him out of sports and other activities in high school; when he began work, he was out for medical reasons one day in three. He also insisted that his mind was affected by alcohol and drugs. Later, he came around to the story that he had not even been living in his home at the time the bodies were discovered, and that the crimes had been committed by someone other than himself.

In late 1972, Santa Cruz, California, seemed like the murder capital of the United States. Every month, there would be the report of another grisly crime—a body found here, a hitchhiker vanished there. There were more such reports, per capita, than in any other locality in the country. Residents were conscious of the murder epidemic; many had bought guns, and security was beefed up at the campus of the University of California at Santa Cruz, from which several women had vanished. Later it would be understood that three multiple murderers were at work in the area at approximately the same time, John Linley Frazier, Herbert Mullin, and Edmund Emil Kemper.

Frazier and Mullin were apprehended, but the killings continued until Easter weekend of 1973. The Tuesday afterward, at three in the morning on April 24, 1973, a call came in to the Santa Cruz police department from a public phone booth in Pueblo, California. The caller said he was Ed Kemper—a highway-department employee well known to the police because he often hung out with them in the bar near the courthouse and in the town's gun shop. Kemper wanted to talk to a particular police lieutenant but settled for the man on duty. He wanted, he said, to confess to the killings of various coeds from the Santa Cruz campus and to the killing of his mother and a friend of his mother's. If someone would come to Pueblo and pick him up, he'd point out where the bodies could be found.

There was some disbelief at the Santa Cruz station; one of those on duty thought Kemper was just pulling the desk man's leg. But Kemper responded to some questions with more intimate knowledge of the details of the coed murders than anyone other than the killer might possess. While Kemper was still on the line, the Santa Cruz department contacted the Pueblo department and asked them to pick up Kemper and hold him until a Santa Cruz man arrived. When the Pueblo department went to the phone booth, they thought at first that it was occupied by two people—Kemper, at six nine and three hundred pounds, was large enough to convey that illusion.

Five years later, when I first talked to Kemper, his size struck me right away. I had known about it, of course, but a man that big gets your attention. He stuck out his hand, shook mine, and immediately wanted to know if in exchange for the interview I could obtain some privileges for him, and some stamps for his correspondence. I said I'd give him the stamps but couldn't offer him anything else. Nonetheless, he was willing to talk, and had pretty good insight into his crimes, having been counseled by mental-health professionals for quite a while, and having spent part of his prison time as a clerk in the psychological section of the institution. He believed his crimes had been precipitated by his hostility toward his mother, who had been oppressive toward him, and that they had stopped when he had finally killed the source of his problems. That was quite a neat and precise explanation of a complex matter, so I asked Kemper where he thought he fit into the *Diagnostic and Statistical Manual of Mental Disorders*, then in its second edition. He said he knew the categories, had read the book, but didn't find a description that fit him, and didn't expect to, until psychiatry had obtained sufficient information to understand people like him. When would that be? When the *DSM* was in its sixth or seventh edition, he answered—and that wouldn't happen until sometime in the next century.

In answering in such a manner, Kemper was trying to tell me how unique he was, and was also reflecting the position of a leading psychiatrist who had spoken to him at length and written a book about him, and who thought that this sort of criminal came along about once in two hundred years. I disagree. Ed Kemper, though certainly remarkable, is not so rare a bird; there are other murderers like him; he differs from them, perhaps, in the degree of his brutality and the depth of what he endured in his childhood.

His size had always been a problem; he had become too large too fast. He never had the opportunity to be a true child, because he was large enough so that people treated him as if he were older. He did not have friends of the same age, and those that were the same size as he were years ahead of him mentally. His size was not an insurmountable obstacle to a productive life; the ranks of professional sports are filled today with outsized men who were once outsized boys, and none of them have become multiple murderers. However, the fact of Kemper's size was combined with the stresses of a severely dysfunctional home, one with an alcoholic and overbearing mother, an absent father, favored sisters, and a grandmother who was in many ways a worse nurturer than the mother. The mother would continually belittle Ed, tell him he was the source of *her* problems, and abuse him mentally in other ways. To me, the most telling event occurred when

Kemper was ten: without his knowledge, his mother and sisters moved him from the second-story bedroom he had occupied down to a spooky old basement room, near the furnace, because he was too big and they considered it unhealthy for him to be around his thirteen-year-old sister or in the same bedroom as his younger sister—they considered him a sexual threat to them. This shocked Kemper and brought his attention to sexual issues; afterward, his fantasies, which had begun at an even earlier age, took a turn for the worse, now entailing bizarre sexual activity with his sisters and his mother, and the killing of these torment-ers. From time to time, at night, Ed would take a knife and hammer and slip into his mother's room and fantasize about killing her.

The move into the basement at age ten came at around the same time as his mother's first divorce, from Kemper's natural father. The mother remarried and divorced twice more between the time Kemper was ten and fourteen. Each time, when the marriage was going badly, Kemper's mother would send him out to live with his grandparents on their farm, and he came to hate that. At the same time, on the farm and in his mother's orbit, he became familiar with firearms. One of his stepfathers was an expert and demanded that Kemper be a good shot and know about guns, safety, ammunition, and the like. As discussed earlier, the grandparents took a gun away from Kemper when he used it—as the stepfather seemed to be urging—to kill small animals. Such a confusion of messages characterized much of what Kemper had to bear.

In 1965, at age fifteen, when his mother was in the throes of yet another marital change, Kemper was sent to the farm. He was miserable, and felt used by his grandmother and ostracized from his schoolmates. One day, Kemper came up behind his grandmother as she was typing a letter at her desk. She had decreed that he must stay around the house and help her with chores that day, when he had wanted to go out into the fields with his grandfather, whom he liked better. He shot his grandmother with a rifle, then stabbed her. Having done this, he next realized that he didn't want his grandfather to see the gruesome sight, so he waited until his grandfather was approaching the house and then shot him, too, before he could enter the house. As if to make clear the connection between this murderous act and the source of his problems, Kemper then went into the house, called his mother at her vacation cottage, and told her that her honeymoon would have to be cut short because he had just killed her parents.

Kemper spent the next four years in the Atascadero State Mental Hospital. During this time, he took dozens of mental tests and did well on them, possibly because he was able to find out the answers that the mental-health personnel found appropriate; later, he would let it be known that he had memorized twenty-eight of the tests and the correct answers. In 1969, the mental-health and correctional professionals at Atascadero State pronounced Kemper to be fit for return to society. He was, after all, still technically a juvenile; over the objections of a state prosecutor, he was released to a California Youth Authority Camp. The next year, at his mother's intercession, he was paroled into her custody—this against the recommendations of the parole board and of some of the psychiatrists at Atascadero.

Looking back, I found rather amazing this parole of Kemper into the custody of the woman who had been the source of his problems. He lived with his mother and worked as a laborer at a Green Giant canning plant. His mother continued to push the justice system to expunge Ed's juvenile offense from his record as he neared adulthood. Though his mother had rescued him, she never stopped abusing Kemper mentally. "Because of you, my murderous son," she would tell him after he returned from Atascadero, "I haven't had sex with a man in five years, because no one wants to be with me out of fear of you."

In terms of sexuality, Kemper himself was still a virgin, and remained so; during the years he might have experimented with sexual contact, he was in a mental institution, and became even more fixated on himself and his fantasies. At an apartment he rented for the times when he was not staying in his mother's house, he gazed at pornography and read detective magazines for erotic—and violent—stimulation. His murderous fantasies had not abated; in fact, they had grown more detailed and intense. Later, he would tell authorities that during his years in Atascadero, he spent a lot of time perfecting a method for disposing of bodies after he had murdered people. No psychologist had been able to elicit from Kemper this sort of information at the time he was an incarcerated teenager; my belief is that Kemper deliberately concealed the fantasy, knowing that to reveal it would surely hinder his release from custody.

Kemper started work for the state highway department in 1971, and then put in an application to become a state trooper. Several law-enforcement agencies turned him down, evidently because of his size, but he began to hang out with the police in Santa Cruz. One friend gave him a training-school badge and a pair of handcuffs. He borrowed a gun from another acquaintance. He had a car that looked somewhat like a police cruiser, with a CB radio and a whip antenna. When he wasn't in that car, he was on a motorcycle. His state credentials, when flashed quickly at a naïve observer, could pass for those of a state trooper. In February of 1971, while riding the motorcycle, he was hit by an automobile and severely injured his arm. He filed a civil suit because the injuries forced him to wear a cast for many months, and in December of 1971, he was awarded an out-of-court settlement of fifteen thousand dollars. The cast on his arm made it impossible for him to do the highway work, so now he had money and time on his hands.

His mother had become a well-liked administrative aide on the campus of the Santa Cruz branch of the state university, and she obtained a car sticker for Kemper so that he could come on campus to pick her up after work. Helpful to students and faculty on campus, she seemed to take out all her frustrations on Kemper. Their relationship worsened. After one horrendous fight in the spring of 1972, Kemper slammed the doors of her home on his way out and vowed that the first good-looking girl he saw that night was going to die.

That victim was never found, and Kemper was never indicted for that killing, about which he furnished few details. He did kill two young women on May 7, 1972, who were later identified. Both were Fresno State College students who had been to see their boyfriends at Berkeley, and were hitchhiking to Palo Alto to visit other friends at Stanford. Kemper went after these victims, he later told me, because they were "hippie girls" of the sort he professed both to admire and despise, and because there were lots of them on the roads; in other words, they were available victims who would probably not be missed for some time.

That same summer of 1972, when Kemper picked up these two potential victims on the highway, a woman researcher named Cameron Smith was picking up female hitchhikers at Berkeley and asking them to fill out a questionnaire. According to a report of her work in Ward Damio's book about the Santa Cruz murders, Ms. Smith discovered that 24 percent of those hitchhikers she interviewed had been raped while hitching, another 18 percent had been attacked, while 27 percent told her they had been subjected to attempted rapes or other perverse acts; only about a third had completed their rides without incident. Despite these frightening odds, young women continued to hitch rides in the Berkeley area, and so by the side of a major highway Ed Kemper was able to pick up two teenaged girls in blue jeans who were carrying overnight bags. He had his handcuffs and badge, as well as a knife and the borrowed gun. Pointing the gun at the girls, he told them he was going to rape them, and pulled off the highway onto a side road. Evidently, the women believed that they were not going to be killed, and therefore decided not to fight back at first. Kemper was able to talk one girl into climbing into the trunk, then he got in the backseat of his car, handcuffed and tied up the second girl, then stabbed and strangled her. He didn't use the gun because bullets from it could be traced. After killing the first girl, he opened the trunk and stabbed the second to death. With the two bodies in the car, he drove to his apartment, and there he decapitated the bodies and cut off their hands.

At the apartment, he cleaned himself up as much as possible. There was still blood on the cast; later, he'd cover this up with white shoe polish until he could convince his doctors to make a new cast for him. The amount of blood and the difficulties Kemper experienced in killing the women with a knife shook him, and he vowed that the next killings would be less messy. That night, he took off all the clothing from the dead bodies and copulated with them. Next morning, he realized that he had made at least three mistakes that could have gotten him caught, and he decided to proceed even more carefully from then on. As he had fantasized doing in Atascadero, that day he dumped and buried the bodies in several different places, the heads in a different spot from the torsos, and the hands in a third location. Anyone who found the torsos would be unable to identify the bodies, because there would be no faces or dental work, and no fingerprints. The burial sites were in a different county from the one where he had picked up the hitchhikers. He disposed of the victims' clothing in remote canyons in the Santa Cruz mountains. The women were reported missing but were not found for several months. In August, the severed head of one girl was discovered. It yielded her identity but absolutely no clues as to how she had died.

By that time, Kemper's mother was lobbying hard to have Ed's juvenile record of the murders of his grandparents sealed by the court. The district attorney objected, saying they should be kept open at least ten more years. A psychiatric examination of Kemper was scheduled for mid-September. Four days before that test, Kemper went out hunting again. He picked up an attractive woman hitchhiking with her twelve-year-old son. As he drove away, he noticed that the woman's friend who saw her off had taken down his license plate number, so he ferried the mother and son to their destination and then returned to the outskirts of Berkeley, nearly desperate to find a victim. This indicates to me that Kemper is a highly organized offender whose intellect is firmly in control of his compulsion to kill. He saw an Asian girl, a fifteen-year-old ballet student, and picked her up.

Told she was being kidnapped, the girl became hysterical, but when he pulled out a new gun borrowed from another friend, she quieted, and he kept her docile by saying that he had problems and wanted to talk to her about them. Stopping the car just north of Santa Cruz, he smothered her until she was unconscious, raped her, then strangled her to death with her own scarf and had intercourse with her corpse. With the body in the trunk of the car, Kemper then decided to go to visit his mother for a while; it was strangely pleasurable for him to chat with her while he had a dead girl in the car.

An important element in the growth of a fantasy can be discerned from Kemper's pleasure in conversing with his mother while he knew he has a dead woman in the car, just a few yards away. Here was something he would add to the ritual, to prolong the excitement of the fantasy. The reality would never become as good as the fantasy, he would later tell me, but he kept on trying to improve both his performance and the elaborate nature of the fantasy.

Among the topics Kemper discussed with his mother that night may have been the forthcoming psychiatric examination; once the records were sealed, Kemper's mother had told him many times, he would be free of the past. Later in the evening, in his apartment, Kemper placed the body in his bed and again had intercourse: In the morning, he spent several hours meticulously dismembering the body, flushing the fluids down the drain and afterward pouring Drano in the drain to remove any evidence from the system. Then he took to the back roads with his burden. He buried the hands in one county, the torso in another, and kept the head in the trunk of his car. The head was still in the trunk of the car when he went to visit one of the psychiatrists appointed by the court. That, too, gave Kemper a kick.

Both psychiatrists who examined him in September of 1972 concluded that he had made excellent progress during his time at Atascadero. One of them wrote:

> If I were seeing this patient without having any history available or without getting the history from him, I would think that we're dealing with a very well adjusted young man who had initiative, intelligence and who was free of any psychiatric illness. . . . In effect, we are dealing with two different people when we talk of the 15 year old boy who

committed the murder and of the 23 year old man we see before us now. . . . It is my opinion that he has made a very excellent response to the years of treatment and rehabilitation and I would see no psychiatric reason to consider him to be of any danger to himself or to any member of society.

The second psychiatrist added:

He appears to have made a good recovery from such a tragic and violent split within himself. He appears to be functioning in one piece now directing his feelings towards verbalization, work, sports and not allowing neurotic buildup within himself. Since it may allow him more freedom as an adult to develop his potential, I would consider it reasonable to have a permanent expunction of his juvenile records. I am glad he has recently "expunged" his motorcycle and I would hope that he would do that ("seal it") permanently since this seemed more a threat to his life and health than any threat he is presently to anyone else.

Since both psychiatrists recommended the sealing of the records so that Kemper could get on with his life, on November 29, 1972, they were officially sealed.

After killing the Asian dancer, Kemper was able to keep a lid on his murderous impulses for the several months before and just after his juvenile records were sealed. With the turn of the new year, however, the urge to kill resurfaced. He returned the guns that he had borrowed from his friends and sought one of his own. Now that his records were sealed, he had a legal right to own a gun. He drove to the town where he had worked at the food factory and purchased a .22 pistol with a long barrel and some hollow-point ammunition that exploded on impact; that same afternoon, in daylight, he picked up another hitchhiker, a rather heavy young girl. He told her he wanted to talk, and she seemed sympathetic. Nonetheless, he killed her with a single bullet from his new gun, then drove to his mother's home. She wasn't there, so Kemper took the body from the car and stashed it in his bedroom closet. After his mother left for work the next morning, he dismembered it. Part of the reason for severing the head was to remove the spent bullet from it; that way, there would be no ballistic evidence to connect him with the crime. He threw the body parts over a remote cliff into the sea. Some of them were found within a few days. The head he buried underneath his mother's window.

By this time, since Kemper and Herbert Mullin were both killing people in the area, many people had become frightened, and security forces were on alert to look for suspicious characters.

Less than a month after killing the heavy girl, and after a particularly heated argument with his mother, in February 1973, Kemper went onto the UCSC campus, picked up two young women, and shot them both before reaching the perimeter of the campus. The students were not quite dead, and one was groaning audibly when Kemper pulled up to the gates where two armed young rookie guards were manning the post. The men looked right into the car but either did not see the dying women or did not understand what they were viewing in the dark interior of the car. Though the exterior of the car was a drab tan, the interior was black. The woman in the front seat, dressed in black, was partially tumbled over into the wheel well, and the one in the back was covered by a blanket that Kemper had purposefully kept in the car for just such an occasion. The guards paid more attention to the campus sticker on the window than to the moaning bundles in the car, and they let Kemper pass. For Ed, it was a moment of triumph.

These bodies, too, he handled boldly when his mother was nearby, seemingly excited by the possibility that she might discover him doing it. He decapitated them in the trunk of the car while it sat in her driveway and took the heads into the house so he could look at them in his bedroom. Masturbation would be a part of this ghastly ritual. He returned the heads to the car in the morning, and kept all the parts in the car for the next day and more, driving the car to the home of some friends, where he had dinner. Later in the evening, he dumped the parts in various places, again taking care to remove the bullets from the heads.

There was a bullet hole in the car, however, and too much blood in the trunk for him to wash away completely, and other such telltale evidence. Kemper seemed aware of these matters, and was a bit skittish. In early April, he bought another gun, a .44 pistol. When a sheriff received the record of the sale of the weapon, he remembered something about Kemper's early conviction, and decided to make a check on it. Finding the record sealed, he nevertheless drove to Kemper's apartment and asked him for the pistol; he would hold it until a court decided whether it was legal for Kemper to own a weapon. Kemper opened the trunk of his car and, without an argument, gave the pistol to the sheriff. The sheriff was satisfied with that and did not search the car thoroughly—and so did not find the .22 murder weapon that was concealed under a seat.

After the sheriff left, however, Kemper started playing what-if games in his mind. What if the sheriff had seen traces of blood or hair in the trunk? What if the sheriff found out about the .22 pistol as he had learned about the .44? What if the authorities came back and searched his car, his apartment, his mother's home? What if there was now a tail on him? Kemper later told the police it was then that he decided he must kill his mother and surrender.

Two weeks after the sheriff picked up the .44, on Good Friday, April 20, 1973, Kemper went to his mother's home. She arrived later, after a faculty meeting, and they had a brief conversation in which his mother was, as usual, sarcastic to him. Once she had fallen asleep, at five in the morning, Kemper took a claw hammer from the kitchen and, as he had done so often in his imagination, went into her bedroom while she slept. This time, he actually brought the hammer down with considerable force on her right temple, then slashed her throat with his pocketknife. Blood was still gushing from her as he decided to sever the head as he had done with his other victims. Another slice removed her larynx, and he threw this part into the disposal unit in the kitchen sink. When the disposal was unable to digest the larynx and spewed it back out, Kemper thought this was poetic justice. He wrapped the body in the bloody sheets and stashed it in the closet.

Later in the morning, he went to the bar that was the police hangout, and to the gun shop, and talked calmly to some friends, even trying to borrow a gun from one of them, who refused. That afternoon, however, he reasoned that since this was a holiday weekend, family members or one of his mother's close friends who also worked at the university might well appear at the house and discover the body. Taking the initiative, he invited his mother's associate Sara Hallett to help him plan a surprise party for her, and when she arrived, he snapped her neck. He left her body on his own bed and spent the night on his mother's. Easter Sunday morning, he stuffed the friend's body in another closet, then piled his guns, the two women's credit cards, and money into the friend's car, and took off on his final journey.

Once in custody, he was determined to give the police the evidence they needed to convict him. He was convinced that they would never have found it on their own, and that if he had simply confessed and not led them point by point to physical evidence, a smart lawyer might later be able to discount the confession and enable

Kemper to escape conviction. And so, in addition to confessing, he told police just where to find the bodies in his mother's home, and, even before the public was made aware of these killings, led police to the dump and burial sites of several of the other victims; still more evidence from the dead girls—a scarf, a textbook, and so on—was found in his mother's home, his apartment, and his car. Part of this evidence was obtained by the police by smart interrogation: They kept complimenting Kemper on his intellect, his powers of memory, his wonderful recall of detail, until he led them to such items as a blood-soaked blanket, with a contemptuous remark such as, "Here's another piece of evidence for your case."

Awaiting trial, Kemper attempted twice to commit suicide by slashing his wrists, and was soon transferred to a solitary cell. The trial itself was rather short. The evidence was there, and it showed clear premeditation. All the psychiatrists called to testify said that Kemper had clearly been sane when he had committed the crimes. During the trial, Kemper was asked why he had killed the hitchhikers. "That was the only way they could be mine," he said, and added, "I had their spirits. I still have them." Kemper was soon convicted of seven murders and sentenced to death. Asked what he thought was the appropriate punishment for his crimes, he replied, "Torture."

He got neither death or active torture; rather, he was put into prison, for although California had embraced the death penalty in principle, no one was being executed in that state at that time. In prison, Kemper calmed down and became a well-behaved inmate, accepted into the prison population, gradually given increasing amounts of privileges, if not freedom, within the institution.

In our interviews, which began five years after his crimes, Kemper concentrated at first on the facts of the murders, in the process telling me a number of things that were of interest to law enforcement; for example, that he had rather consciously tried to have his car appear as if it was a police vehicle, and that he had broken teeth away from the heads of his victims in order to foil attempts at identification. He spoke of the killings in a matter-of-fact way, not to shock, but as if he had been over the territory a million times in his mind and saw it as something unconnected to his everyday self. No one other than a pathologist, he contended, knew more about dead bodies than he did; for instance, he was still amused that one of the medical examiners who had made a report about one of his victims hadn't understood that he had cut her Achilles tendons not because of some strange murderous ritual but to prevent further rigor mortis and to aid in his sexual acts with the body.

He spoke of his childhood, too, not in a way that would allow him to use it to avoid responsibility for the killings, but with a sense of wonderment at what he had experienced. It had not been until his years at Atascadero that he had first begun to realize that the climate in his mother's orbit was abnormal. He was really just recovering when he had been released by the California Youth Authority and plunged back into the cauldron. I asked Kemper whether he had committed any sexual acts with his mother's body after he killed her, and he glared at me and said that he had "humiliated her corpse." He understood that even though he had killed the source of his problems, he was not relieved of them, and would never be fit for life in the outside world again. Equally important, he told me that his fantasies drove these killings, that as time went on, during the months that he was murdering, the fantasies became more and more intricate as well as intense. Nonetheless, in the course of the murders, there was always some detail that didn't happen as planned, or that he felt could have been more perfect. That imperfection pushed him to kill the next time. The actual act of murder, Kemper concluded, was never as good as the fantasy, and never would be.

In 1988, during the satellite broadcast, Kemper and Gacy behaved pretty much as I expected they would. Kemper was totally candid about his crimes, admitting everything, going into gory detail at times, and giving quite a bit of psychological insight into the role that fantasy had played in his murders. His perspective was revelatory to many in the audience. In some ways, Kemper's detailed memories and explanations of his acts were a demonstration of the need to keep even such heinous murderers alive. I believe they should not be executed but, rather, imprisoned and counseled so we can learn from them what we may do to prevent other would-be murderers from following their paths. Executions of such men do not serve any socially useful purpose. They do not deter other would-be serial killers, who are so caught up in their own fantasies that the possibility of being caught and killed themselves does not sway them from their crimes. And actually, executions don't even save the state money, because to kill a prisoner today requires millions of dollars in legal expenses. It's more useful to keep a man such as Ed Kemper alive, so we can study him.

John Gacy used his ninety minutes to try to persuade the watching audience of law-enforcement officials that he was innocent of the crimes for which he had been convicted, and that they, as police experts, should pursue the loose ends and lost witnesses and make it their business to overturn his conviction and see to it that he was set free. An appeal is actually in process for Gacy, and a ruling is expected shortly. Some audience members later were annoyed at me for not verbally pinning Gacy to the wall during that broadcast, for not forcing him to admit his crimes to our forum. I tried to explain that this would have served no real purpose, and that my goal had been to let each of these murderers display his personality for the audience, so that, for instance, they could see for themselves Gacy's perspective, the way he now denied everything, the extent of his brilliance at manipulation. Some still didn't comprehend the point, but I guess that's why we need to have more seminars and continuing education about homicide and the minds of multiple murderers.

12

BROADER HORIZONS

From the time of the formation of the BSU to the present, publicity
has been a two-edged sword for those of us in the unit, and I've always
had it swirling around me. The uproar began back in the era when I
was becoming the senior profiler, taking over from Teten and Mullany.
I was training hostage negotiators in Chicago. Patricia Leeds, a veteran
police-beat reporter in Chicago, was attending the classes in preparation
for writing an article on hostage negotiation. We talked, and I mentioned my interest in William Heirens, whose case she knew very well.
She soon wanted to visit Quantico and prepare an article about profiling
and violent crime. I checked with my superior at Quantico, and with
the public-affairs division, and got a sort of half-approval for her to
come down and interview me and others in the BSU for such an article.

Pat arrived and spent a day, and at the end of it wanted to stay
for a second day. One prerogative that agents at Quantico have is to
allow guests to stay overnight in special guest rooms, so I booked her
into one of those. In the evening, we were chatting in the beer hall
with several Chicago police officers who were at Quantico for a three-
month period. It was late, and I wanted to go home, so I asked the
Chicago men if they would escort Pat back to her room when they
were finished with their beers and conversation. As fate—or the sort
of luck I seem to attract—would have it, Pat was spotted in the beer
hall, without her agent escort, by someone who knew her. He was
John Otto, recently elevated to deputy director of the Bureau, and who
had formerly been the SAC of the Chicago office. Otto was passing
through in the company of a covey of other Bureau big shots, including
Director Webster and Ken Joseph, then in charge at Quantico. Joseph
was annoyed because a guest was loose at the Academy and had no
agent escort.

In the morning, Joseph confronted the Academy's public-affairs officer, who claimed he didn't know what a police reporter was doing at Quantico, nor why she had been allowed to roam around without supervision. By the time I arrived for the day, Joseph was in a state of panic. Who knew what this demon reporter might write about Quantico! What if she wrote about police officers drinking beer on FBI property? About FBI agents whose white shirts were not properly starched? Clearly, there was some reason to believe that J. Edgar Hoover's ghost really did haunt the halls at Quantico.

"Let's not play what-if games," I told Joseph as I sat in his office and listened to this speculation. This was a friendly reporter, engaged in research for what I was certain was going to a positive article. Moreover, I had checked with my superior and with public affairs before allowing her to come to Quantico. If the article came out and it was negative, I said, there would be plenty of reason and time to rake me over the coals; until that eventuality, however, I considered his panic to be unwarranted. As a good friend, Ken Joseph gave way to my view on this matter, but as I left his office, I knew I owed him a favor.

Pat Leeds's front page article in the *Chicago Tribune* on February 15, 1980, was entitled "They Study the Strangest of Slayings," with the subhead "Little-Known FBI Unit Profiles Bizarre Killers." It was as accurate and as flattering as anybody could have wished, and I heard no more paranoid rumblings about unescorted reporters at the Academy. The article was picked up by the wire services and reprinted in many other newspapers, and it led to a flood of other articles, including important ones in *The New York Times, People*, and *Psychology Today*, just to name a few, as well as invitations to me to appear on various television and radio programs. Interest was high because the BSU was unique in law enforcement at the time. Both Los Angeles and New York City had psychologists working for their police departments, but these men did not regularly profile criminals, as we were doing.

Another part of outreach that I pioneered—much more deliberately than the publicity effort—was to the psychiatric and mental-health communities. My outreach to psychiatry was part of an overall thrust of mine to go beyond the bounds of what had traditionally been the purview of the FBI, and to link up with mental-health professionals. I started doing so in the mid-1970s, and have kept it up since then. I certainly felt I could learn something from psychiatrists, psychologists, and other professionals involved in mental health, forensic sciences, prison work, and the like, and many of the mental-health associations, in particular, were delighted to have a participant from the FBI at their gatherings. Invariably, when I appeared on a program as a representative of the FBI, there was a full house. I found that the difference between presenting information about our work to a law-enforcement audience and to a room full of psychiatrists was that the police personnel generally sat, watched, and listened, often with arms folded, almost challenging me to tell them something they didn't already know, while the psychiatrists (perhaps because of their many years of attending classes) invariably took copious notes.

An early, key incident in my outreach to psychiatry happened when at a psychiatric conference I presented the case of Monte Rissell. This case had fascinated me since I first learned about it, principally because had I profiled the unknown rapist and murderer at the time of the crimes, I would have guessed wrong. The number and magnitude of his crimes suggested to me a man in his late twenties or early thirties; if I'd said or written that to the Alexandria, Virginia, police when Rissell was still at large, they would have pursued the wrong sort of suspect. Given what I had come to know of the minds of murderers, I would have believed it improbable that someone still in his teens had been capable of committing a dozen rapes, of which in the last five the victims were also murdered. But that's what Rissell had done.

As a researcher, I had learned to look long and hard at information that challenges preconceptions, including the data about Monte Rissell. Rissell's problems had begun at the same young age as those of many of the offenders sketched earlier in this book, and he had a similar dysfunctional family, but everything else about him seemed to have been accelerated. He began raping women when he was fourteen; convicted, he was sent to a psychiatric facility in Florida, and committed five more rapes during the time he was technically in the charge of that facility: one while on vacation, another during a runaway episode, and others while he was actually living in the institution—in the facility's parking lot, at a public swimming pool, and the like.

Three weeks after coming home from the psychiatric facility, Rissell was charged with an attempted armed robbery that was actually an intended rape. This charge would take a year to work through the courts, and during that time, the judge assigned him to report regularly to a psychiatrist. Unfortunately, this psychiatrist's practice did not normally include violent juvenile offenders.

Rissell saw the psychiatrist on a regular basis and—according to the psychiatrist's reports—made good progress. The progress was an illusion: During this year in which he was receiving treatment, Rissell for the first time murdered one of his rape victims. The crime took place in the vicinity of the apartment complex where he lived. When the year-old attempted robbery case came to trial, Rissell was convicted and sentenced to probation and continued psychiatric counseling. No one at the time of the robbery conviction had traced the murder to him, or even suspected his involvement.

During his probationary period, while still seeing the psychiatrist, Rissell committed four more rape-murders near the apartment complex. There seemed no true pattern to the crimes. The rape victims differed: Some were young, others were in their thirties; some were white, others black; some were single, some married. The police continued to look for an outsider, and Rissell's arrest for these crimes came not as a result of a logical trail leading to his door but, rather, from a chance search of his car. He confessed to the murders, was convicted, and given five life sentences. It was only after spending two years in prison that he told the authorities about the earlier rapes that he had committed while living in the psychiatric facility.

I interviewed Rissell in prison and found him to be quite articulate and forthcoming about his crimes, able to give considerable detail about his motivations and state of mind and to trace these to roots in his childhood. He agreed to become part of our Criminal Personality Research Project, and provided very good data for us. For instance, he recounted that he had let one rape victim go. He had not killed her, because she told him that she had to support a member of her family who had cancer. A member of Rissell's family also had cancer, so he let his victim live. In our terms, he had become personally involved with the victim to such a large degree that he could no longer depersonalize her and kill her.

This sort of information on Rissell is what I was recounting to a forensic psychiatric group in Chicago, in the early 1980s. With Rissell's mug shots on the screen, I was lecturing to an audience of eighty or so mental-health professionals about the case. I was facing the door, and through it I saw a scene that seemed as if it were out of an animated cartoon: A man walked by the door, peered in, and kept going; then, his head came back into the frame, as it were, to look again, and the rest of the body followed. The man came into the lecture hall and took a seat down front near the lectern. He proceeded to watch and listen with rapt attention as I went on with my presentation. During it, I mentioned that Rissell had been seeing a psychiatrist during the time that he was raping and murdering, and that the psychiatrist had not realized that Rissell was lying through his teeth in order to get the doctor to award him a diagnosis of good progress. This, I suggested, was testimony to the manipulative genius of organized murderers. In my view, the problem stemmed from the historic reliance of traditional psychiatry on self-report; that is, that the patient will truthfully tell the doctor everything that has happened and will willingly participate in the healing process. Forensic psychiatry has learned not to rely solely on self-reports, to use outside reports, court records, and the like, and to continually question the accuracy of what a patient-offender discloses about his life and actions.

During my presentation, the man who had come in and sat down was sweating profusely, beginning to look ashen. At the end of my lecture, the lights went on and people started to file out of the room. The sweating, white-faced, obviously troubled man came up and said he had to talk to me.

"I'm a psychiatrist," he said.

"You look like you *need* a psychiatrist," I retorted.

"I'm Dr. Richard Ratner," he said. "I'm the guy who was gulled by Monte Rissell. I've agonized over this case for many years. Can we talk?"

To condense a long story, we did talk and we became friends. I reiterated my contention that he had been fooled by Rissell in much the same way as Rissell's rape and murder victims had, and that he should not blame himself too greatly for that. I went on to urge that in his future forensic work it was imperative that he not rely completely on the self-reports of his patients-offenders.

In recent years, Dr. Ratner has become an active convert to this idea. Still disturbed by the notion that if he had been more astute in the Rissell case, the lives of several people might have been spared, Dr. Ratner lectures to groups and uses himself as an example of a man who was duped by a master manipulator. He has invited me to make grand rounds in psychiatry presentations at various hospitals in the Washington, D.C., area, I've brought him in to Quantico as a guest lecturer, and he has become an adviser to the Criminal Personality Research Project. Of such bonds, one hopes, progress is made in the understanding of the criminal mind.

I had been presenting to psychiatrists for some years when a second important incident occurred. It was at a similar gathering, and I was speaking about what I had come to label "regressive necrophilia." I had on the screen a crime scene slide of a woman from whose vagina one could see a tree branch protruding. I explained that the term regressive necrophilia had been used to describe the insertion of foreign objects into the vagina or anus, something we had observed in cases involving seriously disorganized offenders. We interpreted it as an act that displayed tremendous hostility toward women and, at the same time, the offender's ignorance of consensual sexuality. It is an act that is often misinterpreted by crime-scene analysts as a mutilation, when it is actually a sexual substitution.

One man in the audience, a non-forensic psychiatrist with silver hair, objected vociferously to the slide and to my presentation of the whole subject. He accused me of trying to shock the audience, and insisted that this had to be a most unusual case and that there had never been another like it. He interrupted the lecture to the point that I had to address him directly before I could continue.

I asked the man how many crime scenes he had ever evaluated.

"None," he said. "I'm a psychiatrist, not a police officer."

I stood my ground, saying that we had seen similar behavior in dozens of cases. He continued to say that this was absurd.

Another member of the audience asked the protester to sit down and listen, and said that if he did, perhaps everyone might learn something. The protester could not be appeased, however, and stomped out. Later, other members of the audience suggested to me that he had been on overload, that he was too set in his ways to assimilate new information. They had found the presentation instructive, they said, and, in general, I've had the same positive reaction from the dozens of professional groups to whom I've spoken in the last fifteen or so years.

In the fall of 1991, my attempts to bridge to the psychiatric community were acknowledged when the American Academy of Psychiatry and the Law honored me at their annual conference in Orlando, Florida, with its annual Amicus award, given to the person who as an outsider to the field of psychiatry has done the most to advance its knowledge. No other FBI agent has ever been considered for this award.

From the beginning of my years at Quantico, I was determined that our work would be a two-way street, not one-way, as had been the norm in the old FBI. Toward that end, I was constantly on the lookout to bring people who could help us to the FBI. Dr. Murray Miron, an expert in psycholinguistics, had been brought in as a Bureau consultant by Pat Mullany. My mentors, Mullany and Teten, had also been instrumental in developing people within the Bureau who could assist hypnosis experts, whom we sometimes employed to help witnesses recall in more vivid detail what they had seen in relation to a crime. I reached out to various forensic psychiatrists such as Drs. Park Dietz, James Cavanaugh, Richard Ratner, Robert Simon, and others, and, for my Criminal Personality Research Project, to Dr. Ann Burgess and to such advisers as Dr. Marvin Wolfgang of the University of Pennsylvania, who had done pioneering studies of violent offenders.

A good deal of my time was spent in lecturing to in-service agents and to the police who came to Quantico for courses, and for these courses I always sought outside guest lecturers. Burgess, Dietz, and the others just mentioned, came and spoke, as did Capt. Frank Bolz, who had practically invented hostage negotiation for the New York City police department. I had noticed that no matter how lively our own presentations were, it was these guest lecturers who became the main topic of students' reports back to their superiors.

I went far beyond law enforcement and forensic sciences to find interesting guests. A friend had told me that the patient in *The Three Faces of Eve* case, Chris Sizemore, had recovered from the multiple-personality disorder that had been the basis for a celebrated book, and for a movie starring Joanne Woodward, and had become a dynamite lecturer. I met Chris and determined to have her come to Quantico. The Bureau's general, though unwritten, rule was that you checked such things as unusual lecture guests with your superior. That superior invariably would not object but would inform the agent that he would be acting on his own, and that if anything went wrong, it would be the agent, not the superior, who would face the wrath of the Bureau. I got that standard line from my boss, and more in addition. Wasn't this woman a mental patient? I told him she was fully recovered and not dangerous. He told me it was my rear end on the line, not his; with a deadpan face, I told him that the greatest difficulty with Chris was that since she had three personalities, we'd have to triple our regular honorarium in order to obtain her. He didn't get the joke.

Chris was a big hit, explaining what it was like to have a mental disorder and to recover from it. There had been several headline courtroom cases in which the defense had tried to invoke a defense that involved multiple personalities. Chris spoke convincingly to the effect that if one of a patient's multiple personalities is capable of murder, all are, and that if one is not, neither are the others. In summary, she said that having multiple personalities did not exculpate a murder suspect.

All of the guests contributed in some special way to our growing expertise. Other unusual visiting lecturers included a sculptor, Frank Bender—who specializes in constructing models that show what a suspect might look like after not having been seen in ten or twenty years—and a psychic, Noreen Renier. This woman had been well recommended to me, and had previously worked on some cases with local law-enforcement entities, helping to locate dead bodies and providing similar clues. My superior told me that I was to tell our students that we were just presenting Ranier as an interesting lecturer, not recommending her to local police departments or in any way suggesting that we believed in what she was doing.

She came to Quantico early in 1981, and in her lecture she told us that she was not in control of her powers, that they were sometimes on target and sometimes not. In front of a group of policeman that day, Ranier predicted that an attempted assassination of President Ronald Reagan would take place before the end of the month. She said that the President would be hit in the left chest, that he would not die but would recover, gain a great deal of sympathy from the public, and go on to greater things.

After Reagan was shot, I asked the psychic down for a second appearance at Quantico, and this time she predicted that the President would die in an assassination attempt in November, at the hands of men in foreign uniforms wielding machine guns. This time, I told the Secret Service about her predictions; they were upset that I hadn't brought them the first prediction, which I had initially thought was just a wild guess. She was both right and wrong about the November assassination: It was President Sadat of Egypt who died in October, not November, at the hands of men in foreign uniforms with machine guns.

In another instance, she helped to locate a plane containing the body of a relative of an FBI agent. The psychic also predicted something in my own life. Several days before I was scheduled to leave on a six-week trip to Germany, she told me that I would be coming back shortly, because of something having to do with a dark-haired woman. Three days after I landed in Germany, I was called back to the States because my wife, who had dark hair, had been in a terrible automobile accident.

By this time, however, information that Renier had lectured at

Quantico had gotten out to the media, where it was distorted into a story that announced flatly that the psychic was an FBI consultant. A second story twisted the facts still further, saying that this psychic had been hired by the FBI to predict such things as assassination attempts. The Quantico authorities were incensed at this, and forbade me to invite Renier to lecture again.

A year or two later, we were confronted with a murder case that had happened right on the Quantico base, to the wife of a DEA agent—a case that had us stumped for a long time. While we were still perplexed by it, my superior (a novice to the BSU unit) came to me and asked whether I could invite the psychic down to lecture once more, so he could consult with her and see whether she could help on this murder case. I objected, reminding him that I had been told by higher brass that we were not to use her anymore. He insisted that I bring her down anyway, and agreed to take the heat if her presence became known. After her lecture, he whisked her out of the classroom and allowed her to see and touch the evidence associated with the case, but her input had no bearing on the case, which remains unsolved to this day.

Even though the sort of publicity that Noreen Renier had involved us in was not of the best sort, the BSU continued to be the focus of outside interest. Early in the 1980s, that interest changed from documenting what we did to using it as the basis for fiction.

Writers of articles—and even more so, of fiction—often expand in their work the idea of what the FBI can accomplish through profiling. They make profiling seem like a magic wand that, when available to police, instantly solves the crime. As readers of this book will know by now, magic has nothing to do with it. Profiling is merely the application of sound behavioral science principles, and years of experience, gained in part by evaluating crime scenes and evidence, and also by interviewing incarcerated criminals, with the goal of pointing the police toward the most likely category of suspects. Profiling never catches a killer. Local police do that.

No matter how many times we stressed that point, fiction writers seem to want to have profilers in their own work do more. One day in the early 1980s the public-affairs office of the FBI asked me to take an author around the BSU. His name was Tom Harris, and he had already written one best-selling novel, *Black Sunday*, which had been made into a motion picture. Harris explained to me that he was writing another novel, and that a serial killer would be featured in it. He wanted to know how the FBI would get involved, how a profile was done, how we would assist the local police. He and I spent several hours together, and during it I showed him slides on various cases, among them those on Kemper and Chase. Harris was like a sponge, saying little but absorbing everything. We also discussed my already-lengthy series of prison interviews, and I told him that lately we had been bringing various psychiatrists and other mental-health experts into the Bureau for consultation.

Later, Tom Harris fused the idea of prison interviews with reaching out to psychiatrists and used that in his novel *Red Dragon*, where the FBI agent turns for help to the now-celebrated character of Hannibal Lecter, the psychiatrist and incarcerated serial killer who helps solve the mystery. The character and plot are entirely Harris's, of course, but I am proud to have provided some facts on which his fertile imagination could work.

After *Red Dragon* was published, I asked Harris why he had made his hero a civilian working with the Bureau, and not an agent. He told me that he had wanted the man to have mental problems as a result of his first run-in with Lecter, mental problems that would have disqualified him from being an agent. I thought this was comical, given the weight losses, the pseudo heart attacks, and other problems that many of us in the BSU had experienced.

On a second visit, while he was working on another novel, I spent more hours with Harris and showed him other specific cases, including that of Ed Gein, who became part model for the villain in *The Silence of the Lambs*. I also introduced Harris to the lone female agent who was working with the BSU at the time.

As fiction, both the Harris novels are superb, though they are not truly realistic in their portrayals either of the serial killers or of the heroes and heroines inside the FBI. For instance, in the serial killer of the first book, Francis Dolarhyde, Harris combines attributes of several different sorts of killers, personality dynamics that would be highly unlikely to coexist in one person in the real world. Moreover, FBI agents don't personally go after such killers; we assess crime scenes, make personality profiles, and pass our suggestions on to local law-enforcement agencies, who do the hard field work and ultimately make the arrests.

In the years since Harris came through the BSU, I've served as a source for other major authors writing novels and nonfiction books. Among the most prominent are Mary Higgins Clark, whose novel *Loves Music, Loves to Dance* was based in part on a presentation I made of the Harvey Glattman case (and on some subsequent consultation that I provided to her after I retired from the Bureau), and Ann Rule. Ann Rule became a colleague of mine on the VICAP task force, and I later invited her to lecture at Quantico on Ted Bundy, about whom she had written a book. I introduced her to the case of Jerome Brudos, and she later went to Oregon, did a lot of spadework, and wrote a book about him, called *Lustkiller*.

In recent years, the hue and cry about profiling, and the misinterpretation of it as well as of what the Bureau legitimately does, has continued to increase. The media have come around to lionizing behavioral-science people as supersleuths who put all other police to shame and solve cases where others have failed.

Regrettably, the FBI itself seems to have jumped on this bandwagon. It was most evident in the Bureau's cooperation with the producers of the film *The Silence of the Lambs*. One of the last matters to pass across my desk before I retired was the script for that movie. I objected to several aspects of it. I felt that if the FBI was going to be involved in the filming, to the extent of allowing Quantico to be used as a set, we ought to exert more influence to make the film realistic. For instance, the heroine, played by Jodie Foster in the movie, was an agent-in-training; we would never have placed a trainee in such a position of responsibility or danger, as the script suggested. That detail could easily have been changed without damage to the fictional structure, as could dozens of others such details. They were not changed, however, and some of the scenes at Quantico even include Bureau personnel in extra or cameo roles. The powers that be evidently reasoned that the movie would be such good publicity for the Bureau that it made no difference whether or not the film was accurate.

With the success and wide appeal of the book and movie *The Silence of the Lambs*, there came a frenzy to exploit both serial killers and their profilers. This was most apparent on television. Whereas earlier in the 1980s there had been some legitimate programs about serial killers, the legitimate programming now fell away to the broadcast equivalents of tabloid journalism. My main complaint with most of the recent material is that it is hastily pulled together. For instance, one program that is often helpful to law enforcement is "America's Most Wanted." However, even this program hastened to portray Joe Fisher, in prison in New York, as a man who had killed 150 people. That was Fisher's claim, but while he did kill his wife and perhaps a few other people, he had not murdered hundreds, and a little research would have shown that truth. Fisher, like Henry Lee Lucas, was a drifter and an alcoholic who liked the idea of making huge claims and finding himself featured in newspapers and on television.

The avalanche of publicity has brought with it some strange and upsetting reactions. Several serial killers are now receiving letters in prison from people they do not know, people who write that they want to be just like them and emulate their deeds. I have also been told by individuals at various times that they think it would be interesting to go to a cocktail party and chat with a Ted Bundy or another serial killer. These murderers are awful examples of humanity and should not be idolized or emulated.

Some people still in the BSU have also taken to claiming that they were the models for the FBI characters in the book and movie *The Silence of the Lambs*, though Harris has stated (and I agree) that the characters are entirely his own and not based on any particular individuals. And the problem is seen not only with old BSU hands. New applicants to the BSU are taking Jodie Foster's character as a role model; they, too, want to be supersleuths. If an aspirant to a police force identified too closely with "Dirty Harry" Callahan, we'd have an awful lot of trigger-happy, violent, and dangerous cops. We don't need them, and we don't need FBI supersleuths either. As a society, we seem to be flying too close to the flame, looking for stimulation— we are bored audiences more attuned to fantasy than to reality, in danger of falling completely into the abyss about which Nietzsche warned us.

Since retiring from the FBI, I have worked as an expert witness and a lecturer. Among my recent cases was that of Ricky Greene, a Texas murderer. He had killed a handful of people in seemingly random violence, and was awaiting sentencing. I testified that he could be considered even more dangerous than Ted Bundy, because while Bundy chose his victims by type, Greene demonstrated a willingness to kill almost anyone. I can't tell what effect my testimony, separate from others, had on the outcome, but Greene was sentenced to death.

In a more celebrated case in Rochester, New York, Arthur J. Shawcross was accused of eleven murders of area women, many of whom were prostitutes. Shawcross had previously served fourteen years in a penitentiary for the sexual assault and strangulation murder of an eight-year-old girl. He had also admitted to having killed a young boy, but that charge was dropped in exchange for his guilty plea to the girl's murder. Nonetheless, after fourteen years he had been released and had gone right back to killing.

In the new case, the serial murders of the prostitutes, Shawcross had pleaded not guilty by reason of insanity. Part of his defense was to be based on the notion that he had been sexually, psychologically, and physically abused as a child. Another part was his contention that he suffered from a mental condition of "altered states" akin to multiple personality disorder, and a third strand to the defense was that Shawcross had a Vietnam-related mental illness, Post-Traumatic Stress Disorder.

While my long-term friend and colleague psychiatrist Dr. Park E. Dietz advised the prosecution on how to deal with Shawcross's claims of child abuse and multiple personality disorder, I tackled the PTSD notion. By this time I had put in thirty-five years of active duty and reserve time in Army military police and CID matters, and my experience helped me to quickly debunk Shawcross's PTSD defense. My research showed me that his claim of having witnessed wartime atrocities was patently outrageous and untrue, and my pretrial work in this area was so strong that it shattered the PTSD issue in the case, to the point where the defense did not even seek to make it part of their insanity plea at the trial. The other two areas were similarly countered by Dr. Dietz, and Shawcross was convicted of ten counts of murder in the second degree in one case—and ten consecutive life sentences— and in a second case he was convicted of one count of homicide and sentenced to twenty-five years to life. It is unlikely that he will leave prison alive.

Along with the rest of the world, in the summer of 1991 I read the headlines about Jeffrey Dahmer's arrest in connection with seventeen murders in Milwaukee, Wisconsin, and the details about sexual assaults, mutilation, cannibalism, and necrophilia. In his acts of violence Dahmer seemed to have captured all the horror of serial and sexual killings during the last quarter-century, and rolled them together into one. In fact, he had been sporadically active as a killer during a great deal of that period, as his first homicide had been committed in 1978, when he was eighteen. Near his childhood home in Bath, Ohio, he had picked up a hitchhiker and killed him—rather spontaneously, it appears, without a plan. Nine years went by, and his bizarre and murderous fantasies built up until he began killing again, once in 1987, twice in 1988, once in 1989, four times in 1990, and eight times in 1991, the last several killings separated only by days, before he was caught.

Looking at the case from outside, it was clear to me that Dahmer followed the predictable pattern of serial killers. They begin killing cautiously, frightened of their crimes. Then the pace picks up, and they progress to become effective and efficient killing machines. Eventually, they become cavalier and careless, convinced that they cannot be caught by any mortal. They believe they have ultimate power and authority over others.

As the reader knows, over the years I had conducted hundreds of road shows for the FBI about criminal personality assessment and psychological profiling, a number of them in the Milwaukee area. After my retirement, I was invited to give a similar course in Milwaukee in January of 1991, under the sponsorship of the University of Wisconsin at Milwaukee, and did so in conjunction with Ken Lanning, who had become the Bureau's top expert in crimes entailing the exploitation and sexual assault of children. During my road shows I had developed many contacts among the police officers and attorneys and mental-health professionals in the Milwaukee area. Thus, in a sense it was no surprise that in August 1991 I received a letter from a Milwaukee police detective who had attended my course in January, and who was now actively involved in the Dahmer investigation. "I can't tell you enough how helpful the information you presented was in the recent events here in Milwaukee," the detective wrote. "Knowing what to look for has been of great assistance to both me and to the other investigators involved [in the Dahmer case] as well."

Although I was pleased to receive this endorsement, it saddened me to learn of the actions of certain other officers in the Dahmer case, those who were fired for having allowed a fourteen-year-old Laotian boy to remain in Dahmer's apartment even after they had interviewed Dahmer and observed the highly suspicious circumstances in his apartment. I wished that those officers had had the opportunity to attend the course I'd given, just as the detective had; I felt confident that if they had, the outcome of their initial interview with Dahmer would have been different. Dahmer killed the Laotian boy only minutes after the police had left him in Dahmer's custody. Moreover, Dahmer killed four more males in the next two months before he was apprehended. It is highly likely that five lives could have been saved had those street officers been more alert to the patterns and motives of sexual killers. Had the Milwaukee police in general been more aware of these matters, they might have made Dahmer a suspect even earlier, when a number of young men were disappearing from gay bars in the city. Realistically, though, the Milwaukee police cannot be blamed for such errors in judgment; very few law-enforcement officers in the country have been trained to recognize the complex dynamics of violent offenders. The entire incident renews my belief that more training is needed for the police in this area.

In the fall of 1991, I was contacted by both the prosecution and the defense in the Dahmer case about testifying as an expert witness. My friend Park Dietz was going to work for the prosecution, and, in a strange twist, I eventually determined to appear on the opposite side, for the defense.

For a former FBI agent to appear on the defense side in any case is highly unusual, and might be misunderstood by most lay people, as well as by some of my former FBI and law-enforcement colleagues. However, since leaving the Bureau and becoming a paid consultant and expert witness, I have come to understand that a true expert has but one opinion, and it really doesn't matter which side wants to call upon that opinion, because it is based on facts and experience, and cannot be altered to fit either the defense or the prosecution strategies. That's the basis on which I agreed to work with Gerald P. Boyle, the Milwaukee attorney charged with handling the defense of Jeffrey Dahmer. I could never appear in support of Dahmer's actions or behavior, and I do not condone the outrageous acts of killing seventeen people—but I understand those acts and Dahmer's state of mind. My position is neither for nor against Dahmer, but is most definitely for using my expertise to bring all parties to the correct level of understanding where they can fairly adjudicate the matter at hand. What I'm for is a criminal justice system that can most appropriately handle such difficult things as the Dahmer case.

On January 13, 1992, attorney Boyle announced that Jeffrey Dahmer was prepared to change his plea to each of the fifteen counts of murder for which he had been charged from not guilty by reason of insanity to guilty but insane. "The decision to plead guilty is Mr. Dahmer's, not mine," Boyle said to the press. "This case is about his mental condition. It is his intent to plead guilty." The "guilty but insane" plea is possible under Wisconsin law, though it is not permitted in many other states. I agreed wholeheartedly with the decision to enter this plea. With Dahmer's guilt not in question, he will face an abbreviated trial, a second phase of which will focus only on his mental condition. Regardless of the outcome of that phase, it is a virtual certainty that Dahmer will spend the rest of his life in a secure facility, either a mental institution or a state penitentiary—and that, to my mind, is the correct conclusion to the case. By arranging to have

Dahmer plead guilty, Gerald Boyle has saved the Milwaukee courts many weeks and possibly months of tedious trial testimony, as well as millions of dollars, and has permitted an outcome to the case that will serve the public very well.

In conjunction with Dahmer's defense, I interviewed him for two days. In preparation for this, I delved into the case more deeply. The figure that came to my mind most immediately was the terrible specter of Richard Trenton Chase, the vampire killer whose crimes I detailed in Chapter One. Dahmer, too, consumed blood and human flesh, but he was not as disorganized as Chase had been. This was a man who cruised the gay bars of Milwaukee in his search for victims, and brought them back to his apartment, even though he knew that this course of action would make him vulnerable to police investigation. In this regard, he reminded me of John Gacy. Dahmer kept body parts, such as skeletons and skulls, knowing that these also could be used as evidence against him if they were found. I also learned information that was part of the court record but had not yet become widely known: that Dahmer drank blood, consumed body parts, and preferred sexual contact with the dead and dismembered bodies of his victim. In these last actions, he reminded me of Ted Bundy and of Ed Kemper.

I was astonished to learn that when Dahmer's last victim escaped his apartment in the midst of being attacked, Dahmer calmly waited for the police to arrive and made no effort to destroy or conceal the great amount of evidence that he kept in his rooms. And that evidence was massive, consisting of hundreds of photographs of the victims, both dead and alive, skulls and body parts in the refrigerator and in drums and boxes. Paraphernalia used to restrain and kill the victims was scattered throughout the apartment. I was heartsick to learn that in the months prior to his arrest, Dahmer let outsiders, including his landlord and the police, into his apartment when the paraphernalia were present and in full view in the living room and in adjacent rooms whose doors were open. All the signs of the killer were there, but no one had heeded them.

While Dahmer exhibited many of the characteristics of the organized offender—he hunted victims, lured them to his apartment with promises of money and favors, and after death hid and concealed the evidence of his crimes—he also exhibited many dynamics associated with the disorganized offender: He had sex with his victims after death, consumed their flesh, mutilated their bodies, and kept body-part souvenirs. In our terminology, then, Dahmer was a "mixed" offender. In fact, he encompasses so many usually unrelated dynamics that we may have to make him the prime example of an entirely new category of serial killer.

Is Dahmer sane or insane? After two days interviewing him, I felt only empathy for the tormented and twisted person who sat before me. Dahmer was as candid and as cooperative as any serial murderer whom I have ever confronted, and yet he could not comprehend how he could have committed all of the atrocious deeds that he knew he had done. In the controlled prison environment, he was able to realize the extent to which his compulsions and fantasies had taken over his rational mind, driving him on, murder after murder. He chain-smoked during the entire interview, and suggested that lung cancer might be the solution to his problems. There was no way to view this tormented man as having been sane at the time of his crimes. I was glad that no matter what way the court proceedings would go, he would spend the rest of his life in custody.

I was equally glad that there is no death penalty in the state of Wisconsin, because it would serve no purpose for the state to kill him. The state of Florida spent seven or eight million dollars to execute Ted Bundy, money that might have been better used to build a forensic penal facility devoted to the research and study of people like Bundy, Kemper, Gacy, Berkowitz, and Dahmer, who have so horrendously violated society's trust. Criminologists have long agreed that the death sentence has never deterred violent offenders. It serves only to satisfy the families of victims, and society's general desire for revenge. If, as in the Dahmer case, we can assure the public that these monsters will not be allowed to complete a few years of incarceration and then slip back into our society—if we can agree to keep them in custody for the rest of their lives—then we will have made progress. Precisely where and how they are kept away from society should not be an issue.

The existence of a Jeffrey Dahmer spurs me to press on with my research. There are some murderers in prison cells around the country whom I haven't yet talked to. I am still professionally involved with the Department of Justice's National Institute of Justice and the National Center for Missing and Exploited Children, in the investigation and analysis of those who molest, abduct, and murder children. I maintain faculty affiliation with Michigan State University's School of Criminal Justice, and with Georgetown University's Program on Psychiatry and the Law, and also lecture occasionally at several other universities. Though I will shortly retire from the U.S. Army Reserve and from the CID, I plan to go on training CID agents around the world, so long as the Army wants me to do so. It would be gratifying to believe that all of the work that I have done in regard to violent offenders has made a dent in the incidence of violent crime, but the headlines about terrible murders that crop up regularly in the nation's newspapers, and the routine reports of violence on the nightly news broadcasts, tell me that the fight against monsters goes on and on—and that I must continue to be in the thick of it.

INDEX